Econometrics Computer Program

USER'S REFERENCE MANUAL

VERSION 6.1

Kenneth J. White
Shirley A. Haun
Nancy G. Horsman
S. Donna Wong

McGraw-Hill Book Company
New York St. Louis San Francisco Auckland Bogotá Caracas
Colorado Springs Hamburg Lisbon London Madrid Mexico
Milan Montreal New Delhi Oklahoma City Panama Paris
San Juan São Paulo Singapore Sydney Tokyo Toronto

SHAZAM USER'S REFERENCE MANUAL VERSION 6.1
Copyright © 1988 by Kenneth J. White. All rights reserved. Printed in Canada.
Except as permitted under the United States Copyright Act of 1976, no part of
this publication may be reproduced or distributed in any form or by any means,
or stored in a data base or retrieval systems, without the prior written permis-
sion of the publisher.

ISBN 0-07-069781-7

The editor was Scott D. Stratford.
Ronalds Printing Division of BCE Publitech Inc. was printer and binder.

Acknowledgment

While SHAZAM has been primarily developed by Kenneth J. White, many individuals have aided in improving the program and documentation. In particular, SHAZAM would not have been possible without the assistance of Justin Wyatt, Donna Wong, Mary Beth Walker, Terry Wales, Keith Wales, Eleanor Tao, Gene Savin, David Ryan, Esther Ruberl, Hedley Rees, Angela Redish, Michel Poitevin, Jeff Perloff, Doug Pearce, Charles Nelson, Robert McRae, Mark McBride, Michael McAleer, Stuart Logie, Bert Kritzer, Roger Koenker, Stan Kita, George Judge, Gordon Hughes, Nancy Horsman, Al Horsman, Shirley Haun, Tony Hall, Malcolm Greig, Bill Griffiths, Mark Greene, David Gow, Gene Golub, Debra Glassman, John Geweke, Frank Flynn, Stephen Donald, Katie Diner, Erwin Diewert, John Deegan, John Cragg, Melanie Courchene, Marsha Courchane, James Chalfant, Trudy Cameron, Ray Byron, Linda Bui, Alex Bui, Andrew Brownsword, Peter Berck, Fellini's Espresso Bar, and Duke's Gourmet Cookies.

An appropriate citation for SHAZAM is:

White, K.J., "A General Computer Program for Econometric Methods - SHAZAM," *Econometrica*, January 1978, pp. 239-240.

or

White, K.J., "SHAZAM: A General Computer Program for Econometric Methods (Version 5)," *American Statistician*, February 1987, Vol. 41, No.1, p. 80.

or

White, K.J., "SHAZAM: A Comprehensive Computer Program For Regression Models (Version 6)," *Computational Statistics & Data Analysis*, December 1988.

Additional excellent references on SHAZAM keyed to the popular Econometrics textbooks are:

White, K.J. and Bui, L.T.M., *Basic Econometrics: A Computer Handbook Using SHAZAM*, McGraw-Hill, 1988, ISBN 0-07-834463-8, referred to as the *Gujarati Handbook* in this manual.

and

White, K.J., Haun, S.A., and Gow, D.J., *Introduction to the Theory and Practice of Econometrics: A Computer Handbook Using SHAZAM And SAS*, John Wiley And Sons, 1988, ISBN 0-471-85946-X, referred to as the *Judge Handbook* in this manual.

The above Handbooks contain many SHAZAM examples to accompany the corresponding textbooks.

TABLE OF CONTENTS

"...sound research cannot be produced merely by feeding data to a computer and saying SHAZAM."

Peter Kennedy
A Guide to Econometrics

"A casual reader may wonder whether the names of some of these programs, particularly ORACLE and SHAZAM, reflect in any way the Delphic nature of econometric predictions."

Ivor Francis
Statistical Software: A Comparative Review

"...detailed implementation in concrete computer programs or systems. Hence, names familiar to many such as...GREMLIN, TROLL, AUTOREG, SHAZAM..."

Richard E. Quandt
Handbook of Econometrics

"The easiest solution to an inconclusive bounds test is to use a program such as SHAZAM..."

Judge, Hill, Griffiths, Lütkepohl and Lee
Introduction to the Theory and Practice of Econometrics, 2nd Edition

"In instances where d falls within the inconclusive region the exact critical value d* can be found numerically, providing appropriate computer software [e.g., SHAZAM, White(1978)] is available."

Judge, Griffiths, Hill, Lütkepohl and Lee
The Theory and Practice of Econometrics, 2nd Edition

"Beach and MacKinnon devised an iterative procedure for maximizing Equation (8-77), which has now been incorporated in White's SHAZAM program..."

Jack Johnston
Econometric Methods, 3rd ed.

"Some Computer Programs (e.g. SHAZAM, White (1978)) allow for the estimation of ρ and provide an unconditional covariance matrix."

Fomby, Hill and Johnson
Advanced Econometric Methods

Senator:	"Do you realize that I got a bill passed today that's going to put a million people to work? You know how I did it? I said one word."
Wife:	"SHAZAM?"
Senator:	"No. Subcommittee."

From the movie:
The Seduction of Joe Tynan

1. INTRODUCTION

"I think there is a world market for about five computers."

Thomas J. Watson
Chairman of the Board-IBM, 1943

SHAZAM is a comprehensive computer program for econometricians, statisticians, biometricians, engineers, sociometricians, psychometricians, politicometricians and others who use statistical techniques. SHAZAM is relatively easy to use, has great flexibility, and provides extensive data manipulation capabilities, including matrix operations. The primary strength of SHAZAM is for the estimation of many types of regression models.

Special features of SHAZAM include: Linear or Nonlinear Hypothesis Testing of Regression Coefficients, Linear Restrictions on Coefficients, Confidence Intervals and Ellipses, Bayesian Inequality Restrictions, ARIMA (Box-Jenkins) Models, First and Second Order Maximum-Likelihood or Iterative Cochrane-Orcutt Autoregressive Models, Least Squares Estimation of Higher-order Autoregressive and Moving-average Error Models, First Order Autoregressive Models with a Lagged Dependent Variable, Exact and Higher Order Durbin-Watson Tests, Forecasting, Ridge Regression, Box-Cox and Box-Tidwell Regressions, Box-Cox Autoregressive Models, Autoregressive Models with Missing Observations, Distributed Lags, Nonlinear Regression, Probit, Logit and Tobit Regression, Regression with Non-normal Errors, Robust Regression, Two-Stage Least Squares, Generalized Least Squares, Pooled Cross Section - Time Series, Regression on Principal Components, Iterative Three Stage Least Squares and Seemingly Unrelated Regressions, Principal Components and Factor Analysis, Index Numbers, Stepwise Regression, Plots, Sorting Data and a large variety of Diagnostic Tests.

Users should always be aware of the version of SHAZAM that they are using. This manual describes Version 6.1 of SHAZAM. Some options and commands described in this manual were not available in earlier versions so users should be certain an old version of SHAZAM is not used with this manual.

Presently, SHAZAM has thousands of users in 42 countries and is one of the most popular econometric computer programs in the world. It can be found at the Northernmost (University of Tromso, Norway) and Southernmost (University of Otago, New Zealand) Universities in the world. Questions on SHAZAM use should be referred to: SHAZAM, Department of Economics, University of British Columbia, Vancouver, B.C., V6T 1W5, CANADA, or your local SHAZAM consultant.

WARNING: SHAZAM COMMANDS FROM VERSIONS 1.0-4.6 WILL NOT WORK IN VERSIONS 5.0-6.1. See the chapter *NEW FEATURES IN SHAZAM* for further details.

2. A CHILD'S GUIDE TO RUNNING REGRESSIONS

"Difficult? A child could do it."

Arthur S. Goldberger
Professor of Economics, 1971

If you only need to run Ordinary Least Squares regressions, or if you don't have time to read the entire SHAZAM manual, this CHILD'S GUIDE provides basic information on now to run regressions.

1.   First, you need your data. To enter your data, specify the sample size with the **SAMPLE** command. The sample size is the number of observations in the data. The general format of the **SAMPLE** command is:

SAMPLE *beg end*

where *beg* is the first observation to be used (usually 1), and *end* is the last observation. If your data has 10 observations your **SAMPLE** command will look like this:

SAMPLE 1 10

This **SAMPLE** command sets the sample size to 10 observations and the data will be placed in observations 1 through 10 (because *beg* is specified as 1).

2.   Having set the sample size, you are ready to enter your data. For example, you may enter your data directly following a **READ** command of the form:

READ YEAR CONSUME INCOME PRICE

where YEAR, CONSUME, INCOME and PRICE are the names of the variables for the data you will type in. Normally, data is typed observation by observation. You may use more than one line per observation. If your data is set up variable by variable instead of observation by observation you will have to use the **BYVAR** option on your **READ** command. For details on the **BYVAR** option see the chapter *DATA INPUT AND OUTPUT*. All variables entered on a **READ** command must have an equal number of observations. In the above example, the first number read will be stored in variable YEAR, the next in CONSUME, and so on. In general, the **READ** command will look like this:

READ *vars / options*

where *vars* is a list of variable names for the data and *options* is a list of desired options. Variable names may be up to 8 characters long and must consist only of letters or numbers and start with a letter.

NOTE: Be sure that the number of variables you give on the **READ** command matches the number of variables in your data.

3. If your data is not in free format (numbers are not separated by blanks) you can use a FORTRAN format to specify how you want your data read in. To specify the format in SHAZAM, use a **FORMAT** command. For example:

FORMAT(6X,3F10.0,F5.0,F7.0)

The **FORMAT** command *must* appear *before* the **READ** command. The format must be enclosed in parentheses. In the above example, the first 6 columns are skipped, then 5 variables are read using three fields of 10 columns, one field of 6 columns and one field of 7 columns. To make the **READ** command use this format, you will have to use the **FORMAT** option on the **READ** command. The **READ** command which *follows* the **FORMAT** command will then look like this:

READ *vars* / **FORMAT** *options*

NOTE: Since all data read by SHAZAM is Real Double Precision, you may not use FORTRAN I-Format to read data. Only A, D, E, F, or G-Format should be used. F-Format is most common.

4. Usually, you will want to obtain some basic statistics on your variables. The **STAT** command will print the means, standard deviations, variances, minimums and maximums for the variables listed. The format of the **STAT** command is:

STAT *vars*

where *vars* is a list of variables. There are many options available on the **STAT** command. For details on these options see the chapter *DESCRIPTIVE STATISTICS*.

5. To run an Ordinary Least Squares regression you will need to use the **OLS** command. You should type one **OLS** command for each regression you want to run. The format of the **OLS** command is as follows:

OLS *depvar indeps* / *options*

where *depvar* is the variable name of the dependent variable, *indeps* are the variable names of the independent variables and *options* is a list of options desired (as defined below). A very simple **OLS** command might look like this:

OLS CONSUME INCOME PRICE

This will run a regression of variable CONSUME on variables INCOME and PRICE. No options were required. There are many available options which are described in other parts of this manual. Some common ones are:

ANOVA - Prints the **AN**alysis **Of VA**riance tables
GF - Prints Goodness-of-Fit statistics testing for normality of residuals
LIST - Prints and Plots all Residuals plus residual summary statistics
MAX - The equivalent of **LIST, PCOR, PCOV,** and some others
NOCONSTANT - Suppresses the intercept
PCOR - Prints a **COR**relation matrix of coefficients
PCOV - Prints a **COV**ariance matrix of coefficients
RSTAT - Prints **R**esidual Summary **STAT**istics (Durbin-Watson etc.)

Users should note that the **LIST** or **MAX** options will add substantially to computation costs, particularly if the sample size is large. An example of an **OLS** command with options follows:

OLS CONSUME INCOME PRICE / RSTAT PCOR

This example runs an **OLS** regression of variable CONSUME on variables INCOME and PRICE and prints residual summary statistics and a correlation matrix of coefficients along with the standard output. Do not forget to separate the options from the list of variables by a slash (/). The options may be listed in any order.

6.   The input for a complete SHAZAM run might look like the following example using Theil's [1971, p.102] Textile data:

* I HOPE THIS WORKS!
SAMPLE 1 17
READ YEAR CONSUME INCOME PRICE
```
 1923   99.2   96.7 101.0
 1924   99.0   98.1 100.1
 1925  100.0  100.0 100.0
 1926  111.6  104.9  90.6
 1927  122.2  104.9  86.5
 1928  117.6  109.5  89.7
 1929  121.1  110.8  90.6
 1930  136.0  112.3  82.8
 1931  154.2  109.3  70.1
 1932  153.6  105.3  65.4
 1933  158.5  101.7  61.3
 1934  140.6   95.4  62.5
 1935  136.2   96.4  63.6
 1936  168.0   97.6  52.6
 1937  154.3  102.4  59.7
 1938  149.0  101.6  59.5
 1939  165.5  103.8  61.3
```
STAT YEAR CONSUME INCOME PRICE
OLS CONSUME INCOME PRICE / RSTAT
OLS CONSUME INCOME
STOP

In this simple example there are 4 input variables and 17 observations. The **SAMPLE** command sets the sample size to 17 observations. Two **OLS** regressions are run. Both regressions use variable CONSUME as the dependent variable. The data is read in using free format, but in this case a format could have been specified using first, the **FORMAT** command and then the **FORMAT** option on the **READ** command in the following way:

SAMPLE 1 17
FORMAT(F4.0,3F6.1)
READ YEAR CONSUME INCOME PRICE / FORMAT

The **STAT** command will print means, standard deviations, variances, minimums and maximums for the variables YEAR, CONSUME, INCOME and PRICE. The **STOP** command is a signal to SHAZAM that it has reached the end of the commands.

NOTE: The line in the example beginning with an asterisk (*) is a SHAZAM *comment*. You can insert these at various places in the run, except within the data. Comment lines are printed on the output and sometimes help document the output. Comment lines must begin with an asterisk (*) in column 1. The rest of the line may contain anything.

The output for the first **OLS** command above looks like this: (Note that SHAZAM commands typed by the user appear in SHAZAM output following the symbol |_.)

```
|_OLS CONSUME INCOME PRICE / RSTAT
OLS ESTIMATION
      17 OBSERVATIONS      DEPENDENT VARIABLE = CONSUME
...NOTE..SAMPLE RANGE SET TO:    1,    17

 R-SQUARE =   0.9513     R-SQUARE ADJUSTED =   0.9443
VARIANCE OF THE ESTIMATE =     30.951
STANDARD ERROR OF THE ESTIMATE =    5.5634
MEAN OF DEPENDENT VARIABLE =    134.51
LOG OF THE LIKELIHOOD FUNCTION = -51.6470

MODEL SELECTION TESTS - SEE JUDGE ET.AL.(1985, P.242)
  AKAIKE (1969) FINAL PREDICTION ERROR- FPE =    36.413
    (FPE ALSO KNOWN AS AMEMIYA PREDICTION CRITERION -PC)
  AKAIKE (1973) INFORMATION CRITERION- AIC =    3.5912
  SCHWARZ(1978) CRITERION-SC =    3.7382
```

	ANALYSIS OF VARIANCE - FROM MEAN			
	SS	DF	MS	F
REGRESSION	8460.9	2.	4230.5	136.683
ERROR	433.31	14.	30.951	
TOTAL	8894.2	16.	555.89	

	ANALYSIS OF VARIANCE - FROM ZERO			
	SS	DF	MS	F
REGRESSION	0.31602E+06	3.	0.10534E+06	3403.478
ERROR	433.31	14.	30.951	
TOTAL	0.31646E+06	17.	18615.	

VARIABLE NAME	ESTIMATED COEFFICIENT	STANDARD ERROR	T-RATIO 14 DF	PARTIAL CORR.	STANDARDIZED COEFFICIENT	ELASTICITY AT MEANS
INCOME	1.0617	0.26667	3.9813	0.7287	0.23871	0.81288
PRICE	-1.3830	0.83814E-01	-16.501	-0.9752	-0.98933	-0.78464
CONSTANT	130.71	27.094	4.8241	0.7902	0.0	0.97175

```
DURBIN-WATSON = 2.0185    VON NEUMAN RATIO = 2.1447    RHO = -0.18239
RESIDUAL SUM = -0.96212E-12  RESIDUAL VARIANCE =    30.951
SUM OF ABSOLUTE ERRORS=   72.787
R-SQUARE BETWEEN OBSERVED AND PREDICTED = 0.9513
RUNS TEST:     7 RUNS,    9 POSITIVE,    8 NEGATIVE, NORMAL STATISTIC =-1.2423
COEFFICIENT OF SKEWNESS =  -0.0343 WITH STANDARD DEVIATION OF 0.5497
COEFFICIENT OF EXCESS KURTOSIS =  -0.8701 WITH STANDARD DEVIATION OF 1.0632

        GOODNESS OF FIT TEST FOR NORMALITY OF RESIDUALS -  6 GROUPS
OBSERVED  0.0  2.0  6.0  7.0  2.0  0.0
EXPECTED  0.4  2.3  5.8  5.8  2.3  0.4
CHI-SQUARE =      1.1126 WITH  1 DEGREES OF FREEDOM
```

7.   To run SHAZAM, you will need the appropriate system control commands at your installation. Read the chapter *HOW TO RUN SHAZAM* for this information.

8.   There are three modes of operation in SHAZAM: BATCH, TERMINAL and TALK. BATCH mode occurs when Batch or Background jobs are being run. TERMINAL mode occurs when the user is at a terminal, but the commands are in a separate file assigned to Fortran unit 5 (the input unit). TALK mode is active when the user is at a terminal, but SHAZAM commands are being typed interactively. In BATCH and TERMINAL, the **ECHO** option is automatically set on most systems (see the chapter *SET AND DISPLAY*). In TERMINAL and TALK, the **NOWIDE** option is usually the default setting. In TALK mode, **NOECHO** is set on most systems. On many operating systems these modes are automatically set, however on some operating systems it is necessary to set these modes using a SHAZAM **SET** command. In these cases, the **SET** command would be the first command typed. For further details on setting operating modes see the chapter *SET AND DISPLAY*.

9.   A good way for new users to learn SHAZAM is to run the SHAZAM Demo. To do this, just run SHAZAM at a terminal and type **DEMO**. Then follow the instructions as they appear.

10.   At this point, users may find it helpful to review the *MISCELLANEOUS COMMANDS AND INFORMATION* chapter. It also contains brief descriptions of some of the "rules and regulations" you should follow when running SHAZAM.

3. DATA INPUT AND OUTPUT

"All the waste in a year from a nuclear power plant can be stored under a desk."

Ronald Reagan
1980

This chapter provides complete information on how to **READ**, **PRINT** and **WRITE** data. The **SAMPLE** and **READ** commands are used to input data with SHAZAM. The **SAMPLE** command has the following format:

SAMPLE *beg end*

where *beg* and *end* are numbers specifying which observations should be read in with the **READ** command. For example, to input the first 10 observations of the data with the **READ** command the following **SAMPLE** command should be used:

SAMPLE 1 10

The **SAMPLE** command should not set a sample size larger than the number of observations available in the data.

The **READ** command actually inputs the data and attaches it to the variable names specified. The **READ** command has the following format:

READ *vars / options*

where *vars* is a list of variable names and *options* is a list of desired options (see details below). When working interactively with SHAZAM or when the commands and the data are in the same file, this simple format of the **READ** command is used and the data is typed in directly following the **READ** command. However, if the data is in a separate file, the format is modified slightly to specify the unit number assigned to the data file. The format becomes:

READ(*unit*) *vars / options*

where *unit* is the system unit number assigned to the desired data file. (For further details on assigning files see the chapter *HOW TO RUN SHAZAM.*) On most systems (except IBM mainframe systems) the **FILE** command (described in the chapter *MISCELLANEOUS COMMANDS AND INFORMATION*) can be used to assign files to unit numbers. The read units available for assignment to data files in SHAZAM are 11-49. If no unit is specified unit 5 (the command file) is used. An example of a **READ** command where the data file is assigned to unit 11, and contains 4 variables typed in free format is the following:

FILE 11 *datafilename*
SAMPLE 1 17
READ(11) YEAR CONSUME INCOME PRICE

The following options are available on the **READ** command:

BINARY

This option is used when the data is in Double Precision **BINARY** (unformatted). If the **FILE** command is used to assign the **BINARY** file, follow the instructions for the **FILE** command in the chapter *MISCELLANEOUS COMMANDS AND INFORMATION*. Be sure to include a decimal point (.) after the unit number on the **FILE** command.

BYVAR

This option is used when the data is to be read variable **BY VAR**iable rather than observation by observation. When this option is used, the data for each new variable must begin on a new line. If this option is not used, the data for each new observation must begin on a new line. Observations deleted by the **SKIPIF** command or the expanded form of the **SAMPLE** command are included when this option is used.

CLOSE

This option will **CLOSE** a file that was opened for the **READ** or **WRITE** command. Most operating systems do not require that files be closed, but sometimes it is desirable to do so to free up memory or a unit number. If this option is used, the file will no longer be assigned to the unit number as specified with the **FILE** command or an operating system command.

EOF

The option forces SHAZAM to read to the End Of the data File regardless of the **SAMPLE** command in effect. This is the default if no **SAMPLE** command has been previously specified.

FORMAT

The data will be read in according to the FORTRAN **FORMAT** previously specified on the **FORMAT** command. The format will be stored in a SHAZAM variable called **FORMAT**. (Details on the **FORMAT** command are given later in this chapter.)

LIST

LISTs all variables read in on the given **READ** command. This option is equivalent to a **READ** command together with a **PRINT** command. (Details on **PRINT** are given below.)

REWIND

This option is used to **REWIND** the input data file BEFORE reading any data. The default is NOT to **REWIND** the data file. The **REWIND** option makes it possible to reread a data file. It is also used to read a file created with SHAZAM **WRITE** commands.

BEG=
END=

Sets a sample range for the particular **READ** command which overrides the sample size set on the previous **SAMPLE** command. The sample size set by these options will only be used for the current **READ** command. Subsequent problems will be performed according to the sample range set by the previous **SAMPLE** command.

ROWS =	Specifies the number of **ROWS** and **COL**umn**S** when a matrix is being
COLS =	read in. Only one matrix can be read in on a given **READ** command and
	if a matrix is being read in, no other variables may be read on that **READ**
	command. **SKIPIF** commands are not in effect when a matrix is read.

SKIPLINES =   This option will skip the number of lines specified before reading in any data. It is used if a data file contains a certain number of lines such as labels or comments which need to be skipped before reading in the other data.

To print data with SHAZAM the **PRINT** command is used. The **PRINT** command has the following format:

PRINT *vars / options*

where *vars* is a list of variable names and *options* is a list of desired options. The available options on the **PRINT** command are:

BYVAR   The specified variables will be printed variable **BY VAR**iable rather than observation by observation. If only one variable is printed this option is automatically in effect. It can be turned off with **NOBYVAR**. If **BYVAR** is specified, observations that have been omitted either with **SKIPIF** command or the expanded form of the **SAMPLE** command will also be printed.

FORMAT   The data will be written according to the FORTRAN format previously specified on the **FORMAT** command. The format will be stored in a variable called **FORMAT**.

NEWLINE	These options will start a new line, page or sheet before printing. The
NEWPAGE	**NEWSHEET** option will only work on page printers which use a colon (:)
NEWSHEET	as the new sheet carriage control character.

NONAMES   Omits printing the heading of variable **NAMES**.

| WIDE / | **WIDE** uses 120 columns and **NOWIDE** uses 80 columns. The default |
| NOWIDE | setting is described in the chapter *SET AND DISPLAY*. |

BEG =	Only the observations within the range specified by **BEG =** and **END =**
END =	will be printed. If these are not specified, the range from the **SAMPLE**
	command is used.

It is possible to write selected data from a SHAZAM run into a file by using the **WRITE** command. The **WRITE** command has the following format:

WRITE(*unit*) *vars* / *options*

where *unit* is a FORTRAN unit number (assigned to a file with an operating system command or the SHAZAM **FILE** command), *vars* is a list of variable names and *options* is a list of desired options. The available units for writing data are 11-49. It is important to remember that the assigned file often must be created before it is used on a **WRITE** command. See also the **FILE** command described in the chapter *MISCELLANEOUS COMMANDS AND INFORMATION*. The available options on the **WRITE** command are similar to those available for the **PRINT** and **READ** commands, that is, **BYVAR, CLOSE, FORMAT, NAMES, WIDE, BEG=, END=** and the following additions:

BINARY   The specified variables will be written into the specified file in Double Precision **BINARY**. If the **FILE** command is used to assign the **BINARY** file, follow the instructions for the **FILE** command in the chapter *MISCELLANEOUS COMMANDS AND INFORMATION*. Be sure to include a decimal point (.) after the unit number.

REWIND   This option is used to rewind the output data file before any data is written. Output data files do not rewind by default on the **WRITE** command. The **REWIND** option makes it possible to reuse a data file.

NOTE: The default on the **WRITE** command is **NONAMES**. Therefore, if a heading of variable names is desired the **NAMES** option should be used.

The following examples will illustrate the proper use of options on **READ** and **PRINT** commands as well as present the output that can be expected from the use of these commands. The following is a listing of data typed observation by observation. It is Theil's [1971, p.102] Textile data. The variables are, from left to right, Year, Consumption, Income and Price. For most examples in this manual that use this data, it is assumed that the data is in a separate file assigned to unit 11:

```
1923  99.2  96.7 101.0
1924  99.0  98.1 100.1
1925 100.0 100.0 100.0
1926 111.6 104.9  90.6
1927 122.2 104.9  86.5
1928 117.6 109.5  89.7
1929 121.1 110.8  90.6
1930 136.0 112.3  82.8
1931 154.2 109.3  70.1
1932 153.6 105.3  65.4
1933 158.5 101.7  61.3
1934 140.6  95.4  62.5
1935 136.2  96.4  63.6
1936 168.0  97.6  52.6
1937 154.3 102.4  59.7
1938 149.0 101.6  59.5
1939 165.5 103.8  61.3
```

To input this data, all that is needed is a **SAMPLE** command and a very simple **READ** command:

SAMPLE 1 17
READ(11) YEAR CONSUME INCOME PRICE

Alternatively, this same data could be read using a FORTRAN format statement. The appropriate commands are a **SAMPLE** command, a **FORMAT** command and a **READ** command with the **FORMAT** option:

SAMPLE 1 17
FORMAT(F4.0,3F6.1)
READ(11) YEAR CONSUME INCOME PRICE / FORMAT

To print all or some of these variables the **PRINT** command is used. The following output would result:


```
|_PRINT CONSUME PRICE
    CONSUME          PRICE
    99.20000        101.0000
    99.00000        100.1000
    100.0000        100.0000
    111.6000         90.60000
    122.2000         06.50000
    117.6000         89.70000
    121.1000         90.60000
    136.0000         82.80000
    154.2000         70.10000
    153.6000         65.40000
    158.5000         61.30000
    140.6000         62.50000
    136.2000         63.60000
    168.0000         52.60000
    154.3000         59.70000
    149.0000         59.50000
    165.5000         61.30000
```


```
|_PRINT YEAR INCOME / BEG=1 END=4
     YEAR            INCOME
    1923.000         96.70000
    1924.000         98.10000
    1925.000        100.0000
    1926.000        104.9000
```


The sample size can be reset as many times as desired within a run. The sample size in effect will be the one last specified. This allows extensive manipulation of data. For example, in the following SHAZAM output the sample size is set twice, first to read the entire data file with the **READ** command, and then to print a subset of observations with the **PRINT** command:

```
_SAMPLE 1 17
_READ(11) YEAR CONSUME INCOME PRICE
_PRINT YEAR CONSUME INCOME PRICE
    YEAR            CONSUME          INCOME             PRICE
  1923.000         99.20000        96.70000          101.0000
  1924.000         99.00000        98.10000          100.1000
  1925.000        100.0000        100.0000          100.0000
  1926.000        111.6000        104.9000           90.60000
  1927.000        122.2000        104.9000           86.50000
  1928.000        117.6000        109.5000           89.70000
  1929.000        121.1000        110.8000           90.60000
  1930.000        136.0000        112.3000           82.80000
  1931.000        154.2000        109.3000           70.10000
  1932.000        153.6000        105.3000           65.40000
  1933.000        158.5000        101.7000           61.30000
  1934.000        140.6000         95.40000          62.50000
  1935.000        136.2000         96.40000          63.60000
  1936.000        168.0000         97.60000          52.60000
  1937.000        154.3000        102.4000           59.70000
  1938.000        149.0000        101.6000           59.50000
  1939.000        165.5000        103.8000           61.30000

_SAMPLE 10 17
_PRINT YEAR CONSUME INCOME PRICE
    YEAR            CONSUME          INCOME             PRICE
  1932.000        153.6000        105.3000           65.40000
  1933.000        158.5000        101.7000           61.30000
  1934.000        140.6000         95.40000          62.50000
  1935.000        136.2000         96.40000          63.60000
  1936.000        168.0000         97.60000          52.60000
  1937.000        154.3000        102.4000           59.70000
  1938.000        149.0000        101.6000           59.50000
  1939.000        165.5000        103.8000           61.30000
```

An expanded form of the **SAMPLE** command can also be used to select portions from the larger sample. For example, to select observations 1 through 5 and 12 through 15, the following **SAMPLE** command would be used:

```
_SAMPLE 1 5 12 15
_PRINT YEAR CONSUME INCOME PRICE
    YEAR            CONSUME          INCOME             PRICE
  1923.000         99.20000        96.70000          101.0000
  1924.000         99.00000        98.10000          100.1000
  1925.000        100.0000        100.0000          100.0000
  1926.000        111.6000        104.9000           90.60000
  1927.000        122.2000        104.9000           86.50000
  1934.000        140.6000         95.40000          62.50000
  1935.000        136.2000         96.40000          63.60000
  1936.000        168.0000         97.60000          52.60000
  1937.000        154.3000        102.4000           59.70000
```

It is possible to read in data from more than one file in a single SHAZAM run. If, for example, the Textile data were divided into two portions, 1923-1930 and 1931-1939, and each portion were in a different file, SHAZAM could not only read in both data files, but could also combine the two files so the variables were complete. Since the maximum number of observations of a variable is set by the first **READ** command in the absence of a **SAMPLE** command, it is necessary to first **DIM**ension the size of the variables with the **DIM** command. The **DIM** command will reserve enough space for all the observations from both data files. In this example unit 11 is used for observations 1 to 8 and unit 12 is used for observations 9 to 17:

```
_DIM YEAR 17 CONSUME 17 INCOME 17 PRICE 17
_READ(11) YEAR CONSUME INCOME PRICE / BEG=1 END=8 LIST
    4 VARIABLES AND        8 OBSERVATIONS STARTING AT OBS      1
...SAMPLE RANGE IS NOW SET TO:          1        8
    1923.000        99.20000       96.70000       101.0000
    1924.000        99.00000       98.10000       100.1000
    1925.000        100.0000       100.0000       100.0000
    1926.000        111.6000       104.9000       90.60000
    1927.000        122.2000       104.9000       86.50000
    1928.000        117.6000       109.5000       89.70000
    1929.000        121.1000       110.8000       90.60000
    1930.000        136.0000       112.3000       82.80000
_READ(12) YEAR CONSUME INCOME PRICE / BEG=9 END=17 LIST
    4 VARIABLES AND        9 OBSERVATIONS STARTING AT OBS      9
    1931.000        154.2000       109.3000       70.10000
    1932.000        153.6000       105.3000       65.40000
    1933.000        158.5000       101.7000       61.30000
    1934.000        140.6000       95.40000       62.50000
    1935.000        136.2000       96.40000       63.60000
    1936.000        168.0000       97.60000       52.60000
    1937.000        154.3000       102.4000       59.70000
    1938.000        149.0000       101.6000       59.50000
    1939.000        165.5000       103.8000       61.30000
_SAMPLE 1 17
_PRINT YEAR CONSUME INCOME PRICE
      YEAR          CONSUME          INCOME          PRICE
    1923.000        99.20000       96.70000       101.0000
    1924.000        99.00000       98.10000       100.1000
    1925.000        100.0000       100.0000       100.0000
    1926.000        111.6000       104.9000       90.60000
    1927.000        122.2000       104.9000       86.50000
    1928.000        117.6000       109.5000       89.70000
    1929.000        121.1000       110.8000       90.60000
    1930.000        136.0000       112.3000       82.80000
    1931.000        154.2000       109.3000       70.10000
    1932.000        153.6000       105.3000       65.40000
    1933.000        158.5000       101.7000       61.30000
    1934.000        140.6000       95.40000       62.50000
    1935.000        136.2000       96.40000       63.60000
    1936.000        168.0000       97.60000       52.60000
    1937.000        154.3000       102.4000       59.70000
    1938.000        149.0000       101.6000       59.50000
    1939.000        165.5000       103.8000       61.30000
```

In the above example, the **DIM** command set the length of all four variables to 17. (For further details on the **DIM** command see the chapter *MISCELLANEOUS COMMANDS AND INFORMATION*.) Then, using the **BEG=** and **END=** options, the variables were read in from two data files, one on unit 11 and the other on unit 12. (See *HOW TO RUN SHAZAM* for information on assigning files to unit numbers. On many systems, files can be assigned to unit numbers using the **FILE** command described in the chapter *MISCELLANEOUS COMMANDS AND INFORMATION*.)

When the data is typed variable by variable the **BYVAR** option is needed. The following is a listing of a file which contains the same data as that used above, but it is typed variable by variable rather than observation by observation:

```
 1923   1924   1925   1926   1927   1928   1929   1930
 1931   1932   1933   1934   1935   1936   1937   1938   1939
 99.2   99.0  100.0  111.6  122.2  117.6  121.1  136.0
154.2  153.6  158.5  140.6  136.2  168.0  154.3  149.0  165.5
 96.7   98.1  100.0  104.9  104.9  109.5  110.8  112.3
109.3  105.3  101.7   95.4   96.4   97.6  102.4  101.6  103.8
101.0  100.1  100.0   90.6   86.5   89.7   90.6   82.8
 70.1   65.4   61.3   62.5   63.6   52.6   59.7   59.5   61.3
```

Each variable may extend over more than one line. However, *new variables must start on a new line*. With the **BYVAR** option the **SAMPLE** command is especially important. SHAZAM needs the sample size in order to know when to stop reading observations into the first variable listed on the **READ** command and start reading them into the second, etc.

To input this data a **SAMPLE** command and a **READ** command with the **BYVAR** option are needed:

SAMPLE 1 17
READ(11) YEAR CONSUME INCOME PRICE / BYVAR

Alternatively, this same data could be read by using a FORTRAN format statement. The appropriate commands are a **FORMAT** command and a **READ** command with the **FORMAT** and **BYVAR** options:

SAMPLE 1 17
FORMAT(8F6.0/9F6.0)
READ(11) YEAR CONSUME INCOME PRICE / FORMAT BYVAR

It is also possible to use the **BYVAR** option on the **PRINT** command. The variables will be printed horizontally by variable rather than in columns:

```
|_PRINT YEAR CONSUME / BYVAR
 YEAR
   1923.0    1924.0    1925.0    1926.0    1927.0    1928.0    1929.0    1930.0
   1931.0    1932.0    1933.0    1934.0    1935.0    1936.0    1937.0    1938.0
   1939.0
```

CONSUME
```
   99.20      99.00     100.00     111.60     122.20     117.60     121.10     136.00
  154.20     153.60     158.50     140.60     136.20     168.00     154.30     149.00
  165.50
```

It is often useful to read data as a matrix. To read in a matrix, the **ROWS=** and **COLS=** options are needed on the **READ** command. If the original Textile data were all to be placed in a single matrix named W, the appropriate **READ** command would be:

READ(4) W / ROWS=17 COLS=4

To print W the **PRINT** command is used:

```
|_PRINT W
W
     17 BY       4 MATRIX
   1923.000      99.20000      96.70000      101.0000
   1924.000      99.00000      98.10000      100.1000
   1925.000     100.0000      100.0000      100.0000
   1926.000     111.6000      104.9000       90.60000
   1927.000     122.2000      104.9000       86.50000
   1928.000     117.6000      109.5000       89.70000
   1929.000     121.1000      110.8000       90.60000
   1930.000     136.0000      112.3000       82.80000
   1931.000     154.2000      109.3000       70.10000
   1932.000     153.6000      105.3000       65.40000
   1933.000     158.5000      101.7000       61.30000
   1934.000     140.6000       95.40000      62.50000
   1935.000     136.2000       96.40000      63.60000
   1936.000     168.0000       97.60000      52.60000
   1937.000     154.3000      102.4000       59.70000
   1938.000     149.0000      101.6000       59.50000
   1939.000     165.5000      103.8000       61.30000
```

It is also possible to print only one column of the matrix using the **PRINT** command with the column number of the matrix specified after a colon (:) as follows:

```
|_PRINT W:4
   101.0000    100.1000    100.0000    90.60000    86.50000
   89.70000    90.60000    82.80000    70.10000    65.40000
   61.30000    62.50000    63.60000    52.60000    59.70000
   59.50000    61.30000
```

The above **PRINT** command prints the data occupying the fourth column of the matrix W.

It is possible to read character variables in SHAZAM, using **FORMAT** commands and options. The following example illustrates how to read the names of nine of the provinces of Canada into a variable called PROVINCE and shows that it is possible to read non-character variables on the same **READ** command when the appropriate **FORMAT** is specified (i.e. using a FORTRAN A format to read characters). The data is the unemployment and vacancy rates of each province for January, 1976 as provided by Statistics Canada. Data on the 10th province, Prince Edward Island, was not available.

```
|_SAMPLE 1 9
|_FORMAT(A8,2F5.1)
|_READ PROVINCE UR VR / FORMAT
NEWFOUND    14.9  4.0
NOVA SCO     9.1  5.0
NEW BRUN    12.2  7.0
QUEBEC       9.1  6.0
ONTARIO      7.1  5.0
MANITOBA     6.7  8.0
SASKATCH     4.8  8.0
ALBERTA      5.3 11.0
BRITISH     10.0  4.0
|_PRINT UR VR
      UR                VR
  14.90000          4.000000
  9.100000          5.000000
  12.20000          7.000000
  9.100000          6.000000
  7.100000          5.000000
  6.700000          8.000000
  4.800000          8.000000
  5.300000          11.00000
  10.00000          4.000000
|_FORMAT(1X,A8)
|_PRINT PROVINCE / FORMAT
PROVINCE
NEWFOUND
NOVA SCO
NEW BRUN
QUEBEC
ONTARIO
MANITOBA
SASKATCH
ALBERTA
BRITISH
```

Note, in the above example, that since FORTRAN does not permit printing in column 1, two different **FORMAT** commands are needed, one for the **READ** command and one for the **PRINT** command. Note also that all of the variables PROVINCE, UR and UV could have been printed on the same **PRINT** command if a **FORMAT** command of the form **FORMAT(1X,A8,2F5.1)** had been specified.

Each observation of a character variable may only be 8 characters long, but if the user wishes to have longer character variables, more than one variable name should be specified on the **READ** command and a **FORMAT** command specifying the appropriate A format should also appear. For example, if each observation were to be at most 16 characters long, the appropriate **FORMAT** command would be **FORMAT(2A8)** and 2 variables would be read in on the **READ** command and printed out on the **PRINT** command. The following example illustrates this procedure for the case where 16 characters are permitted:

```
|_SAMPLE 1 9
|_FORMAT(2A8,2F5.1)
|_READ PROV1 PROV2 UR UV / FORMAT
NEWFOUNDLAND      14.9  4.0
NOVA SCOTIA        9.1  5.0
NEW BRUNSWICK     12.2  7.0
QUEBEC             9.1  6.0
ONTARIO            7.1  5.0
MANITOBA           6.7  8.0
SASKATCHEWAN       4.8  8.0
ALBERTA            5.3 11.0
BRITISH COLUMBIA  10.0  4.0


|_FORMAT(1X,2A8,2F5.1)
|_PRINT PROV1 PROV2 UR VR / FORMAT NONAMES
NEWFOUNDLAND      14.9  4.0
NOVA SCOTIA        9.1  5.0
NEW BRUNSWICK     12.2  7.0
QUEBEC             9.1  6.0
ONTARIO            7.1  5.0
MANITOBA           6 7  8.0
SASKATCHEWAN       4.8  8.0
ALBERTA            5.3 11.0
BRITISH COLUMBIA  10.0  4.0
```

Note that some computers will not permit SHAZAM character variables. If this is the case, error messages may appear.

A. *USING THE CITIBASE DATABANK*

The **RESTORE** command is used to restore data from a Databank. At present only the CITIBASE Databank is supported. To use it, the CITIBASE Databank must be available at your installation in its original form as distributed by Citibank. Since this is often on a tape, you must mount the tape and assign it to a FORTRAN unit number from 11-49. You must specify the option **CITIBASE** and the UNIT= number on the **RESTORE** command. In addition you must use the **TIME** command to set the date since the date form of the **SAMPLE** command will be used, (see the chapter *MISCELLANEOUS COMMANDS AND INFORMATION*). In general, the format of the **RESTORE** command is:

RESTORE *vars* / **CITIBASE UNIT**=*unit*

The names on the **RESTORE** command must be CITIBASE names. In the following example it is assumed that the CITIBASE tape has been assigned to unit 11 with a system command and the user wishes to read the annual variables VAR1, VAR2 and VAR3 from the CITIBASE tape for the years 1960 to 1980.

SAMPLE 1 21
TIME 1960 1
SAMPLE 1960.0 1980.0
RESTORE VAR1 VAR2 VAR3 / CITIBASE UNIT = 11
PRINT VAR1 VAR2 VAR3

Since it is very expensive to restore data from the CITIBASE tape you should check your commands carefully. In particular, you should make sure you have typed the variable names correctly or a search of the entire tape will be made looking for a variable that probably does not exist. Once the data has been restored you may want to use the SHAZAM **WRITE** command to put the data in a file for later use.

4. DESCRIPTIVE STATISTICS

"Jupiter's moons are invisible to the naked eye and therefore can have no influence on the earth, and therefore would be useless, and therefore do not exist."

Francisco Sizzi
Professor of Astronomy, 1610

The **STAT** command will print means, standard deviations, variances, minimums and maximums for the variables listed. It can also be used to perform Analysis of Variance, Bartlett's Test and to compute crossproducts, covariances, correlations, medians, modes, frequencies and rank correlation coefficients.

The format of the **STAT** command is:

STAT *vars / options*

where *vars* is a list of variable names and *options* is a list of desired options.

The following options are available on the **STAT** command:

ALL
Statistics are computed for **ALL** the variables in the data. Therefore, no variable names need be specified.

ANOVA
Prints an **AN**alysis **OF VA**riance table and an F-value that tests the null hypothesis that the means of all the variables listed on the given **STAT** command are the same.

BARTLETT
Performs **BARTLETT**'s Homogeneity of Variance Test to test the hypothesis that the variances of all the variables listed are equal.

DN
This option uses N (number of observations) as a divisor rather than N-1 when computing variances and covariances.

MATRIX
Any **MATRIX** or matrices contained in the list *vars* will be treated as a single variable if this option is used. If this option is not specified SHAZAM will treat each column of the matrix as a separate variable.

MAX
Does all of **PCOR, PCOV, PCP, PCPDEV** and **PRANKCOR**.

PCOR
Prints a **COR**relation matrix of the variables listed.

PCOV	Prints a **COV**ariance matrix of the variables listed.
PCP	Prints a Cross**P**roduct matrix of the variables listed.
PCPDEV	Prints a Cross**P**roduct matrix of the variables listed in **DEV**iations from the means.
PFREQ	Prints table of **FREQ**uencies of occurrence for each observed value in the data. Also prints Median and Mode. This option is **not** recommended for large sample sizes with many different possible values since pages and pages of output would result.
PMEDIAN	Prints **MEDIAN** and Mode for each variable. This option could be expensive when the sample size is large.
PRANKCOR	Prints a matrix of Spearman's **RANK COR**relation coefficients.
BEG = **END =**	Specifies the **BEG**inning and **END** observations to be used in the **STAT** command.
COR =	Stores the **COR**relation matrix in the variable specified.
COV =	Stores the **COV**ariance matrix in the variable specified.
CP =	Stores the Cross**P**roduct matrix in the variable specified.
CPDEV =	Stores the Cross**P**roduct matrix in **DEV**iations from the mean in the variable specified.
MAXIM =	Stores the **MAXIM**ums as a vector in the variable specified.
MEAN =	Stores the **MEAN**s as a vector in the variable specified.
MINIM =	Stores the **MINIM**ums as a vector in the variable specified.
RANKCOR =	Stores the **RANK COR**relation matrix in the variable specified.
STDEV =	Stores the **ST**andard **DEV**iations as a vector in the variable specified.

SUMS=   Stores the sum of each variable as a vector in the variable specified.

VAR=   Stores the **VAR**iances as a vector in the variable specified.

WEIGHT=   Specifies a variable to be used as **WEIGHT**s if weighted descriptive statistics are desired.

The following examples using Theil's [1971, p.102] Textile data illustrate some options on the **STAT** command. First, a **STAT** command with the **PCOR** and the **PCOV** options:

```
|_STAT CONSUME INCOME PRICE / PCOR PCOV
NAME     N    MEAN     ST. DEV     VARIANCE    MINIMUM    MAXIMUM
CONSUME  17   134.51   23.577      555.89      99.000     168.00
INCOME   17   102.98   5.3010      28.100      95.400     112.30
PRICE    17   76.312   16.866      284.47      52.600     101.00

CORRELATION MATRIX OF VARIABLES -      17 OBSERVATIONS
CONSUME    1.0000
INCOME     0.61769E-01        1.0000
PRICE     -0.94664            0.17885         1.0000
           CONSUME            INCOME          PRICE

COVARIANCE MATRIX OF VARIABLES -       17 OBSERVATIONS
CONSUME    555.89
INCOME     7.7201             28.100
PRICE     -376.44             15.990          284.47
           CONSUME.           INCOME          PRICE
```

The next example shows the use of the **STDEV=** and **COR=** options. The standard deviations of the variables CONSUME, INCOME and PRICE will be stored in a variable called SD, and will therefore be available for future computations. The correlation matrix will be stored in a variable called CMATRIX and will also be available for future computations:

```
|_STAT CONSUME INCOME PRICE / STDEV=SD COR=CMATRIX
NAME     N    MEAN     ST. DEV     VARIANCE    MINIMUM    MAXIMUM
CONSUME  17   134.51   23.577      555.89      99.000     168.00
INCOME   17   102.98   5.3010      28.100      95.400     112.30
PRICE    17   76.312   16.866      284.47      52.600     101.00
|_PRINT SD CMATRIX
SD
   23.57733        5.300971       16.86623

CMATRIX
   1.000000
   0.6176940E-01    1.000000
  -0.9466377        0.1788467      1.000000
```

It is important to note that options beginning with **P** will merely print the matrix or vector in question, whereas options ending in an equal sign (=) will store the matrix or vector in the variable specified.

The next example uses data from Pindyck and Rubinfeld [1980, p.144]. Each variable contains data for housing expenditure for five families with identical incomes. The income levels are 5, 10, 15 and 20 thousand dollars and will be identified in the following examples by the variable names A, B, C and D. The housing expenditure data corresponding to these levels is:

```
1.8 3.0 4.2 4.8
2.0 3.2 4.2 5.0
2.0 3.5 4.5 5.7
2.0 3.5 4.8 6.0
2.1 3.6 5.0 6.2
```

The following is an example of the use of the **ANOVA** and **BARTLETT** options on the **STAT** command:

```
_SAMPLE 1 5
_READ(11) A B C D
_STAT A B C D / ANOVA BARTLETT
NAME     N   MEAN    ST. DEV   VARIANCE       MINIMUM    MAXIMUM
A        5   1.9800  0.10954   0.12000E-01    1.8000     2.1000
B        5   3.3600  0.25100   0.63000E-01    3.0000     3.6000
C        5   4.5400  0.35777   0.12800        4.2000     5.0000
D        5   5.5400  0.61482   0.37800        4.8000     6.2000
BARTLETTS HOMOGENEITY OF VARIANCE TEST =      9.0525
      APPROXIMATELY CHI-SQUARE WITH    3 DEGREES OF FREEDOM

                   ANALYSIS OF VARIANCE
                 SS         DF        MS            F
BETWEEN       35.346       3.       11.782       81.114
WITHIN         2.3240     16.        0.14525
TOTAL         37.670      19.        1.9826
```

In the following example the housing expenditure data is read in as a matrix, M. If the **MATRIX** option is used on the **STAT** command with M, the matrix M will be treated as a single variable:

```
_SAMPLE 1 5
_READ(11) M / ROWS=5 COLS=4
      5 ROWS AND          4 COLUMNS, BEGINNING AT ROW      1
_STAT M / MATRIX
NAME     N   MEAN    ST. DEV   VARIANCE    MINIMUM    MAXIMUM
M       20   3.8550  1.4081    1.9826      1.8000     6.2000
```

However, if the **MATRIX** option is not specified, each column of M will be treated as a single variable:

DESCRIPTIVE STATISTICS

```
|_STAT M
```

NAME	N	MEAN	ST. DEV	VARIANCE	MINIMUM	MAXIMUM
...NOTE...TREATING COLUMNS OF M				AS VARIABLES		
M	5	1.9800	0.10954	0.12000E-01	1.8000	2.1000
M	5	3.3600	0.25100	0.63000E-01	3.0000	3.6000
M	5	4.5400	0.35777	0.12800	4.2000	5.0000
M	5	5.5400	0.61482	0.37800	4.8000	6.2000

5. PLOTS

"When the President does it, that means it is not illegal."

Richard Nixon
Former U.S. President, 1977

The **PLOT** command will plot variables. In general, the format of the **PLOT** command is:

PLOT *depvars indep / options*

where *depvars* is one or more dependent variables to be plotted against a single independent variable, *indep*, and *options* is a list of desired options.

The available options on the **PLOT** command are:

ALTERNATE   This option alternates the symbols "X" and "O" in plotting columns of the histogram when the **HISTO** option is used. It is especially useful with the **GROUPS=** option described below.

GOAWAY   This option may be used with the **GRAPHICS** option on the Macintosh if you wish the PLOT window to go away after the plot appears on the screen. Alternatively, you can click the GO AWAY box in the upper left corner. The option is in effect except in **TALK** mode. It can be turned off with **NOGOAWAY**.

GRAPHICS /   IBM PC Compatible.
EGA /   These options describe the type of graphics on your system. The
HERCULES /   **TOSHIBA** option is used only for the TOSHIBA Plasma screen. If you do
TOSHIBA   not have an EGA, HERCULES or TOSHIBA graphics monitor try using the **GRAPHICS** options which can be used for CGA monitors. Further details are in the chapter *HOW TO RUN SHAZAM ON THE IBM PC*. See also the **PAUSE** and **PRINT** options discussed below.

GRAPHICS   Macintosh.
This option will display a separate *PLOT* window for the graphics plot. After the plot is displayed the window can be removed by clicking the *GO-AWAY* box in the upper left corner. For further details see the *HOW TO RUN SHAZAM ON THE MACINTOSH* chapter. See also the **GOAWAY** and **PAUSE** options.

GRAPHICS   Available for some mainframe computers.
The option will create a Graphics Plot file on Unit 9 to be sent to the system plotter. The **HOLD, NOBLANK, HISTO, RANGE** and **SYMBOL** options are not used, but the following new options are available: **LINE, LINEONLY** and **DASH**. These options draw a line connecting the symbols, omitting the symbols, and use dashed lines respectively.

HISTO   Plots **HISTO**grams for the variables specified on the **PLOT** command. The histogram could be centered around the mean with a scale of 3 standard deviations on either side of the mean, or, with the use of the **RANGE** option described below, the entire range of the variable(s) could be plotted. The first method is the default and is useful if there are a few outliers which would complicate the scaling of the histogram. However, if all the data must be plotted, the **RANGE** option should be used to get the entire range. A separate histogram is done for each variable in the list. Each histogram takes one page of computer output. If **NOWIDE** is specified the histogram will be half the regular size. See also the **ALTERNATE, RANGE** and **GROUPS=** options.

HOLD   **HOLD**s the printing of the plot. The contents of this plot will be saved for the next **PLOT** command. At that time the plot will be blanked out unless the **NOBLANK** option is used.

LINE   This option is used with the **GRAPHICS, EGA, HERCULES** or **TOSHIBA** option to draw a line connecting the data points and plot a symbol at each point.

LINEONLY   This option is used with the **GRAPHICS, EGA, HERCULES** or **TOSHIBA** option to only draw a line connecting the data points. No symbols at the data points will be plotted.

NOBLANK   Prevents the plot from being initialized with blanks, to allow the plot to be imposed on the plot previously specified with the **HOLD** option. The **HOLD** and **NOBLANK** options would be used if, for example, a plot with different symbols for each part of the sample were desired.

NOPRETTY   SHAZAM attempts to make pretty intervals on the axes by checking the range of the data. This usually works, but sometimes the labels are not acceptable. The **NOPRETTY** option will tell SHAZAM not to attempt to make the axes pretty and just use the range of the data directly.

PAUSE   This option is used with one of the **GRAPHICS** options on IBM-PC Compatible or Macintosh computers to temporarily stop the screen after a graphics plot appears so it can be examined. To resume the run, simply press the RETURN key. This option is automatically in effect in **TALK** mode.

PRINT

This option is used with one of the **GRAPHICS** options on IBM-PC Compatible computers to **PRINT** the plot on a printer. It may not work on some printers. An alternative method is descriped in the chapter *HOW TO RUN SHAZAM ON THE IBM PC*.

RANGE

This option will use the entire **RANGE** of the data for plotting the histogram when the **HISTO** option is used.

SAME /
NOSAME

Plots *depvars* against the *indep* on the **SAME** plot. The two relationships are distinguishable by their differing point symbols. See the **SYMBOL=** option for further details. No more than 8 dependent variables should be plotted against the independent variable on the same plot. The default is **SAME**.

TIME

Plots the listed *depvars* sequentially against **TIME**. In this case, *indep* is not specified.

WIDE /
NOWIDE

NOWIDE reduces the size of the plot in the printed output. All of the reduced plot can be seen on a terminal screen as it takes up less than 80 columns. The default value is explained in the chapter *SET AND DISPLAY*.

BEG=
END=

Sets a sample range for the particular **PLOT** command. This sample size is in effect only for the **PLOT** command with this option. If these options are not specified, the sample range for the current **SAMPLE** command is used.

GROUPS=

When the **HISTO** option is used SHAZAM normally places data into 6 groups. This option can be used to specify up to 60 groups. The values allowed for **GROUPS=** are 2,3,4,5,6,10,12,15,30 or 60.

SYMBOL=

With this option the user can specify the **SYMBOL**s to be used. The default symbols, in order, are * + 0 % $ # ! @.

XMIN=
XMAX=
YMIN=
YMAX=

Specifies the desired range for either the **X** or **Y** axis. If these are not specified the computed **MIN**imum and **MAX**imum for the variables will be used.

The following is an example of the **PLOT** command using Theil's [1971, p.102] Textile data. Each of the variables CONSUME, INCOME and PRICE are plotted against time:

```
|_PLOT CONSUME INCOME PRICE / TIME SAME
         17 OBSERVATIONS
```

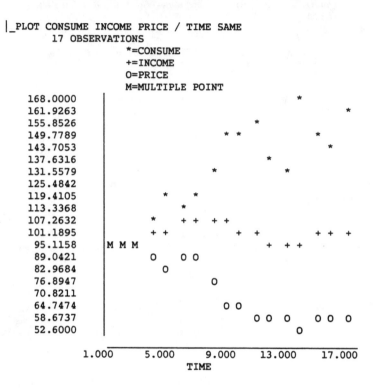

If a **GRAPHICS** option is used on the above **PLOT** command a plot like the following will be obtained:

|_PLOT CONSUME INCOME PRICE / TIME SAME GRAPHICS LINEONLY

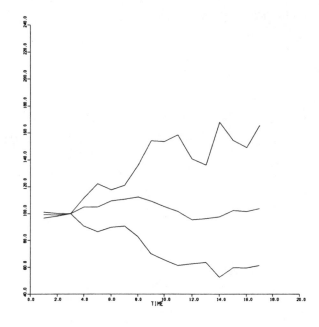

The following example shows the use of the **HOLD** and **NOBLANK** options:

```
|_PLOT CONSUME INCOME / SAME BEG=1 END=9 SYMBOL=X HOLD
         9 OBSERVATIONS
                  X=CONSUME
                  M=MULTIPLE POINT

|_PLOT CONSUME INCOME / BEG=10 END=17 SYMBOL=* NOBLANK
         8 OBSERVATIONS
                  *=CONSUME
                  M=MULTIPLE POINT
    168.0000    |         *                     X
    166.3263    |
    164.6526    |                                 *
    162.9789    |
    161.3053    |
    159.6316    |
    157.9579    |                        *
    156.2842    |                                     X
    154.6105    |
    152.9368    |                     *           *
    151.2632    |
    149.5895    |
    147.9158    |            X    *        X
    146.2421    |                       X
    144.5684    |
    142.8947    |            X
    141.2211    |
    139.5474    |*
    137.8737    |
    136.2000    |X   M    X
                ─────────────────────────────────────────

              95.400    97.875    100.350   102.825   105.300

                               INCOME
```

The **HOLD** and **NOBLANK** options may be used in this way if, for example, the user wished to see if the relationship between two variables changed during a given sample period. Of course, this would only be a visual test of the hypothesis that the relationship had changed and would in no way be conclusive.

6. GENERATING VARIABLES

"The government are very keen on amassing statistics. They collect them, add them, raise them to the nth power, take the cube root and prepare wonderful diagrams. But you must never forget that everyone of these figures comes in the first instance from the village watchman, who just puts down what he damn well pleases."

Anonymous, Quoted in Sir Josiah Stamp,
Some Economic Factors in Modern Life

A. *THE* GENR *COMMAND*

The **GENR** command will create new variables from old ones and do a variety of data transformations. The **SAMPLE** command defines the observation range used in **GENR** commands.

In general, the format of the **GENR** command is:

GENR *newvar* = *equation*

where *newvar* is the name of the new variable to be created and *equation* is any arithmetic equation which involves variables, constants and mathematical functions.

The following mathematical operators may be used:

Priority-level	Operator
1	- (unary)
1	unary functions (see list below)
2	** (exponentiation)
3	* , / (multiplication, division)
4	+ , - (addition, subtraction)
5	.EQ. .NE. .GE. .GT. .LE. .LT. (relations)
6	.NOT. (logical operator)
7	.AND. (logical operator)
8	.OR. (logical operator)

The available unary functions are:

ABS(x)	absolute value
DUM(x)	dummy variable generator
EXP(x)	e^x
INT(x)	integer truncation
LAG(x)	lag a variable one time period
LAG(x,n)	lag a variable n time periods
LGAM(x)	log gamma function, $\log(\Gamma(x))$
LOG(x)	natural logs
MAX(x,y)	maximum of two variables
MIN(x,y)	minimum of two variables
MOD(x,y)	Modulo arithmetic, remainder of x/y
NCDF(x)	normal cumulative density function
NOR(x)	normal random number with standard deviation x
SAMP(x)	draws a random observation from the variable x
SIN(x)	sine
SQRT(x)	square roots
SUM(x)	cumulative sum of variable x starting at observation 1
SUM(x,n)	sum of n observations on variable x
TIME(x)	time index plus x
UNI(x)	uniform random number with range (0,x)

It is possible to select a particular element of a vector by putting that element number in parentheses.

GENR *newvar=oldvar(element)*

For instance, to generate a variable that takes on the value of the third observation of the variable A, the following command is appropriate:

GENR ATHREE = A(3)

The following example illustrates the use of **GENR** commands for a case where Theil's [1971, p.102] Textile data has been read in and a series of new variables needs to be created:

SAMPLE 1 17
READ(11) YEAR CONSUME INCOME PRICE
GENR PRICE = PRICE/100
GENR PCCONS = (CONSUME-LAG(CONSUME))/LAG(CONSUME)
GENR T = TIME(0)

The first **GENR** command is used to change the units of the variable PRICE. The second **GENR** command is used to generate a variable for the percentage change of consumption from the preceding year. Note that observation 1 of PCCONS will not be defined properly since LAG(CONSUME) does not exist for the first observation. A warning message will be printed. The third **GENR** command is used to generate a variable from 1 to 17.

The order of operations of mathematical expressions in SHAZAM conforms to the usual conventions, i.e. first, priority 1, then priority 2, etc. Among operations of the same priority, expressions are executed from left to right. To avoid confusion use as many levels of parentheses as desired.

The LAG(x,n) function will lag the variable x, n times. When only one lag is desired the n can be left off the function (i.e. LAG(x)). The first n observations are undefined when the LAG(x,n) function is used. SHAZAM replaces these observations with zeros. It is not necessary to change the sample size to use the LAG(x,n) function, but warning messages will appear whenever this function is used without proper sample commands. In fact, changing the sample size before generating new variables can cause further sample size problems. However, the sample size should be changed to start at n+1 before estimation. The LAG(x,n) function must be used only on predefined variables and not on functions of variables. So, for example:

GENR X = LAG(SQRT(Y),3)

will result in an error message. To avoid this error two **GENR** commands can be used:

GENR Z = LAG(Y,3)
GENR X = SQRT(Z)

or one:

GENR X = SQRT(LAG(Y,3))

It is possible to lead future variables by using a negative value for n on the LAG(x,n) function. For example:

GENR XT = LAG(X,-1)

Note that in this case the final observation of XT may not be defined.

The TIME(x) function creates a time index. In the example on the second page of this chapter, the TIME(0) function creates a time index so that the first observation is equal to 1 and the rest are consecutively numbered. Similarly, a TIME(1929) function would create a time index so that the first observation is equal to 1930. See the **TIME** command in the chapter *MISCELLANEOUS COMMANDS AND INFORMATION* for an alternate way to create a **TIME** index.

The SUM(x) function creates a cumulative sum of the variable x. So, SUM(2) creates a variable that takes on the values 2,4,6,... This function can be used to create a capital stock series from a net investment series. For example, if the initial Capital Stock is 25.3:

GENR KAPITAL = 25.3 + SUM(INVEST)

The SUM(x,n) function will sum up n successive observations on the variable x. For example, it can be used to convert monthly data to quarterly or yearly data, as in the following case:

SAMPLE 1 10
GENR YCPI = (SUM(MCPI,12))/12

SHAZAM takes the sum of the first 12 observations from MCPI, divides them by 12 and makes this number the first observation in the new variable YCPI. It continues this for subsequent observations in MCPI, until it has created 10 observations for YCPI. The **SAMPLE** command which precedes the **GENR** statement tells SHAZAM the size of the new variable. This is only necessary if the new variable is to have a different length than that specified by the current **SAMPLE** command.

The DUM(x) function will create a dummy variable equal to one when x is positive and equal to zero for observations when x is not positive. For example:

GENR D1 = DUM(3)
GENR D2 = DUM(TIME(0)-6)
GENR D3 = DUM(CONSUME-INCOME-1)

The first of these examples of the DUM(x) function creates a dummy variable that is always equal to one. The second creates a dummy variable that is equal to zero for the first 6 observations and equal to one otherwise. The last example uses the variables CONSUME and INCOME from Theil's [1971, p.102] Textile data and creates a dummy variable equal to one when the relation inside parentheses is positive or zero and equal to zero otherwise. It is also possible to create a matrix of seasonal dummy variables. For information on this procedure, see the chapter *MATRIX MANIPULATION*.

The NCDF(x) function returns the cumulative normal probability of a standard normal variable. The probability will be in the zero-one range. In the following example the use of the NCDF(x) function is illustrated:

```
_SAMPLE 1 21
_GENR Z=(TIME(0)-1)/10
_GENR P=NCDF(Z)
_PRINT Z P
       Z                 P
     0.0           0.5000000
     0.1000000     0.5398278
     0.2000000     0.5792597
     0.3000000     0.6179114
     0.4000000     0.6554217
     0.5000000     0.6914625
     0.6000000     0.7257469
     0.7000000     0.7580363
     0.8000000     0.7881446
     0.9000000     0.8159399
     1.000000      0.8413447
     1.100000      0.8643339
```

1.200000	0.8849303
1.300000	0.9031995
1.400000	0.9192433
1.500000	0.9331928
1.600000	0.9452007
1.700000	0.9554345
1.800000	0.9640697
1.900000	0.9712834
2.000000	0.9772499

In this example, Z is generated to take on the values 0 to 2.0. Then, the NCDF(x) function is used to generate the cumulative normal probability for Z.

If **GENR** commands are used to generate random variables, the random number generators are usually initialized by the system clock. Users can generate all their data if they have none to be read in. In this case, the user specifies the number of observations to be generated on the **SAMPLE** command. For example:

SAMPLE 1 30
GENR X1 = UNI(2)
GENR X2 = 5 + NOR(1)
GENR CHI3 = NOR(1)**2 + NOR(1)**2 + NOR(1)**2
GENR CHI5 = NOR(1)**2 + NOR(1)**2 + NOR(1)**2 + NOR(1)**2 + NOR(1)**2
GENR F35 = (CHI3/3)/(CHI5/5)

The command **SET RANFIX** (described in the chapter *SET AND DISPLAY*) typed before the **GENR** statement will prevent the random number generator from being set by the system clock. In this example all of the data is generated internally. Note that CHI3 and CHI5 have Chi-square distributions and that F35 has an F-distribution with 3 and 5 degrees of freedom. Note also that when the data is generated internally a sample size must be specified with the **SAMPLE** command, otherwise SHAZAM will not know how many observations to generate.

All of the following FORTRAN logical relations are available for use in **GENR** commands:

.EQ., .NE., .GE., .GT., .LE., .LT., .AND., .OR., .NOT..

A value of 1 is generated if an expression is true, and a value of 0 if it is false. Parentheses should be used to ensure the correct order of processing. For example:

GENR X5 = (X1.EQ.X2)
GENR X6 = (X1.LE.X2).OR.(X3.GT.0.5)
GENR X7 = (TIME(0).EQ.18)
GENR X8 = (UNI(1).LE.0.6)
GENR X1 = (X1.GE.0)*X1

The first two examples create dummy variables equal to 1 if the condition is met, and 0 otherwise. The third example creates a dummy variable equal to 1 for observation 18 only. The fourth example creates a binomial random variable from the uniform random number generator. The variable will take on a value of 1 for approximately 60% of the observations and a value of 0 for the rest. Of course, the probabilities are true only for the population and may differ for any sample. The last example will set all negative values of X1 to 0. Note that the old X1 is replaced by the new X1.

The SAMP(x) function can be used to draw a sample (with replacement) from another variable. For example, the variable BIGX might have 100 observations and a new variable of 20 random observations is desired.

SAMPLE 1 20
GENR NEWX = SAMP(BIGX)

This function is quite useful for bootstrapping experiments. See for example Freedman and Peters [1984] and the example in the chapter *PROGRAMMING IN SHAZAM*.

The LGAM(x) function is used to compute the log of the mathematical Gamma function $\Gamma(x)$ which is used in a number of probability distributions, including the Gamma, Chi-square and F distributions.

The MOD(x,y) function is used to compute the remainder of a division. For example: $MOD(15,4) = 3$.

B. *THE* GEN1 *COMMAND*

The **GEN1** command may be used to generate a constant. The **GEN1** command is equivalent to using both a **SAMPLE 1 1** command and a **GENR** command to generate a variable with only one observation. It is faster because it removes the need for the **SAMPLE 1 1** command. **SKIPIF** commands do not affect the **GEN1** command (see Section D of this chapter).

The format of the **GEN1** command is:

GEN1 *equation*

For example:

GEN1 NOB = $N

would save the value of the number of observations from a previous **OLS** regression in the variable NOB. See the chapter *ORDINARY LEAST SQUARES* for a description of the temporary variable $N.

C. *THE* IF *COMMAND*

The **IF** command is a conditional **GENR** command. The format of the **IF** command is:

IF(*expression*)

where *expression* is an expression in parentheses to be evaluated. If the expression is true or positive, the remainder of the **IF** command is executed. For example:

IF(X1.GE.0)X4 = SQRT(X1)
IF(2*X2/6)X2 = X2 + 12
IF(X2)X3 = X2

Note that some observations for a variable may not be defined if the **IF** condition is not true. In this case, the variable will be set to zero when the variable is initially created. For example, for the first **IF** command shown above, the variable X4 is undefined when X1 is less than zero and is thus equal to zero for these observations.

The **IF** command can also be used to conditionally execute any SHAZAM command on the line following the **IF** command. For example, if you only wanted to run an **AUTO** command when the Durbin-Watson Statistic for the **OLS** regression is less than 1.0, you would use:

OLS Y X / RSTAT
IF($DW .LT. 1.0)
AUTO Y X

If the **IF** command is used on a vector of observations (rather than a scalar as in the example above) the command following the **IF** command will be executed if the **IF** condition is true for *any* observation in the sample.

D. *THE* SKIPIF *COMMAND*

The **SKIPIF** command is used to specify conditions under which observations are to be skipped for most commands. (The observations will still be held in memory and in data files.) The format of the **SKIPIF** command is:

SKIPIF *(expression)*

where the *expression* may use arithmetic or logical operators such as those described for **GENR** and **IF** commands. The observation will be skipped if the value of the expression is positive; otherwise, the observation is retained.

Some examples of **SKIPIF** commands are:

SKIPIF (X3 + X4.EQ.X5)
SKIPIF (X3.GT.X12)
SKIPIF ((X4.EQ.0).OR.(X5.EQ.0))
SKIPIF (TIME(0).EQ.0)
SKIPIF (X1)
SKIPIF (LAG(X2 + 3)/12-X4)
SKIPIF (PROVINCE.EQ."MANITOBA")
SKIPIF (ABS(X3 + X4-X5).LE.0.0001)

The above examples should be fairly clear. Users should be aware that the test for equality between two numbers may sometimes fail due to rounding error in the computer. The first example above is a typical case where the problem might occur. The last example gives a possible remedy. Note that if characters are used in the command they must be enclosed in double quotes (") and only upper case comparisons are valid.

Users should take care to express **SKIPIF** commands accurately. A common error is to skip all the observations so that no data is left, for example:

SKIPIF (A.GE.0)
SKIPIF (A.LT.0)

If a large number of consecutive observations are to be skipped at the beginning or end of the data, it is more efficient to omit them with the **SAMPLE** command than with **SKIPIF** commands.

The **SKIPIF** command automatically creates a special variable called SKIP$ and initializes it to be zero for each observation. Then, for any observation to be skipped, SKIP$ is set equal to one.

Note that the SKIP$ variable is set at the time the **SKIPIF** command is executed. For example:

GENR A = 0
SKIPIF(A.EQ.1)
GENR A = 1
PRINT A

would not skip any observations since all observations in A were zero at the time the **SKIPIF** condition was evaluated.

Sometimes the entire data set is required including those observations skipped on **SKIPIF** commands. It is possible to temporarily turn off the **SKIPIF** commands that are in effect. This requires the **SET** command:

SET NOSKIP

To put the **SKIPIF**'s back in effect the **SET** command is again used:

SET SKIP

To permanently eliminate all **SKIPIF** commands in effect, the **DELETE** command is used:

DELETE SKIP$

If the **DELETE** command has been used to eliminate all **SKIPIF** commands it is not necessary to use the **SET SKIP** command to use the **SKIPIF** command again.

SKIPIF commands are in effect for **READ, WRITE** and **PRINT** commands except when a matrix is used or the **BYVAR** option is used.

The **SKIPIF** command will print out messages that tell you which observations have been skipped. If you have many skipped observations you could get many lines of messages. These warnings can be suppressed if you use the **SET NOWARNSKIP** command.

E. *THE* ENDIF *COMMAND*

The **ENDIF** command works like the **IF** command except that when the condition is true for any observation, execution is stopped. If the **ENDIF** command is used inside a **DO**-Loop, the **DO**-Loop is terminated and execution will continue at the statement after **ENDO**. See the chapter *MISCELLANEOUS COMMANDS AND INFORMATION* for information on **DO**-Loops.

The format of the **ENDIF** command is:

ENDIF(*expression*)

For example:

ENDIF(A.LT.0)

7. ORDINARY LEAST SQUARES

"Less is More."

Miës van der Rohe
Architect

The **OLS** command will perform Ordinary Least Squares regressions. In general, the format of the **OLS** command is:

OLS *depvar indeps* / *options*

where *depvar* is the dependent variable, *indeps* is a list of independent variables and *options* is a list of desired options. If any variable in the list of independent variables is a matrix, SHAZAM will treat each column as a separate explanatory variable. If no options are specified the **OLS** command produces R^2, adjusted R^2, the variance and standard error of the regression line, log of the likelihood function, coefficient estimates, standard errors, partial correlation coefficients, standardized coefficients, and elasticities at the sample means. The calculation of the elasticities assumes that all variables are untransformed unless either of the **LINLOG, LOGLIN** or **LOGLOG** options is specified. Users should be aware that the printed elasticities may not be correct if data has been transformed. If you do not understand this, you probably also do not understand the meaning of elasticity.

The available options on the **OLS** command are:

ANOVA
    Prints the ANalysis Of VAriance tables and the F-statistic for the test of no relationship. In some restricted models, the F-test from an **ANOVA** table is invalid. In these cases the F-statistic will not be printed, but may be obtained with the **TEST** command. This option is in effect automatically when running in BATCH mode. In TERMINAL or TALK mode, the **ANOVA** option must be specified if the table is desired. In BATCH mode, if the table is not needed it can be negated with the **NOANOVA** option.

DFBETAS
    This option is used with the **INFLUENCE** option if you also want the **DFBETAS** computed.

DLAG   This option is used when there is a **LAG**ged **D**ependent variable in the regression and Durbin's *h* statistic must be computed. The lagged dependent variable *must* be the first listed independent variable when this option is used. The *h* statistic is a test for autocorrelation when a lagged dependent variable is included in the regression. It is useful since the Durbin-Watson statistic is not valid in such situations. Durbin's *h* statistic cannot always be computed since the square root of a negative number may be required. In such cases, the *h* statistic will neither be computed nor printed. It is essential to remember that when lagged variables have been generated a **SAMPLE** command must be included to delete the beginning observations.

DN   This option will compute the estimated variance of the regression line by **D**ividing the residual sum of squares by **N** instead of n-k.

DUMP   **DUMP**s large amounts of output mainly useful to SHAZAM consultants.

EXACTDW   Computes the **EXACT** **D**urbin **W**atson probability, that is, the probability of rejecting the null hypothesis when it is true. For example, if the Durbin Watson probability is .0437, the null hypothesis that there is no positive autocorrelation is rejected at less than the 5% significance level. This option automatically uses **METHOD = HH**.

GF   Prints **G**oodness of **F**it Tests for normality of residuals when the **MAX, LIST** or **RSTAT** options have been specified. Coefficients of skewness and kurtosis are also computed from the moments. A reference for the Chi-Square Goodness of Fit test is Klein [1974, p. 372]. The calculation of coefficients of skewness and kurtosis of residuals is described in Smillie [1966, p. 95]. This option is automatically in effect when running in BATCH mode. In TALK or TERMINAL mode, the **GF** option must be specified if this output is desired. In BATCH mode, this output can be stopped by specifying **NOGF**.

HETCOV   This option uses White's [1980] **HET**eroskedastic-Consistent **COV**ariance matrix estimation to correct the estimates for an unknown form of heteroskedasticity. This option is not available with **METHOD = HH**. If this option is used, the forecast standard errors computed by the **FC** command will not be correct.

INFLUENCE   This option computes the Belsley-Kuh-Welsch Influence Regression Diagnostics described in Chapter 2 of their book. See also the **DFBETAS** and **HATDIAG=** options. The **INFLUENCE** option is not valid with the **RIDGE=**, **HETCOV, RESTRICT** or Stepwise Regression options.

LINLOG   This option is used when the dependent variable is **LIN**ear, but the
                  independent variables are in **LOG** form. The appropriate adjustments are
                  made to the calculated value of the log-likelihood function and to the
                  elasticities.
                  NOTE: This option does not transform the data. The data must be
                  transformed by the user with the appropriate **GENR** commands.

LIST   **LIST**s and plots the residuals and predicted values of the dependent
                  variable and residual statistics. When **LIST** is specified **RSTAT** is
                  automatically turned on.

LM   Performs certain **L**agrange **M**ultiplier tests for normality on the OLS
                  residuals.

LOGLIN   This option is used when the dependent variable is in **LOG** form, but the
                  independent variables are **LIN**ear. The appropriate adjustments are made
                  to the calculated value of the log-likelihood function and to the elasticities.
                  NOTE: This option does not transform the data. The data must be
                  transformed by the user with the appropriate **GENR** commands.

LOGLOG   This option is used when the dependent variable and all the independent
                  variables are in **LOG** form. The appropriate adjustments are made to the
                  calculated value of the log-likelihood function and to the elasticities.
                  NOTE: This option does not transform the data. The data must be
                  transformed by the user with the appropriate **GENR** commands.

MAX   Prints Analysis of Variance Tables, Variance-covariance matrix,
                  Correlation matrix, Residuals, Residual Statistics and Goodness of Fit Test
                  for Normality. This option is equivalent to using the **ANOVA, LIST,
                  PCOV, PCOR** and **GF** options. Users should be sure the **MAX** output is
                  necessary, otherwise they are paying for output they do not need.

NOCONSTANT   There will be **NO CONSTANT** (intercept) in the estimated equation. This
                  option is used when the intercept is to be suppressed in the regression or
                  when the user is supplying the intercept. This option should be used with
                  caution as some of the usual output may be invalid. In particular, the
                  usual R^2 is not well defined and could be negative. However, when this
                  option is used, a raw moment R^2 is also printed for those who are
                  interested in this statistic. The ANALYSIS OF VARIANCE - FROM
                  MEAN table will not be computed if this option is used.

NOMULSIGSQ   With this option, $(X'X)^{-1}$ is the complete covariance matrix and thus
                  should **NO**t be **MUL**tiplied by σ^2 to get the covariance matrix of
                  coefficients.

NONORM   This option is used with **WEIGHT=** if you do not want normalized weights. Interpretation of output is sometimes difficult when weights are not normalized. Sometimes, the weights can be viewed as a sampling replication factor. Users are expected to know exactly what their weights represent.

PCOR   Prints the **COR**relation matrix of coefficients. This should not be confused with a correlation matrix of variables which can be obtained with a **STAT** command.

PCOV   Prints the **COV**ariance matrix of coefficients. This should not be confused with the covariance matrix of variables which can be obtained with the **STAT** command.

PLUSH   Prints the **LUSH** (Linear Unbiased with Scalar Covariance matrix using Householder transformation) residuals.

REPLICATE This option is used with **WEIGHT=** if your weights indicate a sample replication factor. When this option is specified the **NONORM** option is often desirable. The effective sample size will then be adjusted upward to be equal to the sum of the weights. The **UT** option is automatically in effect.

RESTRICT   This option forces **RESTRICT**ions into the regression. It tells SHAZAM that **RESTRICT** commands follow. An example of this option is shown later in this chapter. Restrictions must be linear. This option may not be used with **METHOD=HH**.

RSTAT   Prints Residual Summary **STAT**istics without printing each observation. The output includes the Durbin-Watson and related residual test statistics. It also includes the Runs Test described in Gujarati, *Basic Econometrics*, Chapter 12. When **LIST** is specified **RSTAT** is automatically turned on.

UT   This option is used with **WEIGHT=** if you want the residuals and predicted values to be UnTransformed so that the estimated coefficients are used with unweighted data in order to obtain predicted values. The regression estimates are not affected by this option. This option is not available with **METHOD=HH**.

BEG=   Specifies the **BEG**inning and **END**ing observations to be used in
END=   estimation. This option overrides the **SAMPLE** command and defaults to the sample range in effect.

COEF=   Saves the **COEF**ficients in the variable specified. If there is an intercept it will be stored last.

COV= Saves the variance-**COV**ariance matrix of coefficients in the variable specified.

FE=, FX= These options allow you to specify the entering and exiting criteria in terms of **F**-values rather than probability levels when running Stepwise regressions. SHAZAM will use the user-supplied values of **FE=** and **FX=** only when no values are supplied for **PE=** or **PX=**. If either **FE=** or **FX=** is not specified, it will be defaulted to the other value. If **FX>FE** then SHAZAM will set **FX** to **FE**. If **FE=0** then all of the step variables will be allowed to enter. If **FX=**infinity (a large number) then all of the step variables may be removed. See the section on *STEPWISE REGRESSION* in this chapter for further details.

HATDIAG= This option is used with the **INFLUENCE** option if you want to save the diagonal elements of the so-called Hat Matrix which is $X(X'X)^{-1}X'$.

IDVAR= The character variable specified on this option will be printed beside its corresponding observation when **LIST** or **MAX** options are specified. For example, the data could consist of one observation for each of the Canadian provinces, in which case the user may identify the residual with the province. For information on reading and printing character variables, see the chapter *DATA INPUT AND OUTPUT*. An example of the **IDVAR=** option in use can be found later in this chapter. Some computers may not permit this option.

INCOEF= This option is used to specify a vector of **COEF**ficients to **IN**put if you know what the coefficients are and do not want to estimate the equation. An example of this option is shown in the chapter *PROGRAMMING IN SHAZAM* for computing the Power of a Test. This option is usually used with the **INSIG2=** option described below.

INCOVAR= This option is used with the **INCOEF=** option if you wish to also specify a covariance matrix. The covariance matrix must be a symmetric matrix stored in lower-triangular form such as that produced by the **COV=** option or the **SYM** function on the **MATRIX** command. When this option is used the **NOMULSIGSQ** option is automatically in effect.

INSIG2= This option is used with the **INCOEF=** option described above to specify a value of σ^2 to be used.

METHOD= Specifies the computational **METHOD** to be used on the **OLS** command. The default is **GS** (Gram Schmidt) as described in Farebrother [1974] and the alternatives are **HH** (Householder Transformations), and **NORMAL** (Choleski solution of Normal equations). All methods should yield nearly identical results with most data, however **GS** is probably the most accurate.

PCINFO=   This option is only used on **OLS** commands in conjunction with the **PC** command. For more information on this option see the chapter *PRINCIPAL COMPONENTS AND FACTOR ANALYSIS.*

PCOMP=   This option is only used on **OLS** commands in conjunction with the **PC** command. For more information on this option see the chapter *PRINCIPAL COMPONENTS AND FACTOR ANALYSIS.*

PE=, PX=   These options are similar to the **FE=** and **FX=** options described above, and are used to specify the Probability levels for Entering (**PE=**) and eXiting (**PX=**) variables that may be stepped into the equation when a Stepwise regression is being run. If a variable is more significant than the **PE** level, it will be included. If at any step a variable becomes less significant than **PX** it will be deleted from the equation. The default values are **PE=.05** and **PX=.05**. If either value is not specified it will be defaulted to the other value. If **PX<PE** then **PX** will be set to equal **PE**. If **PE=1** then all of the step variables will be allowed to enter. If **PX=0** then all of the step variables will be removed. See the section on *STEPWISE REGRESSION* in this chapter for further details.

PREDICT=   Saves the **PREDICT**ed values of the dependent variable in the variable specified.

RESID=   Saves the values of the **RESID**uals from the regression in the variable specified.

RIDGE=   This option specifies a value of k to be used to convert the **OLS** regression to a **RIDGE** regression. This option only permits ordinary **RIDGE** regression where the diagonal elements of the $X'X$ matrix are augmented by k. In order to do a **RIDGE** regression, a value for k must be specified. It may be necessary to run several regressions using different values of k in order to examine the stability of the coefficients. The value of k should be between zero and one. A value of k equal to zero will be an **OLS** regression. The user should be familiar with **RIDGE** regression before using this option. Watson and White [1976] provide good examples of Ridge regression. This option automatically uses **METHOD=NORMAL**. See the *PROGRAMMING IN SHAZAM* chapter for a Ridge Regression example.

STDERR=   Saves the values of the **ST**an**D**ard **ERR**ors of the coefficients in the variable specified.

TRATIO=   Saves the values of the **T-RATIO**s in the variable specified.

WEIGHT=   Specifies a variable to be used as the weight for a **WEIGHT**ed Least Squares regression. The square root of the weight variable will be multiplied by each observation of the dependent and independent variables. **OLS** with the **WEIGHT=** option is similar to a **GLS** regression with a diagonal Omega matrix. The weights are normalized to sum to the number of observations. The log-likelihood function is adjusted to be increased by a term equal to the sum of the LOG(SQRT(WEIGHT)) in order to correspond to the same calculation in **GLS**. Users should also examine the **NONORM, UT** and **REPLICATE** options described above which can be used with the **WEIGHT=** option.

For an example of SHAZAM output from an **OLS** regression see the chapter *A CHILD'S GUIDE TO RUNNING REGRESSIONS*.

A. **OLS** *WITH RESTRICTIONS*

The following is an example of the use of the **RESTRICT** option and **RESTRICT** commands with **OLS** using Theil's [1971, p.102] Textile data:

```
|_OLS CONSUME INCOME PRICE / RESTRICT
OLS ESTIMATION
      17 OBSERVATIONS     DEPENDENT VARIABLE = CONSUME
...NOTE..SAMPLE RANGE SET TO:    1,    17
_RESTRICT INCOME=1
_RESTRICT PRICE=-1
_END
R-SQUARE = 0.8774     R-SQUARE ADJUSTED = 0.8774
VARIANCE OF THE ESTIMATE =     68.159
STANDARD ERROR OF THE ESTIMATE =    8.2558
LOG OF THE LIKELIHOOD FUNCTION = -59.4923
```

VARIABLE NAME	ESTIMATED COEFFICIENT	STANDARD ERROR	T-RATIO 16 DF	PARTIAL CORR.	STANDARDIZED COEFFICIENT	ELASTICITY AT MEANS
INCOME	1.0000	0.66404E-08	0.15059E+09	1.0000	0.22483	0.76563
PRICE	-1.0000	0.83234E-09	-0.12014E+10	-1.0000	-0.71536	-0.56735
CONSTANT	107.84	2.0023	53.855	0.9973	0.0	0.80171

The **RESTRICT** option informs SHAZAM that **RESTRICT** commands are to follow. In this example two **RESTRICT** commands are given. More than one is allowed provided each is typed on a separate line. The **END** command marks the end of the list of **RESTRICT** commands and is required. Each restriction will add one degree of freedom. NOTE: The restrictions *must* be linear.

B. **OLS** *WITH THE* IDVAR= *OPTION*

The following is an example of the use of the **IDVAR=** option on **OLS** using the data that was read and printed in the chapter *DATA INPUT AND OUTPUT*. The variables are the unemployment and vacancy rates for some provinces of Canada for January, 1976 as provided by Statistics Canada:

```
_SAMPLE 1 9
_FORMAT(A8,2F5.1)
_READ PROVINCE UR VR / FORMAT
_OLS UR VR / IDVAR=PROVINCE LIST  WIDE
```

```
OLS ESTIMATION
        9 OBSERVATIONS     DEPENDENT VARIABLE = UR
...NOTE..SAMPLE RANGE SET TO:    1,    9

 R-SQUARE = 0.4300     R-SQUARE ADJUSTED = 0.3486
VARIANCE OF THE ESTIMATE =   6.9981
STANDARD ERROR OF THE ESTIMATE =    2.6454
LOG OF THE LIKELIHOOD FUNCTION = -20.3949
```

	ANALYSIS OF VARIANCE - FROM MEAN			
	SS	DF	MS	F
REGRESSION	36.953	1.	36.953	5.280
ERROR	48.987	7.	6.9981	
TOTAL	85.940	8.	10.743	

	ANALYSIS OF VARIANCE - FROM ZERO			
	SS	DF	MS	F
REGRESSION	733.91	2.	366.96	52.437
ERROR	48.987	7.	6.9981	
TOTAL	782.90	9.	86.989	

VARIABLE NAME	ESTIMATED COEFFICIENT	STANDARD ERROR	T-RATIO 7 DF	PARTIAL CORR.	STANDARDIZED COEFFICIENT	ELASTICITY AT MEANS
VR	-0.93553	0.40712	-2.2979	-0.6557	-0.65574	-0.68511
CONSTANT	14.829	2.7679	5.3575	0.8966	0.0	1.6851

OBSERVATION NO.		OBSERVED VALUE	PREDICTED VALUE	CALCULATED RESIDUAL
1	NEWFOUND	14.900	11.087	3.8132
2	NOVA SCO	9.1000	10.151	-1.0513
3	NEW BRUN	12.200	8.2803	3.9197
4	QUEBEC	9.1000	9.2158	-0.11579
5	ONTARIO	7.1000	10.151	-3.0513
6	MANITOBA	6.7000	7.3447	-0.64474

7 SASKATCH	4.8000	7.3447	-2.5447
8 ALBERTA	5.3000	4.5382	0.76184
9 BRITISH	10.000	11.087	-1.0868

DURBIN-WATSON = 1.9807   VON NEUMAN RATIO = 2.2283   RHO = -0.15456
RESIDUAL SUM = 0.13767E-13 RESIDUAL VARIANCE =   6.9981
SUM OF ABSOLUTE ERRORS=   16.989
R-SQUARE BETWEEN OBSERVED AND PREDICTED = 0.4300
RUNS TEST: 6 RUNS, 3 POSITIVE, 6 NEGATIVE, NORMAL STATISTIC = 0.81650
COEFFICIENT OF SKEWNESS =   0.7266 WITH STANDARD DEVIATION OF 0.7171
COEFFICIENT OF EXCESS KURTOSIS =   -0.4336 WITH STANDARD DEVIATION OF 1.3997

C. OLS AND TEMPORARY VARIABLES

There are many temporary variables available on the **OLS** command. These variables contain useful statistics from the most recent regression command in the SHAZAM run. (For a list of the temporary variables available on each regression command see the chapter *MISCELLANEOUS COMMANDS AND INFORMATION*.)

The available variables defined after the **OLS** command are:

$R2	R-SQUARE
$SIG2	VARIANCE OF THE ESTIMATE (σ^2)
$LLF	LOG OF THE LIKELIHOOD FUNCTION
$RAW	RAW-MOMENT R-SQUARE (Only available when the previous regression was run with **NOCONSTANT**.)
$N	NUMBER OF OBSERVATIONS from the **OLS** regression.

From the ANALYSIS OF VARIANCE - FROM MEAN table in **OLS** output:

$SSR	REGRESSION - SS
$SSE	ERROR - SS
$SST	TOTAL - SS
$K	REGRESSION - DF (Number of parameters in previous **OLS** regression.)
$DF	DEGREES OF FREEDOM
$ANF	F

From the ANALYSIS OF VARIANCE - FROM ZERO table in **OLS** output:

$ZSSR	REGRESSION - SS
$SSE	ERROR - SS
$ZSST	TOTAL - SS
$ZANF	F

If the **RSTAT, LIST** or **MAX** option is used the following statistics are available in temporary variables from the previous **OLS** command:

$DW   DURBIN-WATSON STATISTIC
$R2OP   R-SQUARE BETWEEN OBSERVED AND PREDICTED
$RHO   RESIDUAL AUTOCORRELATION COEFFICIENT

The following example shows one case in which temporary variables would be useful. This example shows the computation of the Chow Test as described in Gujarati (1988, Chapter14.7) to test the hypothesis that the coefficients are the same in the two samples:

```
|_ READ(11) YEAR CONSUME INCOME PRICE
...SAMPLE RANGE IS NOW SET TO:          1         17
|_ ?OLS CONSUME INCOME PRICE
|_ GEN1 CSSE=$SSE
..NOTE..CURRENT VALUE OF $SSE =    433.31
|_ GEN1 DF1=$K
..NOTE..CURRENT VALUE OF $K   =    3.0000
|_ GEN1 DF2=$N-2*$K
..NOTE..CURRENT VALUE OF $N   =    17.000
..NOTE..CURRENT VALUE OF $K   =    3.0000
|_ SAMPLE 1 9
|_ ?OLS CONSUME INCOME PRICE
|_ GEN1 SSE1=$SSE
..NOTE..CURRENT VALUE OF $SSE =    61.671
|_ SAMPLE 10 17
|_ ?OLS CONSUME INCOME PRICE
|_ GEN1 SSE2=$SSE
..NOTE..CURRENT VALUE OF $SSE =    189.35
|_ GEN1 F=((CSSE-(SSE1+SSE2))/DF1)/((SSE1+SSE2)/DF2)
|_ SAMPLE 1 1
|_ PRINT F
    F
   2.662813
|_ DISTRIB F / TYPE=F DF1=DF1 DF2=DF2
                DATA       PDF          CDF         1-CDF
    F
  ROW    1      2.6628    0.78980E-01 0.90020     0.99796E-01
```

In the above example three **OLS** regressions are run. The first is run using all the observations in the sample. This is the combined regression. The second and third are run with the first 9 and last 8 observations in the sample, respectively. The purpose of the Chow test is to the hypothesis that the coefficients are the same in each of the separate samples. The question mark (?) that appears before the **OLS** commands serves to suppress the output, since only the $SSE variables are of interest in this problem. (For details on the ? output suppressor and temporary variables, see the chapter *MISCELLANEOUS COMMANDS AND INFORMATION*.) The contents of the $SSE temporary variable is saved in a permanent variable before another regression is run because only the most recent values of temporary variables are saved. When saving a single variable, like $SSE, the **GEN1** rather than **GENR** command should be used. The variable F contains the Chow Test statistic which has an F-distribution. The Chow Test is represented by the following formula:

$$F=((CSSE-(SSE1+SSE2))/K)/((SSE1+SSE2)/(N1+N2-2K))$$

where SSE1 is the sum of squared errors for the OLS regression using the first 9 observations, SSE2 is the sum of squared errors for the OLS regression using the last 8 observations, CSSE is the sum of squared errors for the combined OLS regression, k is the number of parameters, N1 is the number of observations in the first separate OLS regression, and N2 is the number of observations in the last separate OLS regression.

The next step would be to find the area to the right of the F-test statistic of 2.662813 which has K and N1+N2-2K degrees of freedom. We can do this with the **DISTRIB** command which is described in the chapter *PROBABILITY DISTRIBUTIONS*. We find that this area is .099796 so we can reject the null hypothesis at the 10% level although not at the 5% level. Nevertheless, it might be safe to conclude that the two regressions have different coefficients.

D. *STEPWISE REGRESSION*

Although the use of stepwise regression is generally considered by economists to be a bad practice, it is provided for those who believe it has some redeeming social merit. To do stepwise regression, a slight modification of the **OLS** command is required. The format of the **OLS** command is:

OLS *depvar indeps (stepvars) / options*

where *depvar* is the name of the dependent variable, *indeps* (if present) are the names of the independent variables that are always forced into the equation, *stepvars* are the names of the the variables that may be stepped into the equation, and *options* are the desired options. (See the **FE=, FX=, PE=, PX=** options described above.) The **HETCOV, RESTRICT** and **RIDGE=** options may not be used when stepwise regressions are being run. Stepwise regression automatically uses **METHOD = NORMAL**.

8. HYPOTHESIS TESTING AND CONFIDENCE INTERVALS

"God Himself could not sink this ship."

Titanic deckhand
April 10, 1912

A. *HYPOTHESIS TESTING*

Linear or nonlinear hypothesis testing (**TEST**) on regression coefficients is easily done in SHAZAM. Hypothesis tests are computed by specifying the desired hypothesis. Normally, the regression is run and the hypothesis is tested with a t or an F-test with the **TEST** command. A good discussion of hypothesis testing can be found in Judge, Hill, Griffiths, Lütkepohl and Lee [1988, Ch. 6.3-6.4] and Judge, Griffiths, Hill, Lütkepohl and Lee [1985, Ch. 6.6].

In general, the format of the **TEST** command is:

TEST *equation*

where *equation* is an equation made up of combinations of the variables involved in estimation and represents the hypothesis to be tested. *The equation must be an equality. It must contain an equals (=) sign and must **not** contain logical relations such as .EQ., .NE., .LT., etc. The equation must **not** include any variable other than those in the estimated equation.* If you wish to test models with inequality restrictions see the procedures in the chapter *INEQUALITY RESTRICTIONS*.

Each single hypothesis must be placed on a separate **TEST** command. If a *joint test* is required that involves several hypotheses, these should be grouped together with a blank **TEST** command to introduce them and an **END** command to mark the end of the group. **TEST** commands can also be used to test hypotheses about non-linear constraints, in which case usually only the Wald asymptotic Chi-square statistic is used. For example:

```
OLS CONSUME INCOME PRICE
TEST
TEST INCOME=1
TEST PRICE=-1
END
TEST INCOME=1
TEST INCOME*PRICE=1
```

In the above example, first a joint test is done to test the joint hypothesis that the coefficients on the variables INCOME and PRICE are 1 and -1 respectively and then a single hypothesis test is done to test the hypothesis that the coefficient on the variable INCOME is equal to 1. Finally, a single test is done to test the non-linear hypothesis that the product of the coefficients is equal to 1. Users should know that the value of the test statistic for a non-linear hypothesis is sensitive to the form of the equation (see Gregory and Veall [1985] and Lafontaine and White [1986]).

The SHAZAM output for these commands using Theil's [1971, p.102] Textile data is the following:

```
|_OLS CONSUME INCOME PRICE
OLS ESTIMATION

        17 OBSERVATIONS      DEPENDENT VARIABLE = CONSUME
...NOTE..SAMPLE RANGE SET TO:     1,    17
R-SQUARE = 0.9513      R-SQUARE ADJUSTED = 0.9443
VARIANCE OF THE ESTIMATE =    30.951
STANDARD ERROR OF THE ESTIMATE =    5.5634
LOG OF THE LIKELIHOOD FUNCTION = -51.6471

VARIABLE     ESTIMATED    STANDARD    T-RATIO    PARTIAL STANDARDIZED ELASTICITY
  NAME       COEFFICIENT    ERROR      14 DF      CORR.   COEFFICIENT  AT MEANS

INCOME       1.0617       0.26667      3.9813     0.7287   0.23871      0.81288
PRICE       -1.3830       0.83814E-01 -16.501    -0.9752  -0.98933     -0.78464
CONSTANT     130.71       27.094       4.8241     0.7902   0.0          0.97175
```

The joint test that is used to test the hypothesis that the coefficients on INCOME and PRICE are 1 and -1 respectively gives the following results:

```
|_TEST
_TEST INCOME=1
_TEST PRICE=-1
_END
F STATISTIC   =    10.617224     WITH    2 AND   14 D.F.
WALD CHI-SQUARE STATISTIC   =    21.234448     WITH    2 D.F.
```

The single tests yield the following output, where the t- and F-statistics test the same hypothesis, and where the Wald statistic is an asymptotic Chi-square test statistic that is usually used only for non-linear tests. Output labeled TEST VALUE is the value of the **TEST** equation when all terms are transferred to the left-hand side.

```
|_TEST INCOME=1
TEST VALUE=  0.61710E-01 STD. ERROR OF TEST VALUE =   0.26667
T STATISTIC =  0.23140477    WITH   14 D.F.
F STATISTIC =  0.53548169E-01 WITH    1 AND   14 D.F.
WALD CHI-SQUARE STATISTIC = 0.53548169E-01 WITH    1 D.F.

|_TEST INCOME*PRICE=1
TEST VALUE=  -2.4683     STD. ERROR OF TEST =   0.39456
T STATISTIC =  -6.2559417    WITH   14 D.F.
F STATISTIC =   39.136807    WITH    1 AND   14 D.F.
WALD CHI-SQUARE STATISTIC =   39.136807    WITH    1 D.F.
```

For instructions on doing hypothesis testing on systems of equations, see the chapter *TWO STAGE LEAST SQUARES AND SYSTEMS OF EQUATIONS.*

There are several temporary variables available from the previous **TEST** command. These are \$CHI, \$DF1, \$DF2, \$F, \$STES, \$T and \$VAL as shown on the **TEST** output. For more information on temporary variables see the chapter *MISCELLANEOUS COMMANDS AND INFORMATION.*

B. *CONFIDENCE INTERVALS*

In addition to the **TEST** command described above, SHAZAM can automatically compute confidence intervals for coefficients from a previous estimation with the **CONFID** command. The **CONFID** command can be used anywhere the **TEST** command can be used, and you could have several **TEST** or **CONFID** commands following any estimation command. In general, the format of the **CONFID** command is:

CONFID *coef1 coef2* ... / *options*

where *coef1* and *coef2* are the names of coefficients and *options* is a list of available options. When only 2 coefficients are listed, the **CONFID** command will also compute a plot of the confidence ellipse. The available **PLOT** options are **EGA, GOAWAY, GRAPHICS, HERCULES, HOLD, NOBLANK, PAUSE, PRINT, SYMBOL, TOSHIBA, WIDE/NOWIDE, MODE=, XMAX=, XMIN=, YMAX=** and **YMIN=** as described in the chapter *PLOTS.* Other options available on the **CONFID** command are:

NOFPLOT	The **NOFPLOT** option deletes the joint confidence region plot if two coefficients were specified. This option would be used if you only wanted the individual confidence intervals based on the t- or normal distribution.
NOMID	The **NOMID** option is used when computing the **FPLOT**, but do not want SHAZAM to draw a symbol at the center of the confidence ellipse.
NORMAL	The **NORMAL** option tells SHAZAM that the normal distribution rather than the t distribution should be used in computing confidence regions. Often, we only know that the coefficients are asymptotically normally distributed and the use of the t or F distribution would be inappropriate.
NOTPLOT	The **NOTPLOT** option deletes the computation of the confidence intervals for individual coefficients based on the t or normal distribution. This might be used if only two coefficients were specified and you only want the joint confidence region plot (**FPLOT**). Normally, the t distribution confidence intervals are shown on the joint plot with a plus symbol(+) to show the outline of the confidence rectangle. The **NOTPLOT** option will suppress the drawing of the (+) symbol.
DF=	SHAZAM remembers the degrees of freedom to use from the preceeding regression. However, if a different value is required it can be specified with the **DF=** option.

FCRIT=

This option is similar to the **TCRIT=** option described below and is usually used to complement it. It specifies a critical value from an F-distribution to be used for the joint confidence region plot.

POINTS=

SHAZAM usually constructs the confidence ellipse for the FPLOT by evaluating the ellipse at approximately 200-205 points. The number used can be changed with this option if more or fewer points are desired to obtain a better looking plot.

TCRIT=

SHAZAM computes the critical value of the t distribution by assuming a 95% confidence interval with degrees of freedom from either the previous estimation or the **DF=** option (see next section of this chapter). However, you can compute any confidence interval by specifying the t-distribution critical value found in tables of the t-distribution or from output associated with use of the **DISTRIB** command. This allows the calculation of intervals other than the 95% interval.

The following example shows the output from the **CONFID** command:

```
|_CONFID INCOME PRICE
USING 95% CONFIDENCE REGION
CONFIDENCE INTERVALS BASED ON T-DISTRIBUTION WITH  14 D.F. - TVALUE =    2.145
NAME         LOWER          COEFFICENT        UPPER         STD. ERROR
  INCOME     0.48969         1.0617          1.6337         0.26667
  PRICE     -1.5628         -1.3830         -1.2032         0.83814E-01

CONFIDENCE REGION PLOT FOR INCOME    AND PRICE
 USING F DISTRIBUTION WITH 2 AND    14 D.F.     F-VALUE =    3.740

     1.7911   |                        *
     1.6968   |              *****    * ****
     1.6025   |           +**             ****    +
     1.5083   |         **                 ***
     1.4140   |        **                   ***
     1.3197   |       *                     ***
     1.2255   |       *                      **
     1.1312   |       *                       **
     1.0369   |       *            *           *
    0.94266   |      **                        *
    0.84839   |      *                         **
    0.75413   |       *                        *
    0.65986   |        **                     **
    0.56560   |         ***                  **
    0.47133   |        +   ***            *+*
    0.37706   |             ****         ****
    0.28280   |            * **    *   ***
    0.18853   |
 0.94266E-01  |
-0.24286E-16  |
              _____

              -1.625    -1.500    -1.375    -1.250    -1.125
                                  PRICE
```

If a **GRAPHICS** option is used on the above **CONFID** command then a plot like the following will be obtained:

```
|_CONFID INCOME PRICE / GRAPHICS
```

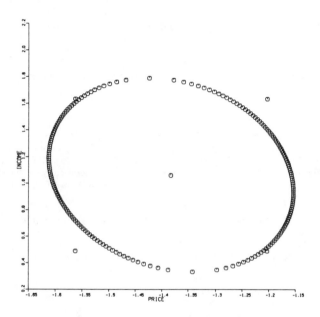

In some cases users would like to compute the confidence region for coefficients that have been estimated in an earlier run and do not wish to re-estimate a model. This is possible for any set of two coefficients where you tell SHAZAM the estimated values of the coefficients, their estimated variances, and the covariance between the coefficients. In this case, the **CONFID** command does not need to follow an estimation command, but the following options *must* be included:

COEF1=   The **COEF1=** option specifies the coefficient estimate for the first coefficient you wish to plot. This coefficient will appear on the Y-axis of the plot.

COEF2=   The **COEF2=** option specifies the coefficient estimate for the second coefficient you wish to plot. This coefficient will appear on the X-axis of the plot.

COVAR12=   The **COVAR12=** option specifies the estimated covariance between the two coefficients.

DF=   The **DF=** option specifies the number of degrees of freedom when the estimation was performed. This will generally be equal to the number of observations minus the number of coefficients estimated. The **DF=** option tells SHAZAM what to use for the t and F values in computing the 95% confidence intervals.

VAR1=   The **VAR1=** option specifies the estimated variance of the first coefficient.

VAR2=   The **VAR2=** option specifies the estimated variance of the second coefficient.

The following example shows the use of the **CONFID** command when you specify the values of the coefficients, their variances, and their covariance. The example uses information from the chapter *TWO STAGE LEAST SQUARES AND SYSTEMS OF EQUATIONS*. Since the coefficients in 2SLS are assumed to be asymptotically normally distributed and the small sample properties are unknown, we use the **NORMAL** option.

```
|_CONFID PLAG P / COEF1=.21623 COEF2=.017302 VAR1=.011506 VAR2=.013936 &
|    COVAR12=-.009571 NORMAL
USING 95% CONFIDENCE REGION
CONFIDENCE INTERVALS BASED ON NORMAL DISTRIBUTION WITH CRITICAL VALUE= 1.960
NAME         LOWER       COEFFICENT      UPPER        STD. ERROR
 PLAG      0.59886E-02   0.21623       0.42647       0.10727
 P        -0.21408       0.17302E-01   0.24868       0.11805
CONFIDENCE REGION PLOT FOR PLAG      AND P
USING CHI-SQUARE DISTRIBUTION WITH CRITICAL VALUE=    5.990
                      M=MULTIPLE POINT
    0.47345     |                    *    *
    0.43801     |             MM        **M**
    0.40256     |             M  +        *MMM                   +
    0.36712     |             M                 MMM
    0.33167     |             MM                   MM
    0.29623     |              MM                   MM*
    0.26078     |              MM                   MM*
    0.22534     |              *M*                   MM
    0.18989     |                MM         *          MM
    0.15445     |                 MM                  MM*
    0.11900     |                *MM                 M*
    0.83560E-01 |                 *MM                M*
    0.48115E-01 |                  MMM                M
    0.12670E-01 |                  MM*                M*
   -0.22775E-01 |          +         *M*M*      +  M
   -0.58220E-01 |                        M**     *M*
   -0.93665E-01 |
   -0.12911     |
   -0.16456     |
   -0.20000     |
                 _____
              -0.400    -0.200    0.       0.200     0.400
                                    P
```

9. INEQUALITY RESTRICTIONS

"However, inequality constrained linear regression is not an option of any of the more popular econometrics software packages. Many practitioners may lack the gall (if not the resources) to determine the solution using ordinary least squares regression packages."

John Geweke, 1986

By following the Bayesian procedure described in Geweke, "Exact Inference in the Inequality Constrained Normal Linear Regression Model", *Journal of Applied Econometrics* [1986] and in Judge, Hill, Griffiths, Lütkepohl and Lee [1988, Chapter 20]; and Chalfant and White [1988], SHAZAM is able to impose inequality restrictions. The method takes a set of coefficients and a covariance matrix from a previous estimation, and generates a large number of replications using Monte Carlo Integration with a randomized distribution of coefficients. Since SHAZAM makes the procedure user-friendly, the user need only specify the inequality restrictions. However, since the method is also computer intensive, be prepared to either (1) spend your whole computer budget, (2) be unpopular with other users of your computer, or (3) let your micro computer run a long time. The **BAYES** command is used to specify the number of replications desired, and is also followed by **RESTRICT** commands that specify the inequality restrictions, and an **END** command. The **BAYES** command must itself follow an estimation command such as **OLS**.

In general, the format of the **BAYES** command is:

BAYES / *options* **NSAMP=**

where *options* is a list of options and **NSAMP=** is the number of replications required.

The available options on the **BAYES** command are:

NOANTITHET　　　This option omits the **ANTITHETIC** replications. The Antithetic procedure draws a vector of random numbers from the appropriate distribution. The antithetic replication simply changes the sign of the vector of random numbers essentially giving an additional replication at low cost and ensuring a symmetric distribtion. See Geweke [1988] for further details.

NORMAL　　　This option assumes the coefficients are normally distributed rather than t distributed.

NSAMP=　　　The **NSAMP** option is required and is used to specify the number of desired replications. This should be a small number (for example 100), while the user is experimenting. Readers of the Geweke ariticle will realize that **NSAMP** is often very high.

OUTUNIT=   This option specifies an output unit to write all the replicated coefficients. The output unit should be assigned with the SHAZAM **FILE** command or an operating systems command. If **NSAMP=** is a large number the resulting file could be quite large.

The following is an example of the **BAYES** command using the Pindyck and Rubinfeld [1981] Housing example in the Geweke article.

```
|_SAMPLE 1 32
|_READ RENT NO RM S DUM
  5 VARIABLES AND        32 OBSERVATIONS STARTING AT OBS        1
|_GENR Y=RENT/NO
|_GENR R=RM/NO
|_GENR SR=S*R
|_GENR OSR=(1-S)*R
|_GENR SD=S*DUM
|_GENR OSD=(1-S)*DUM
|_GENR ONE=1
|_* Run OLS. This gives results from column 1 of Geweke's Table II.
|_* Different machines will yield different results due to the
|_*    Different random numbers
|_DISPLAY CPUTIME
CPUTIME        1.9990
|_OLS Y SR OSR SD OSD / NOANOVA
OLS ESTIMATION
       32 OBSERVATIONS      DEPENDENT VARIABLE = Y

 R-SQUARE =  0.4525    R-SQUARE ADJUSTED =  0.3713
VARIANCE OF THE ESTIMATE =    1395.5
STANDARD ERROR OF THE ESTIMATE =   37.356
LOG OF THE LIKELIHOOD FUNCTION = -158.544
```

VARIABLE NAME	ESTIMATED COEFFICIENT	STANDARD ERROR	T-RATIO 27 DF	PARTIAL CORR.	STANDARDIZED COEFFICIENT	ELASTICITY AT MEANS
SR	103.55	38.473	2.6916	0.4599	1.0083	0.22640
OSR	122.04	37.359	3.2667	0.5322	1.1597	0.52903
SD	3.3151	1.9613	1.6903	0.3093	0.34630	0.55485E-01
OSD	1.1535	0.57143	-2.0187	-0.3621	-0.34802	-0.90010E-01
CONSTANT	38.562	32.223	1.1967	0.2244	0.	0.27909

```
|_DISPLAY CPUTIME
CPUTIME       2.6660
|_* Now use Geweke's method to impose inequality restrictions, and then
|_* run 1000 trials including antithetic replications.
|_* This will give results similar to column 3 of Geweke's Table II.
|_BAYES / NSAMP=1000
BAYESIAN (GEWEKE) INEQUALITY CONSTRAINED ESTIMATION
|_RESTRICT SR.GT.0
|_RESTRICT OSR.GT.0
|_RESTRICT SD.LT.0
|_RESTRICT OSD.LT.0
|_END
NUMBER OF INEQUALITY RESTRICTIONS =    4
NUMBER OF COEFFICIENTS=   5
```

INEQUALITY RESTRICTIONS

```
NUMBER OF REPLICATIONS=      1000
ANTITHETIC REPLICATIONS ALSO INCLUDED
DEGREES OF FREEDOM FOR T DISTRIBUTION =      27
ORIGINAL COEFFICIENT ESTIMATES
   103.55288488897   122.03844729025   3.3151457566017   -1.1535408341482
   38.562062754257
        2000 REPLICATIONS        103 SATISFIED
PROPORTION= 0.05150 NUMERICAL STANDARD ERROR OF PROPORTION= 0.00494
VARIABLE  AVERAGE       STDEV        VARIANCE       NUMERICAL SE
SR         144.35       37.927        1438.5         3.7371
OSR        127.76       40.956        1677.4         4.0355
SD        -0.85167      0.83910       0.70410        0.82679E-01
OSD       -1.1220       0.58368       0.34069        0.57512E-01
CONSTANT   32.519       36.115        1304.3         3.5585
|_DISPLAY CPUTIME
CPUTIME      17.766
 _* Now attempt to impose the restrictions directly using the trick
 _* of squaring a coefficient to force it to be positive. This requires
 _* nonlinear estimation.
 _* This gives results similar to column 2 of Geweke's Table II.
 _NL 1 / NC=5
 _EQ Y=A + (B**2)*SR + (C**2)*OSR - (D**2)*SD - (E**2)*OSD
 _END
    5 VARIABLES IN  1 EQUATIONS WITH  5 COEFFICIENTS
        32 OBSERVATIONS


COEFFICIENT STARTING VALUES
A         1.0000     B         1.0000     C         1.0000
D         1.0000     E         1.0000
     100 MAXIMUM ITERATIONS, CONVERGENCE = 0.000010
INITIAL STATISTICS :
TIME =       0.733 SEC.   ITER. NO.    0   FUNCT. EVALUATIONS    1
LOG-LIKELIHOOD FUNCTION=   -207.0281
COEFFICIENTS
   1.000000      1.000000      1.000000      1.000000      1.000000
GRADIENT
 -0.1960723    -0.1349835    -0.2307822     1.165898      4.093769

FINAL STATISTICS :

TIME =       8.583 SEC.   ITER. NO.   33   FUNCT. EVALUATIONS   45
LOG-LIKELIHOOD FUNCTION=   -160.1530
COEFFICIENTS
   37.63371      11.40220      11.09239    0.8808439E-08  -1.073957
GRADIENT
 -0.6039829E-09 -0.4895324E-08 -0.1394745E-07  0.1627280E-07 -0.6853604E-07

MAXIMUM LIKELIHOOD ESTIMATE OF SIGMA-SQUARED =    1302.0

        COEFFICIENT   ST. ERROR    T-RATIO

A        37.634       30.255       1.2439
B        11.402       1.4500       7.8637
C        11.092       1.5915       6.9697
D      0.88084E-08  0.72146     0.12209E-07
E       -1.0740       0.25274     -4.2492
|_END
```

```
|_* The estimated coefficients are found by squaring each
|_* of the parameters. The TEST command can do this.
|_* The only interesting parts of the TEST output are the
|_* parts labeled 'TEST VALUE' and 'STD. ERROR OF TEST VALUE'
|_* which are the estimated coefficients we want.
|_* Be careful when using these standard errors.  For details
|_* see Lafontaine and White, "Obtaining Any Wald Statistic
|_* You Want", Economics Letters, 1986.
|_TEST B**2
TEST VALUE =    130.01      STD. ERROR OF TEST VALUE    33.066
T STATISTIC =   3.9318297      WITH    32 D.F.
F STATISTIC =  15.459285       WITH     1 AND    32 D.F.
WALD CHI-SQUARE STATISTIC =   15.459285       WITH     1 D.F.
|_TEST C**2
TEST VALUE =    123.04      STD. ERROR OF TEST VALUE    35.308
T STATISTIC =   3.4848358      WITH    32 D.F.
F STATISTIC =  12.144080       WITH     1 AND    32 D.F.
WALD CHI-SQUARE STATISTIC =   12.144080       WITH     1 D.F.
|_TEST -(D**2)
TEST VALUE = -0.77589E-16 STD. ERROR OF TEST VALUE  0.12710E-07
T STATISTIC = -0.61046306E-08 WITH    32 D.F.
F STATISTIC =  0.37266515E-16 WITH     1 AND    32 D.F.
WALD CHI-SQUARE STATISTIC = 0.37266515E-16     WITH     1 D.F.
|_TEST -(E**2)
TEST VALUE =   -1.1534      STD. ERROR OF TEST VALUE  0.54287
T STATISTIC =  -2.1245979      WITH    32 D.F.
F STATISTIC =   4.5139163      WITH     1 AND    32 D.F.
WALD CHI-SQUARE STATISTIC =    4.5139163       WITH     1 D.F.
|_DISPLAY CPUTIME
   CPUTIME      27.650
```

The resulting coefficient estimates satisfy the inequality constraints specified. However, in this example, the probability that the restrictions are true is only .0515. Users should be familiar with the Geweke paper before spending a large amount of computer time with the **BAYES** command. Note, that even with only 1000 replications the cost of the BAYES procedure is high. For example, on a VAX 750 computer unconstrained OLS took only 0.67 seconds of CPUTIME, while the BAYES procedure took 15.1 seconds and the constrained nonlinear procedure took 9.9 seconds. Note, however that only 1000 replications were done on the BAYES procedure here, and Geweke used from 10,000 to 250,000 in his examples. Bayesian inequality regression comes at a relatively high price, but SHAZAM makes it as painless as possible.

10. ARIMA MODELS

"The end of the decline of the Stock Market will ... probably not be long, only a few more days at most."

Irving Fisher, Economist
November 14, 1929

The **ARIMA** command in SHAZAM is used for the Univariate **A**uto**R**egressive, **I**ntegrated, **M**oving **A**verage model and is often called a Box-Jenkins model. A good discussion of Autoregressive, Integrated, Moving Average models can be found in Judge, Hill, Griffiths, Lütkepohl and Lee [1988, Ch. 16.5]; and Nelson [1973].

In general, the format of the **ARIMA** command is:

ARIMA *var / options*

where *var* is the variable to be analyzed and *options* is a list of desired options. Unlike other commands in SHAZAM, the **ARIMA** command has three levels of application — Identification, Estimation and Forecasting — and the options available on this command are therefore restricted by the application level.

IDENTIFICATION PHASE

In the Identification phase, the autocorrelations and partial autocorrelations are computed, and the sample data may be plotted. The following options are available:

ALL   Instructs SHAZAM to difference the data for **ALL** orders up to the order specified with the **NDIFF=** option.

PLOTAC   This option generates a plot of the calculated autocorrelation function. The number of lags specified with the **NLAG=** option is used to determine the order of the autocorrelation function.

PLOTDATA   This option produces a plot of the differenced data.

PLOTPAC   This option is used to plot the partial autocorrelation function. The **NLAGP=** option tells SHAZAM the highest order to plot.

WIDE /   **NOWIDE** tries to fit all the output in 80 columns and **WIDE** assumes 120
NOWIDE   columns are available.

| BEG= | Sets the range for the data being considered. These options override the |
| END= | sample size specified with the **SAMPLE** command. |

NDIFF=   This option tells SHAZAM the order of differencing to transform the data.

NLAG=   Specifies the number of lags being considered in the derivation of the
                  autocorrelations. The default is 24. The maximum is 108.

NLAGP=   Specifies the number of lags being considered in the derivation of the
                  partial autocorrelations. The default is 12. The maximum is 36.

NSDIFF=   Specifies the order of seasonal differencing.

NSPAN=   Specifies the span of the seasonal cycle being considered. For example,
                  NSPAN=4 is used for quarterly data.

The following is an example of **ARIMA** output using the artificial data found in Table 16.3 of Judge, Hill, Griffiths, Lütkepohl and Lee [1988, Ch.16]:

```
|_ARIMA Y / PLOTAC PLOTPAC NLAG=15 NLAGP=15
    ARIMA MODEL
NUMBER OF OBSERVATIONS = 100

      IDENTIFICATION SECTION - VARIABLE=Y
NUMBER OF AUTOCORRELATIONS =  15
NUMBER OF PARTIAL AUTOCORRELATIONS =  15

  NET NUMBER OF OBSERVATIONS =  100
MEAN=   0.54053E-02   VARIANCE=    2.1713      STANDARD DEV.=    1.4735


  LAGS                        AUTOCORRELATIONS                     STD ERR
  1 -12     -.59 0.10 -.02 -.04 0.17 -.18 0.12 -.10 -.00 0.11 -.16 0.08   0.10
 13 -24     0.01 -.03 0.09 0.0  0.0  0.0  0.0  0.0  0.0  0.0  0.0  0.0    0.14


BOX-PIERCE PORTMANTEAU TEST FOR AUTOCORRELATION ADJUSTED FOR DOWNWARD BIAS
                 Q(12)=   52.77, Q(24)=   57.53, Q(36)=

                       PARTIAL AUTOCORRELATIONS                  STD ERR
  1 -12     -.59 -.38 -.29 -.32 -.03 -.07 0.03 -.03 -.15 -.04 -.16 -.23   0.10
 13 -24     -.15 -.15 0.01 0.0  0.0  0.0  0.0  0.0  0.0  0.0  0.0  0.0    0.10
```

```
                                              0     0 0
AUTOCORRELATION FUNCTION OF THE SERIES    (1-B) (1-B )  Y

 1 -.59 .              RRRRRRRRRRRRRRRRRRRRRR       +                    .
 2 0.10 .                         +       RRRR      +                    .
 3 -.02 .                         +       RR        +                    .
 4 -.04 .                         +       RR        +                    .
 5 0.17 .                         +       RRRRRRR+                        .
 6 -.18 .                       +RRRRRRR            +                    .
 7 0.12 .                         +       RRRR      +                    .
 8 -.10 .                         +   RRRR          +                    .
 9 -.00 .                         +       R         +                    .
10 0.11 .                         +       RRRR      +                    .
11 -.16 .                       + RRRRRR             +                    .
12 0.08 .                         +       RRRR      +                    .
13 0.01 .                  +              R                +             .
14 -.03 .                  +              RR               +             .
15 0.09 .                  +              RRRR             +             .


                                                    0     0 0
PARTIAL AUTOCORRELATION FUNCTION OF THE SERIES   (1-B) (1-B  )  Y

 1 -.59 .              RRRRRRRRRRRRRRRRRRRRRR          +                 .
 2 -.38 .              RRRRRRRRRRRRRR                  +                 .
 3 -.29 .              RRRRRRRRRRR                     +                 .
 4 -.32 .              RRRRRRRRRRR                     +                 .
 5 -.03 .                         +       RR           +                 .
 6 -.07 .                         +       RRR          +                 .
 7 0.03 .                         +       RR           +                 .
 8 -.03 .                         +       RR           +                 .
 9 -.15 .                       + RRRRR                +                 .
10 -.04 .                         +       RRR          +                 .
11 -.16 .                       + RRRRR                +                 .
12 -.23 .              RRRRRRRRR                       +                 .
13 -.15 .                       + RRRRR                +                 .
14 -.15 .                       + RRRRR                +                 .
15 0.01 .                         +       R            +                 .
```

ESTIMATION PHASE

The second use of the **ARIMA** command is in the Estimation phase of the modelling process. The options used here deal primarily with specifying the order of the **ARIMA** process and therefore, differ from the options used in the Identification phase. The options used here include:

DN Computes the estimated variance of the regression by dividing the residual sum of squares by N instead of (N-K).

NOCONSTANT Indicates that there is no intercept involved in the ARIMA process being considered.

PITER This option tells SHAZAM to print each iteration of the estimation ARIMA process.

PLOTRES Plots the residuals.

START Tells SHAZAM that the starting values will be read in from the line immediately following the command line in the command file. Otherwise, the value 0.5 will be used for all coefficients.

BEG= Sets the sample range to be used for the Estimation phase. These options
END= override the sample size set on the previous **SAMPLE** command.

COEF= Saves the parameters of the estimated model in the variable specified. They will be used later in the Forecasting phase of the investigation. This option should not be confused with the **COEF=** option used in the Forecasting phase of the ARIMA process. In the Estimation phase **COEF=** saves the coefficients, while in the Forecasting phase, it retrieves those coefficient estimates.

ITER= Specifies the number of iterations. The default is 50.

NAR= Specifies the order of the Autoregressive process.

NDIFF= Specifies the order of differencing to transform the data.

NMA= Specifies the order of the Moving Averages process.

NSAR= Specifies the order of the Seasonal AR process.

NSDIFF= Specifies the order of seasonal differencing.

NSMA=   Specifies the order of Seasonal MA process.

NSPAN=   Specifies the order of the seasonal span.

PREDICT=   Saves the predicted values in the variable specified.

RESID=   Saves the residuals for the parameter estimates in the variable specified.

The **ARIMA** command as used in the Estimation phase requires starting values from which to generate its estimates for the model parameters. If the default value of 0.5 is not suitable, the starting values must be provided on the line immediately following the command line using the following input sequence: AR, MA, SAR, SMA, CONSTANT. For example:

ARIMA Y / NMA=1 NOCONSTANT COEF=COY START
.25 .52

The **ARIMA** command for the Estimation phase *must* specify the order of the ARIMA process being considered or the command will not produce ARIMA estimates. The output for a typical Estimation phase is given here for data found in Chapter 16 of Judge, Hill, Griffiths, Lütkepohl and Lee [1988, Table 16.3]:

```
|_ARIMA Y / NMA=1 NOCONSTANT NOPITER COEF=COY
    ARIMA MODEL
NUMBER OF OBSERVATIONS = 100
NUMBER OF MA PARAMETERS =   1
NO CONSTANT TERM IS IN THE MODEL

ESTIMATION PROCEDURE
STARTING VALUES OF PARAMETERS ARE:
 0.50000

MEAN OF SERIES =  0.5405E-02
VARIANCE OF SERIES =   2.171
STANDARD DEVIATION OF SERIES =   1.474

INITIAL SUM OF SQUARES =       130.4

ITERATION STOPS - RELATIVE CHANGE IN EACH PARAMETER LESS THAN .1E-03

NET NUMBER OF OBS IS  100
DIFFERENCING: 0 CONSECUTIVE, 0 SEASONAL WITH SPAN  0
CONVERGENCE AFTER  6 ITERATIONS
INITIAL SUM OF SQS=       130.4          FINAL SUM OF SQS=      95.77

 R-SQUARE =  0.5545    R-SQUARE ADJUSTED =  0.5500
VARIANCE OF THE ESTIMATE =  0.96657
STANDARD ERROR OF THE ESTIMATE =  0.98314
```

```
          PARAMETER ESTIMATES        STD ERROR    T-STAT
             MA( 1)    0.97220       0.1035E-01    93.96
```

LAGS	AUTOCORRELATIONS OF RESIDUALS	S.E.
1-12	-.16 0.06 0.03 0.06 0.16 -.11 0.02 -.12 -.04 0.04 -.14 0.05	0.10
13-24	0.06 0.04 0.09 -.07 0.07 -.12 0.18 -.07 0.00 0.04 -.27 0.19	0.11
25-36	-.04 0.03 -.12 0.01 0.08 -.05 -.01 0.04 0.05 0.01 -.12 0.04	0.13
37-48	0.03 -.04 -.00 -.16 0.03 -.11 0.01 -.09 -.12 0.05 -.09 -.08	0.13
49-60	-.04 -.05 0.05 0.02 -.04 0.12 -.13 0.07 0.06 0.11 -.09 -.09	0.14

BOX-PIERCE-LJUNG PORTMANTEAU TEST STATISTICS

Q(12)= 11.9 DF=11 P=.369 Q(24)= 35.3 DF=23 P=.049 Q(36)= 42.3 DF=35
P=.186

CROSS-CORRELATIONS BETWEEN RESIDUALS AND DIFFERENCED SERIES

CROSS-CORRELATION AT ZERO LAG = 0.76

LAGS	CROSS CORRELATIONS Y(T),E(T-K)
1-12	-.75 0.14 -.01 0.02 0.07 -.18 0.09 -.09 0.05 0.05 -.12 0.12
13-24	0.01 -.01 0.04 -.11 0.09 -.12 0.19 -.16 0.04 0.02 -.20 0.30
25-36	-.15 0.04 -.10 0.09 0.04 -.09 0.02 0.04 0.01 -.03 -.08 0.11

LEADS	CROSS CORRELATIONS Y(T),E(T+K)
1-12	-.14 0.01 -.01 -.07 0.18 -.09 0.09 -.05 -.05 0.12 -.12 -.01
13-24	0.01 -.03 0.11 -.09 0.12 -.19 0.16 -.04 -.02 0.19 -.30 0.15
25-36	-.04 0.10 -.09 -.05 0.09 -.03 -.03 -.00 0.03 0.08 -.11 0.01

FORECASTING PHASE

The third and final use of the **ARIMA** command is in the Forecasting phase for the ARIMA process where individual forecasts are made. Again, some of the options available for this use of the **ARIMA** command are not valid in the other two phases. The options available include:

LOG	Takes logs of the data.
NOCONSTANT	Indicates that there is no intercept in the equation.
PLOTFORC	Generates a plot of the forecast values, complete with the error bounds associated with each forecast.
COEF=	Provides the coefficient estimates for the ARIMA equation. This should not be confused with the **COEF=** option described for the Estimation phase which saves the estimated coefficient. In the Forecasting phase **COEF=** retrieves those coefficient estimates.
FBEG= **FEND=**	Specify the beginning and ending points for the forecast being made. These options are required.
NAR=	Specifies the order for the Autoregressive process.
NDIFF=	Tells SHAZAM the order of differencing to use when transforming the data.
NMA=	Specifies the order of the Moving Average process.
NSAR=	Specifies the order of the seasonal AR process.
NSDIFF=	Specifies the order of seasonal differencing.
NSMA=	Specifies the order of the seasonal MA process.
NSPAN=	Specifies the span of the seasonal cycle. For example, **NSPAN=4** specifies quarterly data.
PREDICT=	Saves the predicted values in the variable specified.
RESID=	Saves the residuals for the forecast estimates in the variable specified.

Users may sometimes want to use coefficients other than those from the Estimation phase in the Forecasting phase. If other parameter estimates are to be used, place them on the line immediately following the **ARIMA** command. As well, the **FBEG**= and **FEND**= options *must* be specified on the **ARIMA** command for the Forecasting phase so that SHAZAM knows that it is supposed to be making a forecast. Once more, using data found in Judge, Hill, Griffiths, Lütkepohl and Lee [1988, Table 16.3] typical ARIMA output for the Forecasting phase is as follows:

```
|_ARIMA Y / NMA=1 NOCONSTANT FBEG=100 FEND=101 COEF=COY
   ARIMA MODEL
NUMBER OF OBSERVATIONS = 100
NUMBER OF MA PARAMETERS =    1
NO CONSTANT TERM IS IN THE MODEL


   ARIMA FORECAST
NO. OF OBS. USED TO ESTIMATE PARAMETERS           100


          PARAMETER VALUES ARE:

             MA( 1)= 0.97220

FROM ORIGIN DATE 100, FORECASTS ARE CALCULATED UP TO    1 STEPS AHEAD

FUTURE DATE    LOWER      FORECAST        UPPER       ACTUAL        ERROR
   101       -2.05712    -0.132597      1.79192

     STEPS AHEAD     STD ERROR     PSI WT
          1          0.9819        1.0000

VARIANCE OF ONE-STEP-AHEAD ERRORS (RESIDUALS) =  0.9641

MEAN TIME BETWEEN UPCROSSES =    3.000
MEAN TIME BETWEEN PEAKS =    3.000
```

Note that in this example the parameter estimates have been read into the **ARIMA** command using the **COEF**= option.

11. AUTOCORRELATION MODELS

"It can be predicted with all security that in fifty years light will cost one fiftieth of its present price, and in all the big cities there will be no such thing as night."

J.B.S. Haldane
British Scientist, 1927

SHAZAM has some rather powerful capabilities for the estimation of autocorrelation (**AUTO**) models. A good reference on autocorrelation models is Judge, Griffiths, Hill, Lütkepohl and Lee [1985, Ch. 8] or Judge, Hill, Griffiths, Lütkepohl and Lee [1988, Ch. 9].

In the first-order model with autocorrelated errors we have:

$$Y_t = X_t \beta + \epsilon_t$$

and

$$\epsilon_t = \rho \epsilon_{t-1} + v_t$$

where ρ is the autocorrelation parameter and v is a new independent disturbance term. SHAZAM provides four ways for estimating first and second order models. SHAZAM will do a least squares procedure or a maximum likelihood procedure to estimate ρ. The estimates can be obtained by either a Cochrane-Orcutt type iterative procedure or by a grid search. The grid search is more expensive.

In general, the format of the **AUTO** command is:

AUTO *depvar indeps / options*

where *depvar* is the dependent variable, *indeps* is a list of independent variables, and *options* is a list of desired options. As well as **ANOVA, DUMP, GF, LINLOG, LIST, LOGLIN, LOGLOG, MAX, NOCONSTANT, NOWIDE, PCOR, PCOV, RESTRICT, RSTAT, WIDE, BEG=, END=, COEF=, COV=, PREDICT=, RESID=, STDERR=** and **TRATIO=**, as defined for **OLS**, the following options are available on the **AUTO** command:

DLAG   This option can be used with first-order models to tell SHAZAM that the first independent variable is a **LAG**ged **D**ependent variable. With this option the estimated variances will be calculated using Dhrymes [1971, Theorem 7.1]. An example using this method can be found in Savin [1976].

DN This option will compute the estimated variance of the regression line by Dividing the residual sum of squares by N instead of n-k. If the user believes that the model only has good large-sample properties and wants the maximum likelihood estimates of the variances, this option should be used.

DROP This option will **DROP** the first observation in estimation. (In a second-order model, the first two observations will be dropped.) While this yields less efficient estimates, there are cases where this option might be chosen. If this option is not used, the beginning observations are saved with the usual transformation. See any good econometrics text, and Poirier [1978] for discussions of this. If the **DROP** option is used, the **ML** option may not be used.

GS This option will use a Grid Search to estimate ρ. In first-order models, 39 iterations will be required by a grid search. In second-order models, over 100 iterations will be required. The grid search will yield an accuracy of .01.

MISS This option adjusts the maximum likelihood estimates for any **MISS**ing observations that were deleted with **SKIPIF** commands. The method used is described in Savin and White [1978] and in Richardson and White [1979].

ML This option will do a Maximum Likelihood estimation of ρ. If this option is not specified SHAZAM will automatically do the least squares procedure. For a detailed reference on the procedure see Dhrymes [1971, Theorem 4.4]. The **DN** option discussed below is recommended with the **ML** option. If the **GS** option is not also specified, the method used is a modified Cochrane-Orcutt procedure as developed by Beach and MacKinnon [1978].

PAGAN This option may be used with **ORDER = 1** or **ORDER = 2** to estimate the model using Pagan's [1974] procedure.

CONV = This option is used to set a **CONV**ergence criterion when the Cochrane-Orcutt type procedure is being used. The default is .001. This option is ineffective for a grid search.

GAP = This option provides an alternative way to indicate a single **GAP** in the data. It is used when the missing observations were not accounted for in the data. You should specify the observation number immediately before the gap. For example, **GAP = 29** means that a gap exists in the data after observation 29. It will be assumed that only one observation is missing, unless the number of missing observations is specified with the **NMISS =** option.

ITER=   This option may be used when doing an **ITER**ative Cochrane-Orcutt
                         procedure to control the number of iterations. If a value of **ITER=** is
                         specified, this will be the maximum number of iterations allowed. **ITER=**
                         should be a number between 2 and 99. The default is 19.

NMISS=   This option is used with the **GAP=** option to indicate the Number of
                         MISSing observations from the data.
                         For example, **GAP=29 NMISS=3** means that 3 observations were
                         missing from the data after observation 29. This option is not to be
                         confused with the **MISS** option described above.

ORDER=n   This option is used to estimate models with second- or higher-**ORDER**
                         autocorrelation. If **ORDER=2** is specified, an iterative Cochrane-Orcutt
                         procedure is done unless the **GS** option is also specified. With the **GS**
                         option a search is made within the stability triangle by an iterative grid
                         search using initial spacing of .25 for the two values of ρ. The method is
                         not guaranteed to yield a global maximum, particularly in small samples,
                         but it usually works quite well. The **GS** option requires over 100 iterations
                         for the search and can be rather expensive. The missing data options are
                         not valid for **ORDER=1** estimation.

                         If an **ORDER** larger than 2 is specified the model will be estimated using
                         the least squares procedure described in Pagan [1974]. The **DLAG,**
                         DROP, GAP, GS, MISS, ML, NMISS, RESTRICT, RHO and **SRHO**
                         options are not permitted when **ORDER** is larger than 2. Also, the **FC**
                         command will not work after an **AUTO** command that uses this option.

                         Users interested in the maximum likelihood procedure for second-order
                         models should read Box and Jenkins [1976, p.58-65] and Schmidt [1971].
                         A good application of the second-order method can be found in Savin
                         [1978].

ORDER=−n   If a negative **ORDER** is specified the model will be estimated using a moving-average error model instead of an autocorrelation error model. A least squares procedure is used as described in Pagan [1974]. The **MISS, GAP, RHO, SRHO, DLAG, DROP, GS, ML** and **RESTRICT** options are not permitted. The **FC** command will not work after an **AUTO** command that uses this option.

In the first-order model with moving average errors we have:

$$Y_t = X_t \beta + \epsilon_t$$

and

$$\epsilon_t = v_t + \theta v_{t-1}$$

where θ is the moving-average parameter and v is a random disturbance term.

RHO=   This option allows the specification of any value of ρ desired for the regression. With the **RHO=** option neither a Cochrane-Orcutt nor a maximum likelihood estimation is done since SHAZAM already has the value of ρ. This is useful when ρ is already known as it eliminates expensive iterations.

SRHO=   This option is used with the **RHO=** option when the Second-order ρ is to be specified for a second-order model.

An example of the **AUTO** command using the Theil [1971, p.102] Textile example is the following:

```
|_READ(11) YEAR CONSUME INCOME PRICE
...SAMPLE RANGE IS NOW SET TO:          1         17
|_AUTO CONSUME INCOME PRICE / ML DN
DEPENDENT VARIABLE =  CONSUME
..NOTE..R-SQUARE,ANOVA,RESIDUALS DONE ON ORIGINAL VARS
DN OPTION IN EFFECT - DIVISOR IS N

MAXIMUM LIKELIHOOD ESTIMATION              17 OBSERVATIONS
BY COCHRANE-ORCUTT TYPE PROCEDURE WITH CONVERGENCE = 0.00100

     ITERATION              RHO              LOG L.F.              SSE
         1                  0.0             -51.6471             433.31
         2              -0.18491            -51.3982             419.95
         3              -0.19741            -51.3971             419.77
         4              -0.19797            -51.3971             419.77

  LOG L.F. =    -51.3971        AT RHO =     -0.19797
```

	ESTIMATE	ASYMPTOTIC VARIANCE	ASYMPTOTIC ST.ERROR	ASYMPTOTIC T-RATIO
RHO	-0.19797	0.05652	0.23774	-0.83274

R-SQUARE=.9528   R-SQUARE ADJUSTED=.9461
VARIANCE OF THE ESTIMATE =   24.692
STANDARD ERROR OF THE ESTIMATE =   4.9691
LOG OF THE LIKELIHOOD FUNCTION = -51.3971

VARIABLE NAME	ESTIMATED COEFFICIENT	ASYMPTOTIC STANDARD ERROR	T-RATIO --------	PARTIAL CORR.	STANDARDIZED COEFFICIENT	ELASTICITY AT MEANS
INCOME	1.0650	0.20670	5.1525	0.8092	0.23945	0.81543
PRICE	-1.3750	0.64357E-01	-21.366	-0.9850	-0.98364	-0.78012
CONSTANT	129.61	20.876	6.2085	0.8565	0.0	0.96361

Buse's R^2 is defined in Buse [1973] and is shown in Judge, Griffiths, Hill, Lütkepohl and Lee [1985, p. 32, Eq. 2.3.16].

The available temporary variables on the **AUTO** command are: $DF, $DW, $K, $LLF, $N, $R2, $R2OP, $RAW, $RHO, $SIG2, $SSE, $SSR, $SST, $ZDF, $ZSSR and $ZSST.

For more information on temporary variables see the chapter *MISCELLANEOUS COMMANDS AND INFORMATION* and the chapter *ORDINARY LEAST SQUARES*.

12. BOX-COX REGRESSIONS

"No model exists for him who seeks what he has never seen."

Paul Eluard
Artist

Box-Cox (**BOX**) regressions are easily done in SHAZAM. Users not familiar with the Box-Cox transformation should study this before attempting Box-Cox regressions. See Zarembka [1974, Ch. 3]; Judge, Hill, Griffiths, Lütkepohl and Lee [1988, Ch. 12.5]; Magee [1988]; White [1972]; or Savin and White [1978]. The **BOX** command can be used for classical Box-Cox regressions where only the dependent variable is transformed, or in the extended Box-Cox model in which all variables are transformed by the same power transformation. It is possible to restrict the exact power transformation on any of the variables by using the **LAMBDA** command in the manner described below. Any variable in the regression with non-positive values will automatically be restricted to be untransformed.

In general, the format of the **BOX** command is:

BOX *depvar indeps / options*

where *depvar* is the dependent variable, *indeps* is a list of independent variables, and *options* is a list of desired options. Some of the available options on the **BOX** command are slightly different than those for the **OLS** command. In particular, the **NOCONSTANT** option produces a modified transformation (see details below), since the normal transformation requires an intercept in the regression. The **ANOVA, DLAG, GF, LIST, MAX, PCOR, PCOV, RESTRICT, RSTAT, BEG=, END=, COV=, PREDICT=** and **RESID=** options as defined for **OLS** and the **DROP** option as defined for **AUTO**, are available on the **BOX** command.

Some additional options available for use with the **BOX** command are:

ACCUR   Normally, SHAZAM will estimate λ to an **ACCUR**acy of .01. However, if this option is used, SHAZAM will iterate to an **ACCUR**acy of 0.001 at some increase in cost.

ALL   This option is used to extend the Box-Cox model so that **ALL** variables receive the same power transformation (unless restricted). Without this option only the dependent variable is transformed. The extended Box-Cox model is far more expensive to estimate than the classical model. For example, the classical model usually requires only four iterations. The **ALL** option often requires twenty iterations.

AUTO   This option will simultaneously estimate λ and the first-order **AUTO**correlation parameter ρ. The method is that of Savin and White [1978]. This option is very expensive as over 100 iterations are required. An accuracy of 0.01 is obtained for λ and ρ (the **ACCUR** option is not available with this option). When using this option, the **DROP, NMISS=, GAP=** and **RHO=** options described in the chapter on autoregressive models may be used. The λ range for the **AUTO** option is preset at (-2,3.5) and may not be altered. It is important to check for corner solutions.

DN   This option will compute the estimated variance of the regression line by **D**ividing the residual sum of squares by **N** instead of n-k. This option should be used if the user believes that the model has only good large-sample properties, and if the user wants the maximum likelihood estimates of the variances.

DUMP   This option may be used with the **AUTO** option to get some intermediate output on the iterations to be **DUMP**ed. This output is usually of little value, but sometimes contains useful information on the grid search.

FULL   This option will attempt a combined Box-Cox and Box-Tidwell estimation so that all variables in the equation have different λs. This option can be rather expensive as many iterations are required. The above warning on Box-Tidwell regressions also applies for the **FULL** option. In fact, overflows are quite common with this option so it should be used with care. **RESTRICT** commands are not permitted. The **ALL, AUTO, LAMBDA=, LAMS=, LAME=** and **LAMI=** options must not be used with the **TIDWELL** or **FULL** options.

NOCONSTANT   This option will estimate a model with no intercept. Thus, the regression will have **NO CONSTANT**. The user should be aware that the Box-Cox model is not well defined for models without an intercept, and the model is generally not scale-invariant. The transformation that is used on this option is the one suggested by Zarembka [1974], $(X^{**}\lambda/\lambda)$. A further result is that the likelihood function is not continuous at $\lambda = 0$; SHAZAM will use a value of 0.01 instead of 0.0. A Golden Section search algorithm will be used.

TIDWELL	This option will do a Box-**TIDWELL** regression instead of a Box-Cox regression. Only the independent variables will be transformed and each variable will have a different λ. For details on the method see Box and Tidwell [1962]. All independent variables must be strictly positive for this technique. Users should be aware that, quite frequently, the Box-Tidwell method will not converge, thus causing the run to be terminated unsuccessfully. This happens most often in small samples where there is a high variance in one of the λs. If this happens, the run might be successful if the data is scaled to a lower range (for example, divide all variables by 100). If the run is still unsuccessful and the user still wishes to pursue this type of estimation, a SHAZAM consultant should be contacted. **RESTRICT** commands are not permitted. The **ALL, AUTO, LAMBDA=, LAMS=, LAME=** and **LAMI=** options must not be used with the **TIDWELL** or **FULL** options.
UT	The **UT** option will UnTransform the observed and predicted dependent variables for purposes of computing and plotting the residuals. All values will then be in their original form. This is a useful option since the transformed residuals and predicted values usually are difficult to interpret. However, this option will raise costs somewhat since an extra pass through the data is required. In addition, the untransformed residuals will no longer necessarily have a zero mean. Note that this option does not affect the regression results. Only the residual listing will be affected.
COEF=	Saves the **COEF**ficients, the λs for each independent variable and the dependent variable, and ρ if the **AUTO** option is used.
LAMBDA=	This option is used to specify the value of **LAMBDA** desired by the user. Expensive iterations are eliminated with this option.
LAMS= **LAME=** **LAMI=**	These options are used to do a manual grid search of λ. The Starting value of **LAM**bda (**LAMS=**), the Ending value of **LAM**bda (**LAME=**) and an Increment (**LAMI=**) should be specified. When the optimal λ has been determined it can be specified on the **LAMBDA=** option. The manual grid search is rarely needed. It may be necessary if the iterative procedure fails. The manual grid search is not available when using the **AUTO** option.
RHO=	Specifies the **RHO** to be used when the **AUTO** option is specified.

As noted above, SHAZAM uses iterative methods to estimate Box-Cox regressions. In some cases the program will fail during the iterations with a floating-point overflow. If this happens, the data could be scaled by dividing all variables by a constant such as 100 or 1000. This is usually not a problem, however, unless the magnitude of the data is initially very large. Since many iterations are necesary for Box-Cox regressions, the costs will rise substantially for large sample sizes. The user should also be aware that the maximum likelihood methods used here are not for small samples, and the use of these techniques on small samples may yield nonsense results.

An example of the **BOX** command and some of the **BOX** output using Theil's [1971, p.102] Textile data is:

```
|_BOX CONSUME INCOME PRICE / DN ALL NOANOVA

DEPENDENT VARIABLE =CONSUME
DN OPTION IN EFFECT - DIVISOR IS N
```

BOX-COX REGRESSION		17 OBSERVATIONS				
ITERATION	LAMBDA	LOG-L.F.	GRADIENT	R-SQUARE	SSE	SSE/N
1	0.0	-46.586217	0.046633	0.9744	0.13613E-01	0.00080
2	1.000	-51.647054	-5.060837	0.9513	433.31	25.489
17	-0.350	-46.033572	0.023531	0.9766	0.41708E-03	0.00002

```
BOX-COX REGRESSION FOR LAMBDA = -0.350000
 R-SQUARE = 0.9766      R-SQUARE ADJUSTED = 0.9733
VARIANCE OF THE ESTIMATE =   0.24534E-04
STANDARD ERROR OF THE ESTIMATE =   0.49532E-02
LOG OF THE LIKELIHOOD FUNCTION = -46.0336
```

VARIABLE NAME	ESTIMATED COEFFICIENT	ASYMPTOTIC CONDITIONAL STANDARD ERROR	T-RATIO --------	PARTIAL CORR.	STANDARDIZED COEFFICIENT	BOX-COX ELASTICITY AT MEANS
INCOME	1.1535	0.12604	9.1522	0.9256	0.34933	1.2665
PRICE	-0.68995	0.26057E-01	-26.478	-0.9902	-1.0106	-0.84134
CONSTANT	1.2292	0.28096	4.3751	0.7600	0.0	6.8342

If the **ALL** option is used, SHAZAM assumes all the variables are to be transformed by the same λ. At times this may not be desired. In particular, the user might want to restrict some of the λs to be 1.0 or 0.0. The **LAMBDA** command is used to impose restrictions. If the **ALL** option is not in effect, any of the right-hand side variables may be restricted to any λ. Those that are unrestricted will remain untransformed. In general, the format of the **LAMBDA** command is:

LAMBDA *var=value   var=value*

An example is:

BOX MONEY INCOME INTRST / RESTRICT ALL
LAMBDA INCOME=0
END

When the **LAMBDA** command is used to impose retrictions, the **RESTRICT** option must be specified. If **RESTRICT** commands are used they must follow all **LAMBDA** commands. The **END** command should follow all the **LAMBDA** and **RESTRICT** commands. No λs may be restricted if the **TIDWELL** or **FULL** options are being used.

The available temporary variables on the **BOX** command are: $ANF, $DF, $DW, $K, $LLF, $N, $R2, $R2OP, $RAW, $RHO, $SIG2, $SSE, $SSR, $SST, $ZANF, $ZDF, $ZSSR and $ZSST.

For more information on temporary variables see the chapter *MISCELLANEOUS COMMANDS AND INFORMATION* and the chapter *ORDINARY LEAST SQUARES.*

13. DIAGNOSTIC TESTS

"That is a question which has puzzled many an expert, and why? Because there was no reliable test. Now we have the Sherlock Holmes test, and there will no longer be any difficulty."

Holmes to Watson in "A Study in Scarlet"
by A. Conan Doyle

SHAZAM can perform a number of diagnostic tests after estimating a regression model. Some of these tests are recursive residuals, Goldfeld-Quandt, Chow, RESET, and Lagrange Multiplier Tests for heteroskedasticity. Some good references for diagnostic tests are: Godfrey, McAleer, and McKenzie [1988]; Zarembka [1974, Chap. 1]; Breusch and Pagan [1979]; and Pagan and Hall [1983]. The **DIAGNOS** command is used for these tests and many other statistics. While the **DIAGNOS** command can follow most single-equation regression estimations, much of the output is only relevant if used on an OLS regression. The **DIAGNOS** command requires that you first run an **OLS** estimation. The **DIAGNOS** command would normally follow as the next command. In general, the format of the **DIAGNOS** command is:

DIAGNOS / *options*

where *options* is a list of desired options.

The available options on the **DIAGNOS** command are:

ACF Prints the AutoCorrelation Function of residuals and associated test statistics for various orders of autocorrelation.

BACKWARD This option is used with the **RECUR** option to compute **BACKWARD**s recursive residuals.

BOOTLIST This option is used with the **BOOTSAMP=** option to print the entire list of Bootstrapped coefficients for every generated sample. Obviously, this could potentially generate a lot of output.

CHOWTEST Produces a set of sequential **CHOW TEST** statistics and sequential Goldfeld-Quandt Test statistics which split the sample in 2 pieces at every possible point. It also computes Equations 2.10 and 2.12 from Harvey [1981] to test recursive residuals for heteroskedasticity.

HET   This option runs a series of tests for **HET**eroskedasticity by running regressions of squared residuals (E^2) or logs of (E^2) on the predicted values of the dependent variable (YHAT) or the independent variables (X). The regression of (E^2) on all X variables is known as the Breusch-Pagan-Godfrey (B-P-G) Test and the regression of LOG(E^2) all X variables is known as the Harvey Test.

JACKKNIFE   This option runs a series of regressions, successively omitting a different observation to get the **"JACKKNIFE** Coefficient Estimates". An example of JACKKNIFE estimation is in the Appendix to Chapter 9 in the *Judge Handbook*.

LIST   Prints a table of observed and predicted values of the dependent variable, and regression residuals. This gives the same output as the **LIST** option on **OLS** or **FC**.

MAX   Equivalent to specifying the **LIST, RECUR, ACF, RECEST, RECRESID, BACKWARD, CHOWTEST, RESET**, and **HET** options. Obviously, the computation of all these tests can be time consuming.

RECEST /   This option is used with the **RECUR** option to print the **REC**ursive
NORECEST   **EST**imated coefficients.

RECRESID /   This option is used with the **RECUR** option to print the **REC**ursive
NORECRESID   **RESID**uals.

RECUR   Performs **RECUR**sive Estimation by running a series of regressions by adding one observation per regression. It is often used for tests of structural change. Recursive residuals and CUSUM tests are printed along with the tests indicated by Equations 2.10 and 2.12 from Harvey [1981].

RESET   Used to compute the Ramsey **RESET** Specification Test statistics by running three additional regressions of the dependent variable on the independent variables, and on powers of YHAT (the predicted dependent variable - $YHAT^2, YHAT^3, YHAT^4$) included in the same regression. The **RESET** Test is an F test that tests whether the coefficients on the YHAT variables are zero. A description of the RESET Test is contained in Ramsey(1969) and a further example is in Chapter 13 of the *Gujarati Handbook*.

WIDE /   Reduces the width of output to 80 columns. The default value is explained
NOWIDE   in the chapter *SET AND DISPLAY*.

DIAGNOSTIC TESTS

BOOTSAMP= This option will Bootstrap the previous OLS regression. The number of samples desired is specified. A good example of this option can be found in the Appendix to Chapter 9 of the *Judge Handbook*.

BOOTUNIT= This option will write out the generated coefficients for each sample in a Bootstrap experiment on the Unit specified. It is used in conjunction with the **BOOTSAMP=** option. A file should be assigned to the unit with the SHAZAM **FILE** command or an operating system command.

GQOBS= Used with the **CHOWTEST** option to specify the number of observations to be omitted for the Goldfeld-Quandt Test.

MHET= Used with the **CHOWTEST** option to specify M, the number of residuals to use in Harvey's [1981, Equation 2.12] Recursive Residual Exact Heteroskedasticity Test.

RECUNIT= Used with the **RECUR** option if you want to write the **REC**ursive estimates and residuals on the **UNIT** specified. A file should be assigned to the unit with the SHAZAM **FILE** command or an operating system command.

SIGLEVEL= Used with the **RECUR** option to specify the significance level desired for the CUSUM and CUMSUMSQ tests. The available choices are 1, 5, and 10. The default is **SIGLEVEL=5**.

The following is an example of the **DIAGNOS** command using Theil's [1971, p.102] Textile data:

```
|_OLS CONSUME INCOME PRICE
OLS ESTIMATION
        17 OBSERVATIONS      DEPENDENT VARIABLE = CONSUME

 R-SQUARE =  0.9513     R-SQUARE ADJUSTED =  0.9443
VARIANCE OF THE ESTIMATE =   30.951
STANDARD ERROR OF THE ESTIMATE =   5.5634
LOG OF THE LIKELIHOOD FUNCTION = -51.6471
```

VARIABLE NAME	ESTIMATED COEFFICIENT	STANDARD ERROR	T-RATIO 14 DF	PARTIAL CORR.	STANDARDIZED COEFFICIENT	ELASTICITY AT MEANS
INCOME	1.0617	0.26667	3.9813	0.7287	0.23871	0.81288
PRICE	-1.3830	0.83814E-01	-16.501	-0.9752	-0.98933	-0.78464
CONSTANT	130.71	27.094	4.8241	0.7902	0.	0.97175

|_DIAGNOS / MAX

DEPENDENT VARIABLE = CONSUME   17 OBSERVATIONS
REGRESSION COEFFICIENTS
    1.06170929275   -1.38298550222   130.706623949

OBS. NO.	OBSERVED VALUE	PREDICTED VALUE	CALCULATED RESIDUAL				
1	99.200	93.692	5.5076			I	*
2	99.000	96.423	2.5765			I	*
3	100.00	98.579	1.4210			I*	
4	111.60	116.78	-5.1814		*	I	
5	122.20	122.45	-0.25169			*	
6	117.60	122.91	-5.3100		*	I	
7	121.10	123.05	-1.9455			* I	
8	136.00	135.43	0.57462			I*	
9	154.20	149.80	4.3958			I	*
10	153.60	152.06	1.5426			I	*
11	158.50	153.91	4.5946			I	*
12	140.60	145.56	-4.9571		*	I	
13	136.20	145.10	-8.8975	*		I	
14	168.00	161.58	6.4156			I	*
15	154.30	156.86	-2.5614		*	I	
16	149.00	156.29	-7.2887	*		I	
17	165.50	156.14	9.3650			I	*

DURBIN-WATSON = 2.0185   VON NEUMAN RATIO = 2.1447   RHO = -0.18239
RESIDUAL SUM = 0.77804E-12 RESIDUAL VARIANCE =   25.489
SUM OF ABSOLUTE ERRORS=   72.787
R-SQUARE BETWEEN OBSERVED AND PREDICTED = 0.9513
RUNS TEST: 7 RUNS, 9 POSITIVE, 8 NEGATIVE, NORMAL STATISTIC =   -1.2423
COEFFICIENT OF SKEWNESS = -0.0343 WITH STANDARD DEVIATION OF 0.5497
COEFFICIENT OF EXCESS KURTOSIS = -0.8701 WITH STANDARD DEVIATION OF 1.0632

       GOODNESS OF FIT TEST FOR NORMALITY OF RESIDUALS - 6 GROUPS
OBSERVED 0.   4.0 4.0 6.0 3.0 0.
EXPECTED 0.4   2.3 5.8 5.8 2.3 0.4
CHI-SQUARE =   2.7834 WITH 1 DEGREES OF FREEDOM

JARQUE-BERA ASYMPTOTIC LM NORMALITY TEST
CHI-SQUARE =   0.6662 WITH 2 DEGREES OF FREEDOM

HETEROSCEDASTICITY TESTS
  E**2 ON YHAT: CHI-SQUARE =   2.495 WITH 1 D.F.
  E**2 ON YHAT**2 : CHI-SQUARE =   2.658 WITH 1 D.F.
  E**2 ON LOG(YHAT**2) : CHI-SQUARE =   2.303 WITH 1 D.F.
  E**2 ON X (B-P-G) TEST: CHI-SQUARE =   4.900 WITH 2 D.F.
  LOG(E**2) ON X (HARVEY) TEST: CHI-SQUARE =   3.421 WITH 2 D.F.

```
RAMSEY RESET SPECIFICATION TESTS USING POWERS OF YHAT
  RESET(2)=    11.787     - F WITH DF1=   1 AND DF2=  13
  RESET(3)=    5.4877     - F WITH DF1=   2 AND DF2=  12
  RESET(4)=    3.6049     - F WITH DF1=   3 AND DF2=  11


RESIDUAL CORRELOGRAM
LM-TEST FOR HJ:RHO(J)=0, STATISTIC IS STANDARD NORMAL
 LAG      RHO       STD ERR     T-STAT     LM-STAT    DW-TEST
   1    -0.1455     0.2425     -0.5998     0.7014     2.0185
   2    -0.2231     0.2425     -0.9200     1.2257     2.0359
   3     0.1871     0.2425      0.7716     0.9975     1.1956
   4    -0.3002     0.2425     -1.2377     1.7388     2.0133
CHI-SQUARE WITH    4  D.F. IS      3.333

JACKKNIFE COEFFICIENTS

COEFFICIENT    AVERAGE       ST.ERR
   INCOME      1.0259      0.27080
   PRICE      -1.3694      0.91245E-01
   CONSTANT    133.48       28.928


RECURSIVE COEFFICIENT ESTIMATES
   3   0.58599          1.1338         -71.974
   4  -0.54970E-01     -1.2802          233.31
   5  -0.86357         -1.9976          384.60
   6   0.92446E-01     -1.5186          242.54
   7   0.60090         -1.2248          163.09
   8   0.61319         -1.4191          180.66
   9   0.36233         -1.6835          231.55
  10   0.55817         -1.5320          197.07
  11   0.59587         -1.5096          191.07
  12   0.93135         -1.3893          145.05
  13   1.0961          -1.3266          122.07
  14   1.0210          -1.3876          135.31
  15   1.0177          -1.3746          134.45
  16   1.0213          -1.3458          131.41
  17   1.0617          -1.3830          130.71
```

RECURSIVE RESIDUALS

OBS	REC-RES	CUSUM	BOUND	CUSUMSQ
4	0.94469	0.16379	4.0538	0.00206
5	2.2989	0.56238	4.5605	0.01426
6	2.7913	1.04635	5.0673	0.03224
7	3.7605	1.69835	5.5740	0.06487
8	5.2155	2.60263	6.0807	0.12765
9	2.5217	3.03985	6.5875	0.14232
10	-3.5083	2.43157	7.0942	0.17073
11	-0.95105	2.26667	7.6009	0.17282
12	-9.1586	0.67873	8.1076	0.36639
13	-8.5802	-0.80893	8.6144	0.53629
14	7.2539	0.44877	9.1211	0.65773
15	-2.4963	0.01595	9.6278	0.67211
16	-6.5587	-1.12122	10.1345	0.77138
17	9.9530	0.60447	10.6413	1.00000

HARVEY(1981,EQUATION 2.10 RECURSIVE T-TEST =   0.1615 WITH   13 D.F.
HARVEY(1981,EQUATION 2.12 HETEROSKEDASCTICITY TEST =   7.1480 WITH M =   4

BACKWARDS
RECURSIVE COEFFICIENT ESTIMATES

15	6.2400	1.5400	-576.61
14	17.460	-12.984	-853.75
13	2.1880	-2.4999	83.360
12	1.8767	-2.3500	106.17
11	2.0353	-2.2604	85.733
10	2.0944	-2.2117	77.007
9	2.1966	-2.1140	60.963
8	2.1916	-2.0003	54.550
7	2.0917	-1.8616	56.131
6	2.1017	-1.8725	55.789
5	1.8743	-1.7343	70.398
4	1.8319	-1.7090	73.130
3	1.3919	-1.5101	105.21
2	1.2061	-1.4356	119.36
1	1.0617	-1.3830	130.71

BACKWARDS
RECURSIVE RESIDUALS

OBS	REC-RES	CUSUM	BOUND	CUSUMSQ
14	5.6889	1.68609	4.0538	0.07469
13	11.008	4.94850	4.5605	0.35432
12	3.2906	5.92376	5.0673	0.37930
11	4.9015	7.37648	5.5740	0.43475
10	0.98227	7.66761	6.0807	0.43698
9	2.1057	8.29170	6.5875	0.44721
8	1.7982	8.82465	7.0942	0.45467
7	3.0412	9.72601	7.6009	0.47602
6	-0.45786	9.59031	8.1076	0.47650
5	6.4177	11.49238	8.6144	0.57155
4	1.3958	11.90605	9.1211	0.57605
3	9.8188	14.81614	9.6278	0.79854
2	6.4933	16.74061	10.1345	0.89584
1	6.7182	18.73174	10.6413	1.00000

BACKWARDS
HARVEY(1981,EQUATION 2.10 RECURSIVE T-TEST =   5.0063 WITH   13 D.F.
HARVEY(1981,EQUATION 2.12 HETEROSKEDASCTICITY TEST =   0.9855 WITH M =   4

SEQUENTIAL CHOW AND GOLDFELD-QUANDT TESTS

N1	N2	SSE1	SSE2	CHOW	G-Q	DF1	DF2
4	13	0.89245	247.66	2.7256	0.36035E-01	1	10
5	12	6.1774	206.47	3.8048	0.13463	2	9
6	11	13.969	206.26	3.5476	0.18059	3	8
7	10	28.110	197.02	3.3908	0.24969	4	7
8	9	55.312	193.78	2.7117	0.34252	5	6
9	8	61.671	189.35	2.6628	0.27142	6	5
10	7	73.979	188.38	2.3892	0.22440	7	4
11	6	74.883	164.36	2.9744	0.17085	8	3
12	5	158.76	153.53	1.4209	0.22980	9	2
13	4	232.38	32.364	2.3346	0.71803	10	1

CHOW TEST - F DISTRIBUTION WITH DF1=   3 AND DF2=   11

14. DISTRIBUTED-LAG MODELS

"Gentlemen, you have come sixty days too late. The depression is over."

Herbert Hoover
U.S. President, June 1930

Polynomial Distributed Lags (or Almon Lags) are performed by using a special form of notation available only with the **OLS, AUTO, BOX, GLS,** and **POOL** commands. It should *NOT* be used with the **SYSTEM, MLE, NL, PROBIT, LOGIT, TOBIT, ROBUST, ARIMA** or any other estimation command. There are many good references in econometrics textbooks on the use of distributed lags. In particular, see Maddala [1977, p.355-359]; Judge, Griffiths, Hill, Lütkepohl and Lee [1985, Ch.9.3]; Judge, Hill, Griffiths, Lütkepohl and Lee [1988, Ch.17]; Pindyck and Rubinfeld [1980, p.211-224]; and Almon [1965].

SHAZAM allows the user to specify a lag length, order of polynomial and endpoint constraints on any independent variable in the model. Each independent variable may have different order and endpoint constraints. For illustration, the **OLS** command is used here.

In general, the format of the command is:

OLS *depvar indep(first.last,order,endcon) / options*

where *depvar* is the name of the dependent variable and *indep* is the name of an independent variable. Each independent variable may have up to 3 parameters in parentheses which specify the form of the polynomial lag. The first parameter contains two numbers separated by a dot(.). These numbers specify the *first* and *last* periods to use for lags. For example 0.3 means to use the current period (0) and lags t-1, t-2, and t-3. If *order* and *endcon* are not specified an unrestricted lag is used. For example:

OLS CONSUME INCOME(0.3) PRICE

would include INCOME variables for times t-j, j=0,1,2,3 which correspond to the current value of INCOME and the previous 3 lagged values. *Note that no blanks are allowed between the name of the variable and the items in parentheses.* In this example no lags are required for the PRICE variable:

```
|_SAMPLE 1 17
|_OLS CONSUME INCOME(0.3) PRICE
 LAG FOR INCOME   RANGE =   0   3 ORDER= 0 ENDCON=0

OLS ESTIMATION
      14 OBSERVATIONS      DEPENDENT VARIABLE = CONSUME
 ...NOTE..SAMPLE RANGE SET TO:    4,   17

 R-SQUARE =  0.9449     R-SQUARE ADJUSTED =  0.9104
 VARIANCE OF THE ESTIMATE =   30.343
```

```
STANDARD ERROR OF THE ESTIMATE =    5.5084
MEAN OF DEPENDENT VARIABLE =    142.03
LOG OF THE LIKELIHOOD FUNCTION = -39.8357
```

VARIABLE NAME	ESTIMATED COEFFICIENT	STANDARD ERROR	T-RATIO 8 DF	PARTIAL CORR.	STANDARDIZED COEFFICIENT	ELASTICITY AT MEANS
INCOME	1.9286	0.86001	2.2425	0.6213	0.55377	1.4121
INCOME	0.39497E-01	0.82795	0.47705E-01	0.0169	0.11571E-01	0.02884
INCOME	-0.27252	0.86102	-0.31651	-0.1112	-0.82560E-01	-0.19854
INCOME	0.28810	0.71836	0.40104	0.1404	0.91740E-01	0.20906
PRICE	-1.7050	0.16612	-10.264	-0.9641	-1.2699	-0.85421
CONSTANT	57.201	53.674	1.0657	0.3526	0.0	0.40274

An example which imposes a second-order polynomial restriction on the lag parameters for INCOME is:

OLS CONSUME INCOME(0.3,2) PRICE(0.2)

In this case PRICE contains 2 lagged values in addition to the current value, but no polynomial restrictions are placed on the PRICE variable.

```
|_OLS CONSUME INCOME(0.3,2) PRICE(0.2)
 LAG FOR INCOME  RANGE =  0  3 ORDER= 2 ENDCON=0
 LAG FOR PRICE   RANGE =  0  2 ORDER= 0 ENDCON=0

OLS ESTIMATION
     14 OBSERVATIONS    DEPENDENT VARIABLE = CONSUME
...NOTE..SAMPLE RANGE SET TO:    4,   17

 R-SQUARE =  0.9546    R-SQUARE ADJUSTED =  0.9157
VARIANCE OF THE ESTIMATE =    28.547
STANDARD ERROR OF THE ESTIMATE =    5.3429
MEAN OF DEPENDENT VARIABLE =    142.03
LOG OF THE LIKELIHOOD FUNCTION = -38.4739
```

VARIABLE	SUM OF LAG COEFS	MEAN LAG
INCOME	1.7270	-0.22802E-01
PRICE	0.29697	1.6477

VARIABLE NAME	ESTIMATED COEFFICIENT	STANDARD ERROR	T-RATIO 7 DF	PARTIAL CORR.	STANDARDIZED COEFFICIENT	ELASTICITY AT MEANS
INCOME	1.7511	0.83286	2.1025	0.6222	0.50281	1.2822
INCOME	0.16436	0.50007	0.32867	0.1233	0.48150E-01	0.12003
INCOME	-0.36162	0.53513	-0.67576	-0.2475	-0.10955	-0.26345
INCOME	0.17317	0.68318	0.25348	0.0954	0.55143E-01	0.12566
PRICE	-1.9859	0.30902	-6.4266	-0.9247	-1.4791	-0.99495
PRICE	0.10461	0.37377	0.27988	0.1052	0.87352E-01	0.05448
PRICE	0.19236	0.27512	0.69918	0.2555	0.16977	0.10405
CONSTANT	81.250	56.211	1.4455	0.4794	0.0	0.57207

Endpoint constraints may be specified for any polynomial by using the third parameter. This parameter is defined as follows:

0= No ENDPOINT constraints;
1= ENDPOINT constraints on the left side of the polynomial;
2= ENDPOINT constraints on the right side of the polynomial;
3= ENDPOINT constraints on both left and right sides.

An example is:

OLS CONSUME INCOME(0.3,2,1) PRICE(0.2,3,3)

In this case INCOME has 3 lags in addition to the current period, with a second degree polynomial and endpoint constraint on the left side. The PRICE variable will have two lags in addition to the current period with a third-degree polynomial and endpoint constraints on both sides. This yields the following output:

```
|_OLS CONSUME INCOME(0.3,2,1) PRICE(0.2,3,3)
 LAG FOR INCOME   RANGE =  0  3 ORDER= 2 ENDCON=1
 LAG FOR PRICE    RANGE =  0  2 ORDER= 3 ENDCON=3

OLS ESTIMATION
        14 OBSERVATIONS       DEPENDENT VARIABLE = CONSUME
...NOTE..SAMPLE RANGE SET TO:    4,    17

 R-SQUARE =  0.9051     R-SQUARE ADJUSTED =  0.8630
 VARIANCE OF THE ESTIMATE =    46.427
 STANDARD ERROR OF THE ESTIMATE =   6.8137
 MEAN OF DEPENDENT VARIABLE =    142.03
 LOG OF THE LIKELIHOOD FUNCTION = -43.6375
```

VARIABLE	SUM OF LAG COEFS	MEAN LAG
INCOME	1.0562	-0.39209
PRICE	-1.5214	-0.35099

VARIABLE NAME	ESTIMATED COEFFICIENT	STANDARD ERROR	T-RATIO 9 DF	PARTIAL CORR.	STANDARDIZED COEFFICIENT	ELASTICITY AT MEANS
INCOME	0.61093	0.21953	2.7829	0.6801	0.17542	0.44732
INCOME	0.71655	0.25162	2.8478	0.6885	0.20992	0.52329
INCOME	0.31686	0.14652	2.1626	0.5848	0.95994E-01	0.23084
INCOME	-0.58814	0.35478	-1.6578	-0.4837	-0.18729	-0.42679
PRICE	-1.4841	0.29196	-5.0833	-0.8612	-1.1053	-0.74354
PRICE	-0.60855	0.73453E-01	-8.2850	-0.9403	-0.50815	-0.31673
PRICE	0.57127	0.25947	2.2017	0.5917	0.50418	0.30899
CONSTANT	138.71	46.606	2.9762	0.7043	0.0	0.97662

SHAZAM will automatically delete the necessary number of observations at the beginning of the data, so this should not be done with the **SAMPLE** command. In the above example the original data and sample size were set for observations 1 thru 17. However, since 3 observations are lost due to lags SHAZAM will only use observations 4 thru 17. Note that other programs (TSP, for instance) may use a different method to specify the degree of the polynomial. In particular the order may be equal to the SHAZAM definition plus 1.

Since the Almon method imposes restrictions on the coefficients, the number of degrees of freedom is increased by the number of restrictions. The number of restrictions for a lagged variables is equal to the number of coefficient estimates for that variable minus the order of the polynomial minus one. Each endpoint constraint will also increase the number of restrictions.

15. FORECASTING

"The 1976 Olympics could no more lose money than I could have a baby."

Mr. Jean Drapeau
Mayor of Montreal, 1973

Forecasting is very easy to do in SHAZAM. The **FC** command just uses a set of regression coefficients for a single equation and a set of data to compute predicted values of the dependent variable and compare the predictions to the actual values. The procedure is exactly the same as that used to compute predicted values in regressions. In addition, the Forecast standard errors are available from the preceding **OLS** command or the **AUTO** and **POOL** commands assuming first-order autocorrelation. The calculation of the forecast standard errors does not make any adjustments if lagged dependent variables are present. The advantage of the **FC** command is that the estimated coefficients can be taken from a previous regression and predicted values can be generated over any chosen set of observations. There is also the option to use any set of coefficients desired.

In general, the format of the **FC** command, when the estimated coefficients from the immediately preceding regression are being used, is:

FC / *options*

while the format when reading in all the coefficients is:

FC *depvar indeps* / *options* **COEF=**

where *depvar* is the variable name of the dependent variable, *indeps* is a list of variable names of the independent variables, **COEF=** is a required option used to specify the name of the variable in which the coefficients are stored, and *options* is a list of desired options.

When the coefficients from the previous regression are being used the variables must not be specified since SHAZAM remembers them. However, when a new set of coefficients is being specified SHAZAM must be told which variables to use and the variable in which the coefficients have been saved must be specified on the **COEF=** option. The FC command is similar to the **OLS** command except no estimation is done. If the **PREDICT=** or **RESID=** options are used, the variable used for the results must have been previously defined with the **DIM** command.

As well as the **GF, LIST, BEG=, END=, PREDICT=** and **RESID=** options as defined for **OLS**, the following options are available:

AFCSE   This option is used with the **BLUP** or **IBLUP** option if Equation 8.3.14 in Judge, Griffiths, Hill, Lütkepohl and Lee [1985] is desired instead of Equation 8.3.13. This formula can also be found as Equation 7.11 in Harvey [1981] and is based on Baillie [1979].

BLUP, **IBLUP**	These options are used in autoregressive models when the user wishes the predicted values to be adjusted with the lagged residual, to give the Best Linear Unbiased Predictions. **BLUP** only uses information from the first observation specified while **IBLUP** uses information from the Immediately preceding observation. Forecast standard errors are computed for the **BLUP** and **IBLUP** cases using the square root of Equation 8.3.13 in Judge, Griffiths, Hill, Lütkepohl, and Lee [1985]. This is the same formula as Equation 7.10 in Harvey[1981]. Note, that correct forecast standard errors are only available for the first-order autocorrelation model.
DYNAMIC	Performs **DYNAMIC** forecasts for models with a lagged dependent variable. It is assumed that the lag variable is the first independent variable listed.
MAX	This option is equivalent to the **LIST, GF** and **RSTAT** options.
CSNUM =	Specifies which cross-section to use on a Pooled Cross-Section Time-Series model.
ESTEND =	Specifies the last observation of the estimation for AUTO and POOL models.
FCSE =	This option is available to save the Forecast standard errors in the variable specified. The option is only available when the coefficients from the previous regression are used for forecasting. The variable to be used for the Forecast standard errors must be defined before the estimation with the **DIM** command. Note that if the **HETCOV** option was used on the previous OLS command, the Forecast standard errors are incorrect.
NC =	Specifies the number of cross-sections in a Pooled Cross-Section Time-Series model.

When a set of coefficients is being read in, the following options may also be included:

ALL	This option is used with the **MODEL = BOX** and **LAMBDA =** options when transformation of **ALL** variables, dependent and independent, is desired. When this option is used restrictions may be implemented on the λs with the **LAMBDA** command.
NOCONSTANT	No intercept is included in the regression. In this case, a value for the intercept should not be included.
RESTRICT	If **LAMBDA** commands are specified, the **RESTRICT** option must be used.

UPPER	This option is used when **MODEL=TOBIT** is specified on the **FC** command. For details on this option see the chapter *TOBIT REGRESSION*.
LAMBDA=	This option is used to specify a value of **LAMBDA** if the **MODEL=BOX** option is specified.
LIMIT=	This option is used when **MODEL=TOBIT** is specified on the **FC** command. For details on this option see the chapter *TOBIT REGRESSION*.
MODEL=	This option is used to tell SHAZAM what **MODEL** is used. The available models are **AUTO, BOX, LOGIT, OLS, POOL, PROBIT** and **TOBIT**. When **MODEL=TOBIT** is used the *normalized* coefficients (including the one on the dependent variable) must be read in. The default is **MODEL=OLS**. When **MODEL=POOL** is used, the forecast must be done for only one Cross-Section. The relative position of the Cross-Section is specified with theCSNUM= and NC= options.
ORDER=	This option specifies the **ORDER** of the model for **MODEL=AUTO**.
POOLSE=	Specifies the standard error of the cross-section in a Pooled Cross-Section Time-Series model when **MODEL=POOL**.
RHO=	This option is used to specify a value of the first-order autoregressive parameter for the regression when **MODEL=AUTO** or **MODEL=BOX** or **MODEL=POOL** is specified.
SRHO=	When **MODEL=AUTO** and **ORDER=2** this option is used with the **RHO=** option to specify a value of the Second-order **RHO**.

Useful references for forecasting are Salkever [1976] and Pagan and Nichols[1984].

Some examples of the use of the **FC** command are:

1. **SAMPLE 1 17**
    OLS CONSUME INCOME PRICE / LIST
    FC / LIST

2. **SAMPLE 1 10**
    OLS CONSUME INCOME PRICE
    FC / LIST BEG=11 END=17

3. **FC GNP INVEST CONSUME GOVT / LAMBDA=.7 COEF=VECTOR MODEL=BOX**

4. **SAMPLE 1 40**
    AUTO GNP INVEST / MAX
    FC / BLUP BEG=34 END=50 LIST ESTEND=40
    FC / IBLUP BEG=1 END=50 LIST ESTEND=40

5. **SAMPLE 1 32**
    AUTO CONSUME INCOME PRICE / ML MAX
    FC / BLUP BEG=30 END=50 LIST ESTEND=32

Note that, in the first example, the **FC** command would reproduce the residual listing of the **OLS** command, which would not be very useful. The second example specifies a sample range to use for the forecasting. The third example reads in a set of coefficients; no listing of the predicted values is done, but the summary forecast statistics will be given. In the fourth example, a first-order autoregressive model is run. The listing on the two **FC** commands will differ only because of the use of the **BLUP** and **IBLUP** options. In the last example, another autoregressive model is run and forecasts are made with the **BLUP** option. Note that **BEG=30** is specified since the last two observations for the estimation period are required.

The output will include mean error, mean square error, root mean square error, and the Theil U-statistic [1966], which has a range from zero to infinity. See also Maddala [1977, p.342-347].

The following is the output of the second example above using the Textile data:

```
|_SAMPLE 1 10
|_OLS CONSUME INCOME PRICE
OLS ESTIMATION
      10 OBSERVATIONS     DEPENDENT VARIABLE = CONSUME
...NOTE..SAMPLE RANGE SET TO:     1,   10

 R-SQUARE =  0.9810     R-SQUARE ADJUSTED =  0.9755
VARIANCE OF THE ESTIMATE =    10.568
STANDARD ERROR OF THE ESTIMATE =    3.2509
MEAN OF DEPENDENT VARIABLE =    121.45
LOG OF THE LIKELIHOOD FUNCTION = -24.1954

MODEL SELECTION TESTS - SEE JUDGE ET.AL.(1985, P.242)
  AKAIKE (1969) FINAL PREDICTION ERROR- FPE =    13.739
    (FPE ALSO KNOWN AS AMEMIYA PREDICTION CRITERION -PC)
  AKAIKE (1973) INFORMATION CRITERION- AIC =   2.6012
  SCHWARZ(1978) CRITERION-SC =   2.6920
```

VARIABLE NAME	ESTIMATED COEFFICIENT	STANDARD ERROR	T-RATIO 7 DF	PARTIAL CORR.	STANDARDIZED COEFFICIENT	ELASTICITY AT MEANS
INCOME	0.55817	0.24556	2.2730	0.6517	0.14623	0.48339
PRICE	-1.5320	0.10980	-13.953	-0.9825	-0.89763	-1.1060
CONSTANT	197.07	32.439	6.0751	0.9168	0.0	1.6226

```
|_FC / LIST BEG=11 END=17

DEPENDENT VARIABLE = CONSUME              7 OBSERVATIONS
REGRESSION COEFFICIENTS
   0.558165798286       -1.53203247506        197.070728749
   OBS.   OBSERVED      PREDICTED    CALCULATED  STD. ERROR
   NO.     VALUE         VALUE        RESIDUAL
   11     158.50        159.92       -1.4226      4.8628                 *I
   12     140.60        154.57      -13.968       5.7288          *       I
   13     136.20        153.44      -17.241       5.4723          *       I
   14     168.00        170.96       -2.9628      6.1911                 *I
   15     154.30        162.76       -8.4646      4.8977              *   I
   16     149.00        162.62      -13.624       5.0160          *       I
   17     165.50        161.09        4.4053      4.6130                  I *
```

SUM OF ABSOLUTE ERRORS=   62.088
R-SQUARE BETWEEN OBSERVED AND PREDICTED = 0.6833
RUNS TEST: 2 RUNS,   1 POSITIVE,   6 NEGATIVE, NORMAL STATISTIC =-1.5811
MEAN ERROR =   -7.6111
SUM-SQUARED ERRORS =   779.82
MEAN SQUARE ERROR =   111.40
MEAN ABSOLUTE ERROR=   8.8697
ROOT MEAN SQUARE ERROR =   10.555
THEIL INEQUALITY COEFFICIENT U = 0.650
  DECOMPOSITION
      PROPORTION DUE TO BIAS = 0.51999
      PROPORTION DUE TO VARIANCE = 0.29305
      PROPORTION DUE TO COVARIANCE = 0.18696
  DECOMPOSITION
      PROPORTION DUE TO BIAS = 0.51999
      PROPORTION DUE TO REGRESSION = 0.12868
      PROPORTION DUE TO DISTURBANCE = 0.35133

16. GENERALIZED LEAST SQUARES

"50 years hence...we shall escape the absurdity of growing a whole chicken in order to eat the breast or wing, by growing these parts separately under a suitable medium."

Winston Churchill
Member of British Parliament, 1932

The **GLS** command in SHAZAM performs Generalized Least Squares regressions. A good discussion of Generalized Least Squares can be found in Judge, Hill, Griffiths, Lütkepohl and Lee [1988, Ch. 8]. The **GLS** estimator can be written as:

$$\hat{\beta} = (X'\Omega^{-1}X)^{-1}X'\Omega^{-1}Y$$

and

$$V(\hat{\beta}) = \hat{\sigma}^2(X'\Omega^{-1}X)^{-1}$$

where:

$$\hat{\sigma}^2 = (\epsilon'\Omega^{-1}\epsilon)/(n-k)$$

and

$$V(\epsilon) = \hat{\sigma}^2\Omega$$

and Y is the dependent variable, X is the matrix of exogenous variables, $\hat{\beta}$ is the vector of estimated coefficients, $V(\hat{\beta})$ is the covariance matrix of coefficients, $\hat{\sigma}^2$ is the variance of the regression line, $V(\epsilon)$ is the covariance matrix of disturbances, n is the sample size, k is the number of regressors, and ϵ is the vector of residuals. The Ω matrix can be decomposed so that $P'P = \Omega^{-1}$. The definition of R^2 is found in Buse [1973] and also shown in Judge, Griffiths, Hill, Lütkepohl and Lee [1985, p. 32, Eq. 2.3.16].

In general, the format of the **GLS** command is:

GLS *depvar indeps / options*

where *depvar* is the dependent variable, *indeps* is a list of the independent variables, and *options* is a list of desired options. One of **OMEGA=**, **OMINV=** or **PMATRIX=** is required to tell SHAZAM which matrix to use for estimation. For example, to give SHAZAM the Ω matrix the **OMEGA=** option is used.

As well as **ANOVA, DLAG, DN, GF, LIST, MAX, NOCONSTANT, PCOR, PCOV, RSTAT, BEG=, END=, COEF=, COR=, COV=, PREDICT=, STDERR=** and **TRATIO=**, as defined for **OLS**, the following options are available on the **GLS** command:

BLUP

With this option the predicted values are adjusted using information obtained from previous period residuals according to the transformation specified by the P matrix. This option is not effective in forecasts using the **GLS** coefficients.

DUMP

This option will print out the Ω, Ω^{-1} and P matrices. It is important to be aware that each of these matrices is of the order n X n and in large samples could require many pages of printout. The **DUMP** option is useful for checking to see if the input of the matrix has been done correctly.

FULLMAT

If the **FULLMAT** option is not specified, SHAZAM assumes that the specified matrix contains the diagonals of Ω (**OMEGA=**), Ω^{-1} (**OMINV=**) or the P matrix (**PMATRIX=**).

NOMULSIGSQ

With this option, $(X'X)^{-1}$ is the complete covariance matrix and thus will **NO**t be **MUL**tiplied by $\hat{\sigma}^2$ to get the covariance matrix of coefficients.

UT

With this option, the estimated coefficients will be used with the original data to compute predicted values and residuals that are UnTransformed. Without this option, the residual output and predicted values given are transformed.

PMATRIX=
OMEGA=
OMINV=

These options specify which matrix is to be used for estimation, the **P MATRIX**, the **OMEGA** matrix or the **OM**ega **INV**erse matrix. One of these options *must* be specified on each **GLS** command. The **FULLMAT** option must be used if the complete matrix, rather than just the diagonals of the matrix, is given.

RESID=

Saves the **RESID**uals in the variable specified. For details on which residuals are saved see the **UT** and **BLUP** options.

The following is an example of **GLS** output using Theil's [1971, p.102] Textile data to estimate a first-order autoregressive model:

```
_DIM P 17 2
_SAMPLE 2 17
_GENR P:1=1
_SAMPLE 1 1
_GENR P:1=SQRT(1-.8*.8)
_SAMPLE 1 17
_GENR P:2=-.8
```

```
|_PRINT P
P
    17 BY      2 MATRIX
 0.6000000     -0.8000000
 1.000000      -0.8000000
 1.000000      -0.8000000
 1.000000      -0.8000000
 1.000000      -0.8000000
 1.000000      -0.8000000
 1.000000      -0.8000000
 1.000000      -0.8000000
 1.000000      -0.8000000
 1.000000      -0.8000000
 1.000000      -0.8000000
 1.000000      -0.8000000
 1.000000      -0.8000000
 1.000000      -0.8000000
 1.000000      -0.8000000
 1.000000      -0.8000000
 1.000000      -0.8000000
|_READ(11) YEAR CONSUME INCOME PRICE
    4 VARIABLES AND        17 OBSERVATIONS STARTING AT OBS 1
|_GLS CONSUME INCOME PRICE / PMATRIX=P
...WARNING..ASSUMING P         CONTAINS DIAGONALS
GLS ESTIMATION
    17 OBSERVATIONS     DEPENDENT VARIABLE = CONSUME
...NOTE..SAMPLE RANGE SET TO    1,   17
R-SQUARE DEFINITIONS BASED ON BUSE, AMSTAT(1973)
LOG-LIKELIHOOD FUNCTION =   -55.9037
 R-SQUARE = 0.7652     R-SQUARE ADJUSTED = 0.7316
VARIANCE OF THE ESTIMATE =    48.091
STANDARD ERROR OF THE ESTIMATE =   6.9348
LOG OF THE LIKELIHOOD FUNCTION = -55.9037
```

VARIABLE NAME	ESTIMATED COEFFICIENT	STANDARD ERROR	T-RATIO 14 DF	PARTIAL CORR.	STANDARDIZED COEFFICIENT	ELASTICITY AT MEANS
INCOME	1.1240	0.55952	2.0089	0.4730	0.25271	0.86057
PRICE	-1.6577	0.25249	-6.5655	-0.8688	-1.1859	-0.94051
CONSTANT	148.12	59.598	2.4853	0.5533	0.0	1.1012

Note above the use of the **DIM** command and the colon (:) function to create the **PMATRIX** variable. First, P is dimensioned to be the size of the **PMATRIX** for this problem. Next, the second to the seventeenth observations of the first column are given a value of one and the first observation of this column is given a value of SQRT(1-.8*.8). Finally, the second column is given a value of -.8. The **GENR** command is used to fill the matrix P. This should all make sense if it is understood how **GLS** can be used to estimate a first-order autoregressive model. The **DIM** command is explained in the chapter *MISCELLANEOUS COMMANDS AND INFORMATION*.

The available temporary variables on the **GLS** command are: $ANF, $DF, $DW, $K, $LLF, $N, $R2, $R2OP, $RAW, $RHO, $SIG2, $SSE, $SSR, $SST, $ZANF, $ZDF, $ZSSR and $ZSST.

For more information on temporary variables see the chapter *MISCELLANEOUS COMMANDS AND INFORMATION* and the chapter *ORDINARY LEAST SQUARES*.

17. MAXIMUM LIKELIHOOD ESTIMATION OF NON-NORMAL MODELS

"It's the work of a madman."

Ambroise Vollard
French art dealer, 1907
(viewing a Picasso painting)

The **MLE** command does Maximum Likelihood Estimation of some types of regression models with non-normal errors. If regressions with Multivariate-t errors are desired see the chapter in this manual titled *ROBUST ESTIMATION*. If the desired form of the model is not listed with the **TYPE=** option described below see the **LOGDEN** option in the chapter *NONLINEAR REGRESSION* where a user-specified density function may be estimated. This command should only be used if this type of regression model is fully understood. For a good description of some of these see Cameron and White [1988].

In general, the format of the **MLE** command is:

MLE *depvar indeps / options*

where *depvar* is the dependent variable, *indeps* is a list of independent variables, and *options* is a list of desired options. It is possible to specify the distribution of the errors when using the **MLE** command with the **TYPE=** option. The **ANOVA, DUMP, GF, LIST, MAX, NOCONSTANT, PCOR, PCOV, RSTAT, BEG=, END=, COEF=, COR=, COV=, PREDICT=, RESID=, STDERR=, TRATIO=, WEIGHT=** and **NONORM** options, as defined for **OLS**, are available on the **MLE** command. When the **WEIGHT=** option is specified the method explained under the **REPLICATE** option in **OLS** is used. Also, the **CONV=, ITER=, PITER=, OUT=** and **IN=** options described in the chapter *NONLINEAR REGRESSION* may be used on the **MLE** command. In addition, the following options are available:

LM
This option will perform a Lagrange Multiplier Test of some models against a less restricted model. If **TYPE=EXP** is used, two **LM** Tests for the **GAMMA** or **WEIBULL** models will be done. If **TYPE=WEIBULL** or **TYPE=GAMMA** is used the **LM** Test of a Generalized Gamma distribution is performed.

METHOD=
Specifies the nonlinear algorithm to use. The choices are **BFGS** (the default) or **DFP**. These **METHODS** are described in the chapter *NONLINEAR REGRESSION*.

TYPE=
Specifies the **TYPE** of distribution to be assumed for the errors. The available **TYPE**s are **WEIBULL, EWEIBULL, GAMMA, EGAMMA, GG, EGG** (Generalized Gamma), **LOGNORM** (Lognormal), **BETA, EXP** (Exponential) and **EXTREMEV** (Extreme Value Distribution). The default is **TYPE=EXP**. The types **EWEIBULL, EGAMMA, EGG** and **EXTREMEV** are used when the dependent variable is in log form. They correspond to the **WEIBULL, GAMMA, GG,** and **EXP** forms respectively.

The following is an example of **MLE** output using Theil's [1971, p.102] Textile data. Since no type is specified the default (**EXP**) is used:

```
|_MLE CONS INCOME PRICE / LM
EXP        REGRESSION    17 OBSERVATIONS

  QUASI-NEWTON METHOD USING BFGS UPDATE FORMULA
INITIAL STATISTICS :
TIME =    0.007 SEC.   ITER. NO.    1 FUNCTION EVALUATIONS    1
LOG-LIKELIHOOD FUNCTION=   -100.0802
COEFFICIENTS
    1.061710      -1.382985      130.7066
GRADIENT
 -0.1963726E-01 -0.3026842E-01 -0.2327427E-03
FINAL STATISTICS :
TIME =    0.012 SEC.   ITER. NO.    2 FUNCTION EVALUATIONS    2
LOG-LIKELIHOOD FUNCTION=   -100.0797
COEFFICIENTS
    0.9188552     -1.348463      142.7181
GRADIENT
 -0.1911042E-02 -0.1817677E-02 -0.1911540E-04

LM TEST OF EXP      AGAINST WEIBULL
  LM GRADIENT
 -0.1911042E-02 -0.1817677E-02 -0.1911540E-04  -16.97903
  LM SECOND DERIVATIVES
    10.898
     8.6995       7.2588
    0.10593       0.84822E-01  0.10323E-02
    5.6534        4.3493        0.54957E-01   20.051
CHI-SQUARE =   16.931      WITH 1 D.F.
LM TEST OF EXP      AGAINST GAMMA
  LM GRADIENT
 -0.1911042E-02 -0.1817677E-02 -0.1911540E-04  -9.801741
  LM SECOND DERIVATIVES
    10.898
     8.6995       7.2588
    0.10593       0.84822E-01  0.10323E-02
   -0.19110E-02  -0.18177E-02 -0.19115E-04   10.964
  CHI-SQUARE =    8.7628     WITH 1 D.F.
  R-SQUARE = 0.9499      R-SQUARE ADJUSTED = 0.9428
VARIANCE OF THE ESTIMATE =    26.204
STANDARD ERROR OF THE ESTIMATE =    5.1190
LOG OF THE LIKELIHOOD FUNCTION = -100.080
```

VARIABLE NAME	ESTIMATED COEFFICIENT	ASYMPTOTIC STANDARD ERROR	T-RATIO --------	PARTIAL CORR.	STANDARDIZED COEFFICIENT	ELASTICITY AT MEANS
INCOME	0.91886	5.9965	0.15323	0.0409	0.20659	0.70351
PRICE	-1.3485	1.8624	-0.72405	-0.1900	-0.96463	-0.76505
CONSTANT	142.72	642.62	0.22209	0.0593	0.0	1.0611

The available temporary variables on the **MLE** command are: $DF, $DW, $K, $LLF, $N, $R2, $R2OP, $RAW, $RHO, $SIG2, $SSE, $SSR, $SST, $ZDF, $ZSSR and $ZSST.

For more information on temporary variables see the chapter *MISCELLANEOUS COMMANDS AND INFORMATION* and the chapter *ORDINARY LEAST SQUARES*.

18. NONLINEAR REGRESSION

"It may be safely asserted...that population, when unchecked, increases in geometrical progression of such a nature to double itself every twenty-five years."

Thomas Malthus
British Economist, 1830

SHAZAM will estimate nonlinear regressions by a maximum likelihood procedure. It is assumed that the errors are additive and normally distributed. The algorithm is a Quasi-Newton method. Nonlinear estimation in SHAZAM is not difficult, but is frequently rather slow. It is very important for users to give SHAZAM good starting values of the coefficients. In theory, there is no limit to the number of equations that can be estimated as a nonlinear, seemingly unrelated, regressions system.

NOTE: Users should be familiar with nonlinear estimation before attempting this procedure. Some simple basic information can be found in Maddala [1977]. A more rigorous treatment of nonlinear estimation can be found in Judge, Griffiths, Hill, Lütkepohl and Lee [1985, Ch 6, Appendix B]; Judge, Hill, Griffiths, Lütkepohl and Lee [1988, Chapter 12]; and in Amemiya [1983] and Gallant [1987].

To set up a nonlinear model in SHAZAM, it is necessary to tell SHAZAM some basic information as well as give it an **EQ** command indicating the form of each equation in the model. In addition, the desired starting values should be specified on **COEF** commands or placed in a vector and specified with the **START=** option.

In general, the format for nonlinear estimation is:

NL *neq* / **NCOEF=** *options*
EQ *equation*
COEF *coef value coef value*
END

where *neq* is the number of equations, and *options* is a list of desired options.

One **EQ** command is required for every equation in the model. Coefficients that appear in one equation may also appear in other equations. **RESTRICT** commands are not permitted. No forecasting options are available.

As well as **LIST, PCOR, RSTAT, BEG=, END=, COEF=, COR=, COV=, STDERR=** and **TRATIO=** as defined for **OLS**, the available options are:

ACROSS   This option corrects for autocorrelation **ACROSS** equations as well as
                  within a single equation. With the **ACROSS** option a full matrix (NEQ x
                  NEQ) of autocorrelation coefficients is estimated. The values of the RHO
                  coefficients will be printed in column order (VEC(R)), corresponding to the
                  R matrix shown in equation 12.3.3 of Judge, Griffiths, Hill, Lütkepohl, and
                  Lee [1985]. This option can be computationally slow.

AUTO   This option will correct the equations for first-order **AUTO**correlation. The
                  method is described in Pagan [1974].

DRHO   Normally, when the **AUTO** option is specified SHAZAM gives the same
                  value of ρ to each equation. With the **DRHO** option a Different value of
                  RHO is given to each equation. When the order of autocorrelation is
                  specified as higher than one on the **ORDER=** option the **DRHO** option
                  will also give more than one ρ for each equation.

DUMP   This option will **DUMP** the internal code that SHAZAM has generated for
                  the **EQ** commands. This option is only useful for SHAZAM consultants.
                  As noted above, if **DUMP** is specified with **EVAL** there will be a large
                  amount of output.

EVAL   This option **EVAL**uates the likelihood function for the starting values and
                  prints out the answer. If **ITER=0** is also specified no estimation will be
                  done. This is useful for experimentation purposes. If **EVAL** and **DUMP**
                  are specified all the data in the nonlinear system is dumped along with the
                  computed residuals and derivatives of the function with respect to all
                  parameters. First, the data for each observation will be printed. Then the
                  residual for each equation and the derivatives of each equation with
                  respect to each parameter will be printed, and finally, the derivatives for
                  the equations will be printed consecutively. This option may not be used
                  with the **NUMERIC** option.

GENRVAR   This option will take the vector of coefficients and generate a set of scalar
                  variables using the same names as those used for the coefficients on the
                  EQ command. These scalar variables can then be used for the rest of the
                  SHAZAM run. This is an alternative to the **COEF=** method for saving
                  the coefficients.
                  NOTE: A large number of variables may need to be generated if the model
                  is large. The coefficient names used may not be used on any **EQ** command
                  later in the same run.

LOGDEN   This option is used to tell SHAZAM that the equation given on the **EQ**
                  command is the LOG-DENSITY for a single observation rather than a
                  regression equation. SHAZAM will then compute a complete likelihood
                  function by summing the log-densities. This option allows maximum
                  likelihood estimation of a large variety of functions. A specific example is
                  contained in Chapter 12.3 of the *Judge Handbook*.

NUMCOV   This option will use numeric differences to compute the covariance matrix after estimation. If this option is NOT specified SHAZAM uses a method based on the Davidon-Fletcher-Powell algorithm which builds up the covariance matrix after many iterations. This method may not be accurate if the model only runs for a small number of iterations. The numeric method is more expensive and also may not necessarily be accurate. The differential to be used in numeric differences can be controlled with the **STEPSIZE=** option.

NUMERIC   This option will use the **NUMERIC** difference method to compute derivatives in the algorithm. SHAZAM normally computes analytic derivatives which are more accurate. However, in some models with many equations and parameters, considerable savings in required memory will result if the **NUMERIC** option is used to compute numeric derivatives. In some cases the **NUMERIC** option may even be faster.

OPGCOV   This option will use the outer-product of the Gradient method to compute the covariance matrix. It is not valid with the **NUMERIC** option.

PCOV   The **PCOV** option will Print an estimate of the **COV**ariance matrix of coefficients after convergence. This estimate is based on an estimate of the Hessian which SHAZAM computes internally. SHAZAM estimates the Hessian by building it up after repeated iterations. Therefore, if the model converges immediately, SHAZAM will have a very poor estimate of the Hessian or none at all. In this case, the covariance matrix will just be an identity matrix.

SAME   The **SAME** option will run the previous **NL** regression without repeating the **EQ** commands. This should only be used in TALK mode at a terminal.

CONV=   This option is used to specify the **CONV**ergence criterion for the coefficients. This value will be multiplied by each coefficient starting value to compute the convergence condition for each coefficient. The default is **CONV=.00001**.

IN= *unit*   This option will read back the values of the coefficients and log-likelihood fuction that were saved with the **OUT=** option. This option is only useful when there is something to **IN**put from a previous run. This option may be combined with the **OUT=** option to insure that the **IN=** file always contains the values of the coefficients from the most recent iteration. The **COEF** command should only be used with the **IN=** option if the starting values of some of the coefficients are to be modified. When both **OUT=** and **IN=** are used the same unit number is usually used. A binary file should be assigned to the unit with the SHAZAM **FILE** command or an operating system command.

ITER=   The **ITER=** option is used to specify the maximum number of **ITER**ations. The default is 100.

METHOD=   The default is a Davidon-Fletcher-Powell algorithm. An alternative
                    METHOD=BFGS, Broyden-Fletcher-Goldfarb-Shanno (BFGS), is
                    described in Belsley [1980]. Another alternative is a slightly different
                    D-F-P algorithm which can be obtained with **METHOD=DFP**.

NCOEF=   Specifies the Number of different **COEF**ficients to be estimated. This
                    option is required.

ORDER=   Specifies the **ORDER** of autocorrelation to be corrected when the **AUTO**
                    option is used. The default is **ORDER=1**.

OUT=_unit_   This option will write **OUT** on the unit specified the values of the
                    coefficients and log-likelihood function after each iteration. This is quite
                    useful for restarting the model in another run with the **IN=** option
                    described above. When this option is used, a file must be assigned to the
                    output unit as described in the chapter _HOW TO RUN SHAZAM_. The
                    values will be written in double precision in unformatted (binary) all on one
                    line. Units 11-49 are available for use.

PITER=   Specifies the frequency with which **ITER**ations will be **P**rinted in the
                    output. The default **PITER=15** indicates that one out of every 15
                    iterations will be printed.

START=   This option will use the values in the specified variable as starting values
                    for the estimation. The order of the parameters should be the same as
                    normally printed by the SHAZAM **NL** command, namely, the order that
                    they appear on the **EQ** commands. In some cases this may be an easier
                    way to input starting values than by using the **COEF** command. Be
                    careful to make sure that the length of the START vector is equal to the
                    number of coefficients specified with the **NCOEF=** option.

STEPSIZE=   Specifies the stepsize to use with the **NUMCOV** option to control the
                    differential in numeric derivatives. The default is **STEPSIZE=1E-4**. The
                    calculated covariance matrix may be very sensitive to this value.

The following example shows how to set up a nonlinear estimation of the Theil [1971, p.102]
Textile data equation. The model has one equation and three coefficients:

```
_NL 1 / NCOEF=3
_EQ CONSUME=A+B*INCOME+C*PRICE
_COEF A 1 B 1 C 1
   3 VARIABLES IN  1 EQUATIONS WITH  3 COEFFICIENTS

COEFFICIENT STARTING VALUES
A          1.0000      B          1.0000      C          1.0000
      100 MAXIMUM ITERATIONS, CONVERGENCE = 0.000010
INITIAL STATISTICS :
```

```
TIME =   0.022 SEC.   ITER. NO.      0   FUNCT. EVALUATIONS    1
LOG-LIKELIHOOD FUNCTION=   -93.81530
COEFFICIENTS
    1.000000        1.000000        1.000000
GRADIENT
    0.2139579       22.19384        19.30445
INTERMEDIATE STATISTICS :
TIME =   0.068 SEC.   ITER. NO.     15   FUNCT. EVALUATIONS   23
LOG-LIKELIHOOD FUNCTION=   -51.80821
COEFFICIENTS
    139.0081        0.9593592       -1.351122
GRADIENT
    0.1261540       11.53399        14.20190
FINAL STATISTICS :
TIME =   0.087 SEC.   ITER. NO.     23   FUNCT. EVALUATIONS   31
LOG-LIKELIHOOD FUNCTION=   -51.64705
COEFFICIENTS
    130.7066        1.061710        -1.382985
GRADIENT
   -0.9900047E-09 -0.1060253E-06 -0.7260919E-07
MAXIMUM LIKELIHOOD ESTIMATE OF SIGMA-SQUARED =    25.489
         COEFFICIENT   ST. ERROR    T-RATIO
A          130.71       24.902       5.2488
B          1.0617       0.24568      4.3216
C         -1.3830       0.76302E-01 -18.125
|_END
```

Note that the **EQ** command supplies names for the coefficients to be estimated. The **EQ** command can be continued on additional lines if there is an ampersand (&) typed at the end of the line to be continued. An equation with continuation lines may contain a total of 1024 columns. **EQ** commands are similar to **GENR** commands except **EQ** commands only permit functions LOG() and EXP(). SHAZAM will assume that anything in the equation that has not already been defined as a variable will be an estimated coefficient.

In the above example, the coefficients are A, B and C; the variables are CONSUME, INCOME and PRICE. The **COEF** command immediately follows the **EQ** command. If the **COEF** command is omitted, SHAZAM uses a starting value of 1 for all estimated coefficients. In the above example, starting values of 1 are specified on the **COEF** command, but this is not necessary. Notice that this example is identical to that illustrated in the chapter *ORDINARY LEAST SQUARES*. The **NL** command gives the same estimated coefficients as the **OLS** command, but the cost of running **NL** regressions is much higher. An **END** command should follow the **COEF** command.

The following example shows how to set up a nonlinear estimation of the CES production function model described in Judge, Griffiths, Hill, Lütkepohl and Lee [1985, p. 210]. The model has one equation and 4 coefficients.

READ K L Q
GENR LOGQ=LOG(Q)
NL 1 / NCOEF=4 PCOV
EQ LOGQ=LOG(GAM)-(V/P)*LOG(DEL*K(-P)+(1-DEL)*L**(-P))**
COEF
3.0 .8 .5 .5
END

In this example, the coefficients are GAM, V, P and DEL; the variables are LOGQ, K and L. The **COEF** command immediately follows the **EQF** command. If the variable names are not specified on the **COEF** command, SHAZAM assumes that the starting values appear in the same order as they appear on the **EQ** command (i.e. GAM V P DEL). Alternatively, the **COEF** command could include the name of the coefficient followed by its starting value:

COEF V .5 GAM 3.0 DEL .8

If no starting value is assigned to a coefficient, a value of 1.0 is assumed.

The next example shows how to set up a nonlinear estimation of the Linear Expenditure System. In this system it is assumed that consumers can spend their income on 4 goods. The variables E1, E2, E3 and E4 will be the expenditures on the goods, and the variables P1, P2, P3 and P4 are the prices. Total income Y is the sum of all the expenditures. In the Linear Expenditure System, the coefficients to be estimated are the marginal budget shares (BETA1, BETA2, BETA3) along with the subsistence quantities (GAMMA1, GAMMA2, GAMMA3 and GAMMA4). Since this is a complete system of demand equations, it is well known that only 3 of the 4 equations need to be estimated (BETA4 = 1-BETA1-BETA2-BETA3). Thus, there are 3 equations and 7 coefficients to estimate. The SHAZAM job might look like:

```
SAMPLE 1 45
READ(11) E1 E2 E3 E4 P1 P2 P3 P4
GENR Y=E1+E2+E3+E4
NL 3 / NCOEF=7 ITER=300 CONV=.001 PCOV
EQ
E1=P1*GAMMA1+BETA1*(Y-P1*GAMMA1-P2*GAMMA2-P3*GAMMA3-P4*GAMMA4)
EQ
E2=P2*GAMMA2+BETA2*(Y-P1*GAMMA1-P2*GAMMA2-P3*GAMMA3-P4*GAMMA4)
EQ
E3=P3*GAMMA3+BETA3*(Y-P1*GAMMA1-P2*GAMMA2-P3*GAMMA3-P4*GAMMA4)
COEF BETA1 .4 BETA2 .2 BETA3 .3
COEF GAMMA1 1050 GAMMA2 2048 GAMMA3 50 GAMMA4 500
END
```

It is important to remember to eliminate 1 equation from the model when estimating systems of demand equations so that the system is not overdetermined.

Users experienced with nonlinear estimation will be aware that there is no guarantee that the model will converge. If it does, convergence to a local rather than a global maximum is likely. For this reason, the model should always be re-estimated with different starting values to verify that the global maximum has probably been achieved. Since the costs of nonlinear estimation are extremely high it is often useful to attempt to get good starting values by first estimating a linear simplification of the model.

19. POOLED CROSS-SECTION TIME-SERIES

"Branch banking...will mean, I suggest in all humility, the beginning of the end of the capitalist system."

John T. Flynn
Business writer, 1933

SHAZAM will perform a Pooled Cross-Section and Time-Series estimation under certain model specifications and conditions. A Generalized Least Squares procedure is used on the model described in Kmenta [1986, pp.616-625]. This model is also described briefly in Judge, Griffiths, Hill, Lütkepohl and Lee [1985, p.518]. SHAZAM provides three ways to specify the model. The default is the Cross-sectionally Heteroskedastic and Time-wise Autoregressive Model discussed in Kmenta [1986, pp.618-622]. A slight variation of this model is to restrict all cross-sections to have the same autoregressive parameter as described in Kmenta [1986, Eq.12.32]. SHAZAM also provides an option to do the full Cross-sectionally Correlated and Time-wise Autoregressive Model described in Kmenta [1986, pp.622-625]. In all cases SHAZAM modifies the Kmenta procedure to keep the first observation of each cross-section. The transformation used to keep the first observation is identical to the one used in first-order autoregressive models.

It will be assumed that the data is arranged to conform to the Kmenta model. The data should be arranged so that all observations of a particular cross-sectional unit are together. A cross-sectional unit is, for example, a household or a region. Therefore, SHAZAM will require a complete time-series for the first group followed by a time-series for the second group, etc. If the data is not set up in this fashion it must be sorted before estimation of the model. In some cases the SHAZAM **SORT** command will help to rearrange the data. It will be assumed that there are n cross-sectional units and each one has t observations in the time-series. The total number of observations will then be n x t. Each cross-sectional unit must have the same number of observations in the time-series.

The format of the **POOL** command is:

POOL *depvar indeps* / **NC=** *options*

where *depvar* and *indeps* are the names of the dependent and independent variables. The **NC=** option **must** specify the number of cross-sectional units (for example, households) in the data. SHAZAM will then figure out the number of time periods from the total number of observations. Most of the options from the **OLS** command are available. The definition of R^2 is found in Buse [1973] and is also shown in Judge, Hill, Griffiths, Lütkepohl and Lee [1985, p. 32, Eq. 2.3.16].

As well as the **ANOVA, DLAG, DUMP, GF, LIST, MAX, NOCONSTANT, PCOR, RSTAT, BEG=, END=, COEF=, COV=, PREDICT=, RESID=, STDERR=** and **TRATIO=** options, as defined for **OLS**, and the **UT** option defined for **GLS**, the following options are available on the **POOL** command:

CORCOEF   The **CORCOEF** option estimates ρ using the correlation coefficient form, the alternative method described by Kmenta [1986, Eq.12.26]. This method confines the estimate of ρ to the interval [-1,+1].

FULL   The **FULL** option will estimate the **FULL** Cross-sectionally Correlated and Time-wise Autoregressive Model. As described in Kmenta [p.512-514], the model is modified by the usual transformation to retain the first observation. The **FULL** model takes longer to estimate than the other models.

MULSIGSQ   The estimated covariance matrix of coefficients is calculated using equation 12.39 in Kmenta [1986, p.623]. However, some econometricians believe that this matrix should be multiplied by the overall estimate of σ^2. The **MULSIGSQ** option does this multiplication. This option is the default, but could be turned off with the **NOMULSIGSQ** option.

PCOV   The **PCOV** option prints the covariance matrix of coefficients just as on other regression commands. In addition it prints the PHI matrix shown on the next page if NC is greater than 8. IF NC is less than 8 the PHI matrix is always printed.

SAME   The **SAME** option will force all the values of ρ to be equal for each of the cross-sectional units. This value is estimated by Kmenta [1986, Eq.12.32]. Following this restriction, the Cross-sectionally Heteroskedastic and Time-wise Autoregressive Model is estimated.

NC=   Specifies the number of cross-sectional units in the data. This option is required.

RHO=   Specifies a value of ρ to use instead of the estimated values. When this option is used the **SAME** option is automatically in effect. This option is commonly used with **RHO=0** to suppress the autocorrelation correction so that only the heteroskedastic correction is performed.

The following is an example of the **POOL** command using the cross-section data found in Judge, Griffiths, Hill, Lütkepohl and Lee [1985, p.553]:

```
|_POOL Y X / NC=4 FULL CORCOEF
POOLED CROSS-SECTION TIME-SERIES ESTIMATION
     4 CROSS-SECTIONS AND      10 TIME-PERIODS
 DEPENDENT VARIABLE = Y
OLS COEFFICIENTS
   1.2600      5.1222
```

```
RHO VECTOR
   0.11231        0.66390E-03  0.71514      -0.19030
CONSTANT RHO =  0.40119
VARIANCES
   22.369         26.734       49.119        14.279
PHI MATRIX
   22.369
   13.969         26.734
  -16.065        -13.283       49.119
  -4.4654         7.9856       -2.8788       14.409
FINAL COEFFICIENTS
   1.1701         9.1403
FINAL SSE =    30.758
LOG-LIKELIHOOD FUNCTION =     -116.664
 BUSE R-SQUARE = 0.9444       BUSE RAW-MOMENT R-SQUARE = 0.9949
 VARIANCE OF THE ESTIMATE =  0.80942
 STANDARD ERROR OF THE ESTIMATE =  0.89968
```

VARIABLE NAME	ESTIMATED COEFFICIENT	STANDARD ERROR	T-RATIO 38 DF	PARTIAL CORR.	STANDARDIZED COEFFICIENT	ELASTICITY AT MEANS
X	1.1701	0.51212E-01	22.849	0.9655	0.82651	0.81338
CONSTANT	9.1403	1.5946	5.7322	0.6810	0.0	0.22156

The available temporary variables on the **POOL** command are: $ANF, $DF, $DW, $K, $LLF, $N, $R2, $R2OP, $RAW, $RHO, $SIG2, $SSE, $SSR, $SST, $ZANF, $ZDF, $ZSSR and $ZSST.

For more information on temporary variables see the chapter *MISCELLANEOUS COMMANDS AND INFORMATION* and the chapter *ORDINARY LEAST SQUARES*.

20. **PROBIT AND LOGIT REGRESSION**

"The deliverance of the saints must take place some time before 1914."

Charles Taze Russell
American religious leader, 1910

"The deliverance of the saints must take place some time after 1914."

Charles Taze Russell
American religious leader, 1923

SHAZAM will do a multiple Probit or Logit regression on a single equation where the dependent variable is a 0-1 dummy variable. Before attempting Probit or Logit regression the user should be familiar with the technique. Some basic references are Chow [1983, Ch.8]; Hanushek and Jackson [1977, Ch.7]; Judge, Griffiths, Hill, Lütkepohl and Lee [1985, Ch.18]; Judge, Hill, Griffiths, Lütkepohl and Lee [1988, Ch.19]; Maddala [1977, Ch.7]; Maddala [1983, Ch.7]; and Pindyck and Rubinfeld [1980, Ch.8]. A simple example of the multiple Probit model using SHAZAM can be found in White [1972]. A simple example of the Logit model can be found in Cameron and White [1986].

In the Probit Model, an Index I is created which is a linear function of the right-hand side variables:

$$I = X \beta$$

The index I, which has a range from minus infinity to plus infinity, is then translated to a 0-1 range by the use of the cumulative normal distribution. Therefore, an $I=0$ would be translated to a 0.5 probability, and the regular cumulative normal table could be used to interpret various values of I. Clearly, while the index I is a linear function of X, the probabilities are not; therefore, the coefficients must be interpreted carefully.

In the Logit model, the dependent variable is transformed using the logistic function:

$$Y = 1 / (1 + \exp(-X\beta))$$

The Probit and Logit algorithms use fast iterative methods which usually converge in 4 or 5 iterations. The routines are based on computer programs originally written by John Cragg. A maximum likelihood estimation method is used so hypothesis testing is usually done via a likelihood ratio test. **RESTRICT** commands are not permitted.

In general, the formats of the **PROBIT** and **LOGIT** commands are:

PROBIT *depvar indeps / options*
LOGIT *depvar indeps / options*

where *depvar* is the dependent variable, *indeps* is a list of independent variables, and *options* is a list of desired options. As well as **MAX, NOCONSTANT, NONORM, PCOR, BEG=, END= COEF=, COV=** and **WEIGHT=**, as defined for **OLS**, the following options are available on the **PROBIT** and **LOGIT** commands:

DUMP
This option will **DUMP** the matrix of second derivatives and possibly some other output that the user normally does not want to see.

LIST
The **LIST** option will **LIST**, for each observation, the value of the index I, the predicted and observed values of the dependent variable, and a plot of the predicted values. It will also print the residual statistics obtained with **RSTAT**. Note that the predicted values, rather than the residuals, are plotted with the **LIST** option in the Probit and Logit models since a plot of the residuals is not very informative.

PCOV
The **PCOV** option will **P**rint the estimated asymptotic **COV**ariance matrix of the coefficients. The matrix is the inverse of the negative of the matrix of second derivatives of the likelihood function. In a large sample the coefficients will be normally distributed.

RSTAT
The **RSTAT** option yields usual **R**esidual **STAT**istics, but no listing of the observations. While many of the usual statistics are printed (for example, Durbin-Watson), they should be used with care since they may not be valid for the Probit and Logit models.

CONV=
This option is used to set the **CONV**ergence criterion for the log-likelihood function. The default is .001.

IMR=
The **IMR=** option saves the computed Inverse Mill's Ratio in the variable specified. This is sometimes used after a Probit estimation for use in a second stage equation. The Ratio is defined as $f(X\beta) / F(X\beta)$ if $Y=1$ and $f(X\beta) / (F(X\beta)-1)$ if $Y=0$ where $f()$ is the standard normal density function and $F()$ is the cumulative standard normal density function. The ratio is discussed in Heckman [1979, p.156]. Numerous applications can be found in Maddala [1983, Ch. 8-9].

INDEX=
The **INDEX=** option saves the computed **INDEX** in the variable specified.

ITER=
This option may be used to set the maximum number of **ITER**ations allowed. The default is 25.

PITER=
Specifies the frequency with which the **ITER**ations will be **P**rinted. The default is **PITER=1**. To prevent any information from being printed **PITER=0** must be specified.

PREDICT=
Saves the **PREDICT**ed probabilities in the variable specified.

If the **WEIGHT=** option is used, the method used follows that described for the **REPLICATE** option in **OLS**.

The output from the **PROBIT** and **LOGIT** commands includes the following statistics:

Weighted aggregate elasticity - sum of individual elasticities
    weighted by the probabilities. (See Hensher and Johnson [1981, Eq.3.44].)
Likelihood ratio test. (See Maddala [1983, p.40].)
Maddala R-square. (See Maddala [1983, Eq.2.44].)
Cragg-Uhler R-square. (See Maddala [1983, Eq.2.50].)
McFadden R-square. (See Hensher and Johnson [1981, Eq.3.32].)
    Adjusted for degrees of freedom. (See Hensher and Johnson [1981, Eq.3.33].)
    Approximately F distributed. (See Chow [1983, Eq.49].)
Chow R-square. (See Chow [1983, Eq.47].)
Prediction of success table. (See Maddala [1983, Table 3].)
Sum of squared residuals. (See Amemiya [1981, Eq.2.54].)
Weighted sum of squared residuals. (See Amemiya [1981, Eq.2.56].)

The following example of **LOGIT** output uses the voting data set from Pindyck and Rubinfeld [1980, Table 10.10]. The variables are PUB12, PUB34, PUB5, PRIV, YEARS, SCHOOL, LOGINC, PTCON and YESVM:

```
|_LOGIT YESVM PUB12 PUB34 PUB5 PRIV YEARS SCHOOL LOGINC PTCON/PITER=1
 LOGIT ANALYSIS     DEPENDENT VARIABLE =YESVM    CHOICES =  2
          95. TOTAL OBSERVATIONS
          59. OBSERVATIONS AT ONE
          36. OBSERVATIONS AT ZERO
       25 MAXIMUM ITERATIONS
 CONVERGENCE TOLERANCE =0.00001

 LOG OF LIKELIHOOD WITH CONSTANT TERM ONLY =    -63.037
 BINOMIAL  ESTIMATE = 0.6211

 ITERATION  5      LOG OF LIKELIHOOD FUNCTION =    -53.303

 ITERATION  6 ESTIMATES
   0.58364       1.1261       0.52606      -0.34142      -0.26127E-01  2.6250
   2.1872       -2.3945      -5.2014
```

VARIABLE NAME	ESTIMATED COEFFICIENT	ASYMPTOTIC STANDARD ERROR	T-RATIO	ELASTICITY AT MEANS	WEIGHTED AGGREGATE ELASTICITY
PUB12	0.58364	0.68779	0.84857	0.93986E-01	0.91051E-01
PUB34	1.1261	0.76821	1.4659	0.11827	0.96460E-01
PUB5	0.52606	1.2693	0.41444	0.73664E-02	0.69375E-02
PRIV	-0.34142	0.78300	-0.43604	-0.11952E-01	-0.12037E-01
YEARS	-0.26127E-01	0.26934E-01	-0.97004	-0.73996E-01	-0.68592E-01
SCHOOL	2.6250	1.4105	1.8610	0.10109	0.28999E-01
LOGINC	2.1872	0.78787	2.7761	7.2529	6.7561
PTCON	-2.3945	1.0813	-2.2144	-5.5262	-5.1745
CONSTANT	-5.2014	7.5506	-0.68887	-1.7298	-1.6137

```
LOG-LIKELIHOOD(0)  =   -63.037    LOG-LIKELIHOOD FUNCTION  =   -53.303
LIKELIHOOD RATIO TEST  =    19.4681   WITH    8  D.F.

MADDALA R-SQUARE              0.1853
CRAGG-UHLER R-SQUARE         0.25218
MCFADDEN R-SQUARE            0.15442
    ADJUSTED FOR DEGREES OF FREEDOM         0.75759E-01
    APPROXIMATELY F-DISTRIBUTED     0.20544      WITH    8  AND    9  D.F.
CHOW R-SQUARE                0.17197
```

PREDICTION SUCCESS TABLE

		ACTUAL	
		0	1
PREDICTED	0	18.	7.
	1	18.	52.

```
NUMBER OF RIGHT PREDICTIONS =        70.0
PERCENTAGE OF RIGHT PREDICTIONS =    0.73684

EXPECTED OBSERVATIONS AT 0  =        36.0   OBSERVED =     36.0
EXPECTED OBSERVATIONS AT 1  =        59.0   OBSERVED =     59.0
SUM OF SQUARED "RESIDUALS" =         18.513
WEIGHTED SUM OF SQUARED "RESIDUALS" =     86.839
```

HENSHER-JOHNSON PREDICTION SUCCESS TABLE

	PREDICTED	CHOICE	OBSERVED COUNT	OBSERVED SHARE
ACTUAL	0	1		
0	17.591	18.409	36.000	0.379
1	18.409	40.591	59.000	0.621
PREDICTED COUNT	36.000	59.000	95.000	1.000
PREDICTED SHARE	0.379	0.621	1.000	
PROP. SUCCESSFUL	0.489	0.688	0.612	
SUCCESS INDEX	0.110	0.067	0.083	
PROPORTIONAL ERROR	-0.000	-0.000		
NORMALIZED SUCCESS INDEX			0.177	

21. **ROBUST ESTIMATION**

"39..This appears to be the first uninteresting number, which of course
makes it an especially interesting number, because it is the smallest number
to have the property of being uninteresting. It is therefore also the first
number to be simultaneously interesting and uninteresting."

David Wells, 1986
The Penguin Dictionary of Curious
and Interesting Numbers

SHAZAM can perform the Robust Estimation methods described in Judge, Hill, Griffiths, Lütkepohl and Lee [1988, Chapter 22]. Extensive examples are provided in Chapter 22 of the *Judge Handbook*. The methods for detecting Influential Observations outlined in that chapter can be obtained using the **INFLUENCE** and related options on the **OLS** command.

The estimation methods available with the **ROBUST** command are: Least Absolute Errors, Regression with multivariate-t errors (either the uncorrelated or independent error case is allowed), Regression Quantiles and Trimmed Least Squares.

The coefficients in these models do not necessarily follow a t-distribution, so hypothesis testing must be done carefully. Often the distribution is unknown.

The multivariate-t regression model specifes an error distribution with fatter tails than those in OLS. The difference between the uncorrelated and independent error cases is described in detail in Kelejian and Prucha [1985].

The method of Regression Quantiles is described further in Koenker and Bassett [1978] and in Koenker and D'Orey [1987]. In the Regression Quantile method, given a value of θ, the θth sample regression quantile is found by minimizing the function:

$$\sum_{Y \geq X\beta} \theta \, |Y\text{-}X\beta| \quad + \quad \sum_{Y < X\beta} (1-\theta) \, |Y\text{-}X\beta|$$

The value of the above formula is printed in the output as OBJECTIVE FUNCTION. The output also includes a statistic labelled EMPIRICAL QUANTILE FUNCTION AT MEANS which is defined as the predicted value at the mean values of the independent variables.

When $\theta = .5$ the method is a least absolute errors (LAE) estimator, also known as minimum absolute deviations (MAD), least absolute values (LAV) or the L1 estimator. The covariance matrix for the LAE estimator is defined in Chapter 22.4.1 of Judge, Hill, Griffiths, Lütkepohl and Lee [1988].

The Trimmed Least Squares method takes the quantiles a and $(1-a)$ and constructs the estimators $\beta(a)$ and $\beta(1-a)$. Then, observations where $Y\text{-}X\beta(a) \leq 0$ or $Y\text{-}X\beta(1-a) \geq 0$ are discarded. Ordinary Least Squares is then applied to the remaining observations with a covariance matrix as described in Chapter 22.4.3 of Judge, Hill, Griffiths, Lütkepohl and Lee [1988]. In general, the format of the **ROBUST** command is:

ROBUST *depvar indeps / options*

where *depvar* is the dependent variable, *indeps* is a list of independent variables, and *options* is a list of options.

In addition to the **LINLOG, LIST, LOGLIN, LOGLOG, MAX, PCOR, PCOV, RSTAT, BEG=, END=, COEF=, COV=, PREDICT=, RESID=, STDERR= and TRATIO=** options described on the **OLS** command, the available options on the **ROBUST** command are:

FIVEQUAN
This option uses the five quantile values (.1, .25, .5, .75, .9) in computing regression quantiles. The corresponding weights are (.05, .25, .4, .25, .05) See Chapter 22.4.2 in Judge, Hill, Griffiths, Lütkepohl and Lee [1988].

GASTWIRT
This option uses the Gastwirth weighting scheme in computing regression quantiles. This scheme uses the quantile values (.33, .5, .67) with corresponding weights (.3, .4, .3). See Chapter 22.4.2 in Judge, Hill, Griffiths, Lütkepohl and Lee [1988].

LAE
This option is the default method and specifies that the Least Absolute Error model is desired.

TUKEY
This option uses the Tukey Trimean weighting scheme in computing regression quantiles. This scheme uses the quantiles (.25, .5, .75) with corresponding weights of (.25, .5, .25). See Chapter 22.4.2 in Judge, Hill, Griffiths, Lütkepohl and Lee [1988].

UNCOR
This option is used with the **MULTIT=** option described below to specify that the *uncorrelated* error model is requested. If this option is **not** used the *independent* error model is assumed.

CONV=
This option is used with the **MULTIT=** option described below to specify a convergence criterion to stop the iterative procedure used to obtain the estimates. The iterations will stop when the difference in $\beta'\beta$ between two sucessive iterations is less than the value specifed with **CONV=**. The default is **CONV=.01**.

DIFF=   This option is used with the **LAE** option described above to specify a value of d to use for equation 22.4.10 in Judge, Hill, Griffiths, Lütkepohl and Lee [1988]. The parameter d tells what differential to use when selecting which ordered residual to use in computing the covariance matrix. The default is DIFF=(N-K-1)/6 where N is the number of observations and K is the number of coefficients. In small samples this default may be too large to compute the quantiles so SHAZAM will adjust it downward. See also Siddiqui[1960] and Bofinger[1975] for a more precise determination of d.

ITER=   This option is used with the **MULTIT=** option described below to specify the maximum number of iterations allowed in the iterative procedure used to obtain the estimates. The default is **ITER=10**.

MULTIT=   This option specifies that the Multivariate-t method described in Judge, Hill, Griffiths, Lütkepohl and Lee [1988, Chapter 22.3] should be used.

THETA=   This option specifies a single value of θ to use for the Regression Quantile method.

THETAB=,
THETAE=,
THETAI=   These options specify beginning, ending, and increments to be used for a grid search over θ values for the Regression Quantile method. If these options are specified the **THETA=** option is ignored.

TRIM=   This option specifies that Trimmed Least Squares is desired as described in Chapter 22.4.3 of Judge, Hill, Griffiths, Lütkepohl and Lee [1988]. The value specified for the trimming proportion (a) should be between 0 and .5. A listing of the observation numbers for the deleted observations is printed unless the **SET NOWARN** command has been used.

Only one method is permitted on any **ROBUST** command. Hence users must chose the Least Absolute Error (**LAE**), Multivariate-t (**MULTIT=**), Trimmed Least Squares (**TRIM=**) or Regression Quantile (**FIVEQUAN, GASTWIRT, TUKEY, THETA=, THETAB=, THETAE=, THETAI=**) option. The default is the **LAE** method. Note that calculations of R-SQUARE are not well defined in these models. Users may prefer to use the one that is reported with the **RSTAT** option. The following is an example of the **ROBUST** command to obtain the LAE estimates for the textile data.

```
|_ROBUST CONSUME INCOME PRICE / LAE RSTAT
LEAST ABSOLUTE ERRORS REGRESSION
OBJECTIVE FUNCTION  =   35.244
NUMBER OF SIMPLEX ITERATIONS =   5.0000
EMPIRICAL QUANTILE FUNCTION AT MEANS =   136.24
SUM OF ABSOLUTE ERRORS =   70.487
   USING DIFF=  2 FOR COVARIANCE CALCULATIONS
```

```
VARIANCE OF THE ESTIMATE =    68.326
STANDARD ERROR OF THE ESTIMATE =    8.2659
MEAN OF DEPENDENT VARIABLE =    134.51
```

VARIABLE NAME	ESTIMATED COEFFICIENT	STANDARD ERROR	T-RATIO 14 DF	PARTIAL CORR.	STANDARDIZED COEFFICIENT	ELASTICITY AT MEANS
INCOME	0.69851	0.39622	1.7629	0.4262	0.15705	0.53480
PRICE	−1.4421	0.12453	−11.581	−0.9516	−1.0316	−0.81819
CONSTANT	174.36	40.256	4.3313	0.7567	0.0	1.2963

```
DURBIN-WATSON = 1.5333    VON NEUMAN RATIO = 1.6291    RHO =  0.19972
RESIDUAL SUM =  -29.562      RESIDUAL VARIANCE =    40.782
SUM OF ABSOLUTE ERRORS=    70.487
R-SQUARE BETWEEN OBSERVED AND PREDICTED = 0.9435
RUNS TEST:  7 RUNS, 10 POSITIVE, 7 NEGATIVE, NORMAL STATISTIC =  -1.1583
```

22. **TOBIT REGRESSION**

"That the automobile has reached the limit of its development is suggested by the fact that during the past year no improvements of a radical nature have been introduced."

Scientific American
January 2, 1909

Tobit regression is used for regressions with limited dependent variables. The model is fully described in Tobin [1958, p.24-36]. Other references are Goldberger [1964, p.248-255]; Maddala [1977, Ch. 9.7]; Judge, Hill, Griffiths, Lütkepohl and Lee [1988, Ch. 19]; and Maddala [1983, Ch. 6]. A simple example of the Tobit model using SHAZAM can be found in Deegan and White [1976, p.127-135].

In the Tobit model an Index I is created. This index is a linear function of the right-hand side variables:

$$I = Xa$$

where a is a vector of *normalized* coefficients corresponding to the coefficient vector a in the Tobin article. Through the use of the normal density function and the cumulative normal distribution function, the index I is transformed to a predicted limited dependent variable. The coefficient vector a is transformed into the regression coefficient vector β by multiplying all elements of a by the calculated standard error of the estimate.

Interpretation of the Tobit model is complicated by the fact that all computations are performed on the *normalized* a vector, and the estimated standard errors of the coefficients are those of the a vector and not the β. However, it is quite easy to perform hypotheses on the regression coefficients β by working on the a vector in the manner described in the Tobin article. Users should note that other computer programs may use a different transformation than that found in the Tobin article. SHAZAM will print both the a and β vectors, labelled as *normalized* coefficients and *regression* coefficients, respectively. The Tobit algorithm in SHAZAM is based on a computer program originally written by John Cragg.

A maximum likelihood estimation procedure is used so that hypothesis testing can be done with a likelihood ratio test. **RESTRICT** commands are not permitted.

In general, the format of the **TOBIT** command is:

TOBIT *depvar indeps* / *options*

where *depvar* is the dependent variable, *indeps* is a list of independent variables, and *options* is a list of desired options. As well as **MAX, NOCONSTANT, NONORM, BEG=, END=, COEF=, COV=** and **WEIGHT=** as defined for **OLS**, the following options are available on the **TOBIT** command:

DUMP   This option will **DUMP** the matrix of second derivatives, the moment matrices of limit and non-limit observations, and some other output that is probably not useful to the average user.

LIST   This option will **LIST**, for each observation, the value of the index I, the density and cumulative probabilities corresponding to the index I, and the observed, expected and conditional values of the dependent variable. No plot is produced.

PCOR   This option will Print the **COR**relation matrix of the *normalized* coefficients.

PCOV   The **PCOV** option will Print the estimated asymptotic **COV**ariance matrix of the *normalized* coefficients. The matrix is the inverse of the negative of the matrix of second derivatives of the likelihood function. In a large sample the *normalized* coefficients will be normally distributed.

UPPER   This option is used if the limit is an **UPPER** limit rather than a lower limit.

CONV=   This option is used to set the **CONV**ergence criterion for the log-likelihood function. The default is .00000001.

INDEX=   The **INDEX=** option saves the computed **INDEX** in the variable specified.

ITER=   This option may be used to set the maximum number of **ITER**ations allowed. The default is 25.

LIMIT=   This option is used to specify the **LIMIT**ing value of the dependent variable. The default is **LIMIT=0**.

PITER=   Specifies the frequency with which **ITER**ations are to be Printed. The default is **PITER=1**. If **PITER=0** is specified, no iterations are printed.

PREDICT=   Saves the **PREDICT**ed expected values in the variable specified.

If the **WEIGHT=** option is used the method performed follows that described for the **REPLICATE** option in **OLS**.

The following is an example of a **TOBIT** run using data found in Judge, Hill, Griffiths, Lütkepohl and Lee [1988, Table 19.3]:

```
|_TOBIT Y X2 / PCOV PITER=0

TOBIT ANALYSIS, LIMIT=  0.          25 MAX ITERATIONS
        6 LIMIT OBSERVATIONS
       14 NON-LIMIT OBSERVATIONS

 FIRST DERIVATIVES OF LOG OF LIKELIHOOD FUNCTION EVALUATED AT MAXIMUM
  -0.33306691E-14  -0.13877788E-15   0.59952043E-14

NUMBER OF ITERATIONS =  3

 DEPENDENT VARIABLE = Y
 STANDARD ERROR OF ESTIMATE =   3.6310
```

<table>
<tr><td></td><td></td><td>ASYMPTOTIC</td><td></td><td></td><td></td><td></td></tr>
<tr><td>VARIABLE</td><td>NORMALIZED
COEFFICIENT</td><td>STANDARD
ERROR</td><td>T-RATIO</td><td>REGRESSION
COEFFICIENT</td><td>ELASTICITY
OF INDEX</td><td>ELASTICITY
OF E(Y)</td></tr>
<tr><td>X2</td><td>0.24820</td><td>0.58959E-01</td><td>4.2096</td><td>0.90120</td><td>1.9458</td><td>1.9970</td></tr>
<tr><td>CONSTANT</td><td>-1.5786</td><td>0.60413</td><td>-2.6130</td><td>-5.7319</td><td></td><td></td></tr>
<tr><td>Y</td><td>0.27541</td><td>0.53292E-01</td><td></td><td></td><td></td><td></td></tr>
</table>

```
THE PREDICTED PROBABILITY OF Y > LIMIT GIVEN AVERAGE X (I) = 0.8479
 THE OBSERVED FREQUENCY OF Y > LIMIT IS = 0.7000
 AT MEAN VALUES OF ALL X(I), E(Y) =       4.0177

VARIANCE-COVARIANCE MATRIX OF COEFFICIENTS
X2         0.34762E-02
CONSTANT -0.29497E-01  0.36497
Y          0.19654E-02 -0.68295E-02  0.28400E-02
              X2          CONSTANT        Y

LOG-LIKELIHOOD FUNCTION= -41.255240
MEAN-SQUARE ERROR=  8.0589568
MEAN ERROR=-0.40295353E-02
```

In the SHAZAM **TOBIT** output the ELASTICITY OF INDEX is the elasticity of the index computed at the mean using the regression coefficients. The ELASTICITY OF E(Y) is the elasticity of E(Y) as given in Maddala [1983, Eq. 6.37] and computed at the mean. The EXPECTED VALUE OF THE DEPENDENT VARIABLE (given when the **LIST** or **MAX** options are specified) is described in Maddala [1983, Eq. 6.37]. The CONDITIONAL EXPECTED VALUE OF THE DEPENDENT VARIABLE is given in Maddala [1983, Eq. 6.36] and is computed only for the non-limit observations.

23. TWO-STAGE LEAST SQUARES AND SYSTEMS OF EQUATIONS

"You won't have Nixon to kick around anymore - because, gentlemen, this is my last press conference."

Richard M. Nixon
November 7, 1962
(after losing the California Governor Election)

A. 2SLS *OR INSTRUMENTAL VARIABLE ESTIMATION*

Two-Stage Least Squares is normally done in SHAZAM with the **2SLS** command. Users should read about 2SLS in any standard econometrics textbook before attempting this procedure. A good reference is Judge, Hill, Griffiths, Lütkepohl and Lee [1988, Ch. 14-15]. An alternative to Two-Stage Least Squares is the Limited Information Maximum Likelihood (LIML) method described in the chapter *PROGRAMMING IN SHAZAM*. Since 2SLS is a single equation technique for estimating equations in a simultaneous equation model, each equation is estimated separately and it is not necessary to estimate all equations in the model. As is the case with most multiple equation methods, it is necessary to know which variables are endogenous and which are exogenous. The 2SLS estimator and variance are:

$$\hat{\beta} = [Z'X(X'X)^{-1}X'Z]^{-1}Z'X(X'X)^{-1}X'Y$$

and

$$V(\hat{\beta}) = \hat{\sigma}^2[Z'X(X'X)^{-1}X'Z]^{-1}$$

where:

$$\hat{\sigma}^2 = (y-Z\hat{\beta})'(y-Z\hat{\beta})/(n-k)$$

and

$$R^2 = 1-(e'e)/(y'y)$$

and y is the dependent variable, Z is the matrix of right-hand side variables in the equation, X is the matrix of all exogenous variables in the system, $\hat{\beta}$ is the vector of estimated coefficients, $V(\hat{\beta})$ is the covariance matrix of coefficients, $\hat{\sigma}^2$ is the estimated variance of the regression line, n is the sample size and k is the number of right-hand side variables in the equation. The **2SLS** command can be used for any instrumental variables estimation. In this case, X is the matrix of instrumental variables. You can type the command name **INST** instead of **2SLS**, but the output will be identical.

Note that the denominator in the calculation of $\hat{\sigma}^2$ is (n-k). Some econometricians would argue that the denominator should just be n, since the **2SLS** estimator is only consistent when the small sample distribution is unknown. If it is preferable to the user that the estimates be done by dividing by n instead of n-k, the **DN** option should be used on the **2SLS** command. The **DN** option is described later in the chapter. The estimated coefficients are not affected in either case, but all the variances and t-ratios will be. Users should note that R^2 in **2SLS**, and in many other models, is not well defined and could easily be negative. In fact, the lower bound is minus infinity. This usually indicates that the equation does not fit the data very well. Many econometricians would prefer to use the squared-correlation coefficient between the observed and predicted dependent variable instead for these models. That value is obtained with the RSTAT and is available as R-SQUARE BETWEEN OBSERVED AND PREDICTED. It is also available in the temporary variable $R2OP.

In general, the format of the **2SLS** command is:

2SLS *depvar rhsvars (exogs) / options*

where *depvar* is the dependent variable, *rhsvars* is a list of all the right-hand side variables in the equation, *exogs* is a list of all the exogenous variables in the system, and *options* is a list of desired options.

Note that the list of *exogs* must be enclosed in parentheses, and that SHAZAM automatically includes a constant in the list of exogenous variables. In addition, the sample size should exceed the number of *rhsvars* and the number of degrees of freedom. If there are not more exogenous variables than right-hand side variables, the equation will be underidentified. While most of the **OLS** options are also available as *options* on **2SLS**, the user should be aware that hypothesis testing in 2SLS is complicated by the unknown distributions, so the normal t and F tests are invalid. At best these can be interpreted as being asymptotically Normal and Chi-Square. The F test from an Analysis of Variance table is invalid, and the printed R^2, which is defined as 1 minus the unexplained proportion of the total variance, may not coincide with that obtained by using other programs which do the calculation differently.

The following **OLS** options may be used on the **2SLS** command: **DUMP, GF, LIST, MAX, NOCONSTANT, PCOR, PCOV, RESTRICT, RSTAT, BEG=, END=, COEF=, COV=, PREDICT=** and **RESID=**.

An example of a **2SLS** command and the resulting SHAZAM output using the first equation of the Klein model [Theil, 1971] is the following:

```
|_2SLS C PLAG P WGWP (WG T G TIME PLAG KLAG XLAG) / DN PCOV RSTAT
 TWO STAGE LEAST SQUARES - DEPENDENT VARIABLE = C
   7 EXOGENOUS VARIABLES
       21 OBSERVATIONS
 DN OPTION IN EFFECT - DIVISOR IS N

  R-SQUARE =   0.9767     R-SQUARE ADJUSTED =   0.9726
 VARIANCE OF THE ESTIMATE =   1.0441
 STANDARD ERROR OF THE ESTIMATE =   1.0218
 MEAN OF DEPENDENT VARIABLE =   53.995
```

		ASYMPTOTIC				
VARIABLE NAME	ESTIMATED COEFFICIENT	STANDARD ERROR	T-RATIO --------	PARTIAL CORR.	STANDARDIZED COEFFICIENT	ELASTICITY AT MEANS
PLAG	0.21623	0.10727	2.0158	0.4392	0.12695	0.06558
P	0.17302E-01	0.11805	0.14657	0.0355	0.10643E-01	0.00541
WGWP	0.81018	0.40250E-01	20.129	0.9797	0.89225	0.62241
CONSTANT	16.555	1.3208	12.534	0.9499	0.0	0.30660

```
VARIANCE-COVARIANCE MATRIX OF COEFFICIENTS
PLAG        0.11506E-01
P          -0.95710E-02    0.13936E-01
WGWP       -0.53085E-03   -0.15260E-02    0.16200D 03
CONSTANT   -0.47520E-02   -0.15344E-01   -0.32733E-01      1.7445
                 PLAG           P            WGWP        CONSTANT

 DURBIN-WATSON = 1.4851     VON NEUMAN RATIO = 1.5593     RHO =   0.20423
 RESIDUAL SUM =  0.81712E-13  RESIDUAL VARIANCE =    1.0441
 SUM OF ABSOLUTE ERRORS=   17.866
 R-SQUARE BETWEEN OBSERVED AND PREDICTED = 0.9768
 RUNS TEST:  9 RUNS,  9 POSITIVE,  12 NEGATIVE, NORMAL STATISTIC =   -1.0460
```

B. **SYSTEMS** *OF EQUATIONS*

SHAZAM provides a procedure for estimating systems of simultaneous equations or sets of Seemingly Unrelated Regressions. The Seemingly Unrelated Regressions case is also known as Zellner estimation, Iterative Zellner estimation, or Multivariate Regression. The simultaneous equation problem is usually called Three-Stage Least Squares or Iterative Three-Stage Least Squares. SHAZAM will estimate a set of equations and do a joint generalized least squares procedure by using the covariance matrix of residuals across equations. As an option, SHAZAM will iterate on this covariance matrix until convergence. If a list of exogenous variables is provided, a Three-Stage Least Squares or Iterative Three-Stage Least Squares procedure is done. All equations must be linear. Some good references on systems of equations are Theil [1971, Ch. 7,9,10], Judge, Hill, Griffiths, Lütkepohl and Lee [1988, Ch. 11 and 15], and Judge, Griffiths, Hill, Lütkepohl and Lee [1985, Ch. 12] and Srivastava and Giles [1987].

SHAZAM can also impose linear restrictions on the coefficients within or across equations. Linear or nonlinear hypotheses may also be tested. Estimation of systems of equations can be rather slow, especially if there are many equations or variables in the system. Imposing restrictions on the coefficients will also slow the estimation. In large models, it is quite possible for SHAZAM to run out of memory. For information on how to proceed in this case, see the **PAR** command discussed in the chapter *HOW TO RUN SHAZAM* or the chapter *MISCELLANEOUS COMMANDS AND INFORMATION*.

To set up a system for estimation, the following commands are used:

SYSTEM *neq exogs / options*
OLS *depvar indeps*
.
.
.
OLS *depvar indeps*
RESTRICT *restriction*
END
TEST *equation*

where *neq* is the number of equations, *exogs* is a list of the exogenous variables and *options* is a list of desired options. Do NOT use *options* on the **OLS** commands. They must only be used with the **SYSTEM** command. **The** *exogs* **must ONLY be included for Three Stage Least Squares and not for Zellner estimation.** After the **SYSTEM** command there should be an **OLS** command for each equation in the system. If restrictions are desired, type the **RESTRICT** commands followed by **END**. Note that when **RESTRICT** commands are used the **RESTRICT** option on the **SYSTEM** command must be specified. **TEST** commands may follow the **END** command.

The available options on the **SYSTEM** command are:

DN This is a useful option and its use is strongly recommended. With this option the fact that the estimation procedure has good asymptotic properties is recognized. The covariance matrix is computed using N as the Divisor, rather than the alternative measure (which provides a dubious degrees of freedom adjustment). The use of the **DN** option is consistent with Theil's development. Without the **DN** option, the degrees of freedom correction for the covariances is MT/(MT-K), where M is the number of equations, T is the number of observations, and K is the number of free parameters in the system.

DUMP This option will **DUMP** a lot of intermediate output after each iteration, including the system $X'X$ matrix and its inverse, and the inverse of the residual covariance matrix (SIGMA). This option is primarily of interest to SHAZAM consultants.

FULL This option is used to get **FULL** equation output. This output is similar to that of regular **OLS** regressions. **FULL** is automatically in effect except in TALK mode. It can be turned off with the **NOFULL** option.

LIST These options are used as on **OLS** commands to control output. They
RSTAT should only be used when full output is required for each equation. Users
MAX should be aware when interpreting the equation-by-equation output that
GF some statistics printed are not valid in system estimation. If systems analysis is properly understood the questionable statistics are easily identified. Since the analysis of variance F-test is invalid it is not printed; if it is desired, TEST commands should be used.

NOCONSTANT Normally, SHAZAM will automatically put an intercept in each equation in the system. If there are some (or all) equations in which no intercept is desired the **NOCONSTANT** option should be specified. Then, an intercept should be created by generating a variable of ones (1) with a **GENR** command and this variable should be included in each equation in which an intercept is desired. Without the **NOCONSTANT** option the intercept will only be printed in the **FULL** equation-by-equation output, and the variances of the intercepts will only be approximate unless the model converges.

PCOR These options will Print the CORrelation and COVariance matrices of all
PCOV coefficients in the system after convergence. If these options are specified the matrices will also be printed for each equation in the equation-by-equation output. Users should be aware when interpreting the equation-by-equation output that some statistics printed are not valid in system estimation. Since it is assumed estimation of systems of equations is understood by the user it is also assumed that the questionable nature of some of these statistics is understood.

PINVEV This option will Print the INVerse of the Exogenous Variables matrix when the **3SLS** system is being used. This option is rarely needed.

PSIGMA This option will **P**rint the residual covariance matrix (**SIGMA**) after each iteration. If this option is not used the matrix will be printed for the first and final iterations. This option can add pages of output if there are many equations in the system and, thus, should not be specified unless this information is specifically needed.

RESTRICT This option is used when **RESTRICT** commands are to be used. The **RESTRICT** commands follow the **OLS** commands. Only linear restrictions are permitted. Users should be aware that iterative estimates may not necessarily be maximum likelihood estimates if restrictions on the intercepts of the equation are imposed.

COEF= Saves the values of the **COEF**ficients in the variable specified. The values for all equations will be in a single vector. No values for the equation intercepts will be saved so if these are required the directions above for the **NOCONSTANT** option should be followed.

COEFMAT= Saves the values of the **COEF**ficients in the variable specified in MATRIX form with each column of the matrix representing one equation. Equation intercepts will also be saved. This is useful if the coefficients for a single equation need to be specified on the **FC** command.

CONV= This option is used to specify a **CONV**ergence criterion to stop the iterative procedure (subject to the maximum number of iterations specified with the **ITER=** option). The criterion is the maximum desired percentage change in each of the coefficients. The default is .001.

COV= Saves the **COV**ariance matrix in the variable specified. No values for the variances and covariances of equation intercepts will be saved so if these are required the directions above for the **NOCONSTANT** option should be followed.

ITER= This option is used to specify the maximum number of **ITER**ations performed if an iterative procedure is desired. If this option is not specified, one iteration is done. If **ITER=0** is specified, the system is estimated without the Generalized Least Squares procedure which uses the covariance matrix of residuals. This would be equivalent to running separate **OLS** regressions (or **2SLS**), but more expensive. **ITER=0** would be appropriate only if there were restrictions across equations or hypothesis testing across equations.

OUT= *unit* **IN**= *unit*	These options are used to **OUT**put a dump of useful information on the unit specified at each iteration, so that the system can be restarted in another run at the same point by **IN**putting the dump. This can be very useful in expensive models to avoid re-estimation of already calculated data in the event that a time limit is reached. With the **OUT**= option, the information from the most recent iteration will be written on the specified unit. **OUT**= and **IN**= are usually assigned to the same unit so the latest information replaces existing information. Units 11-49 are available and may be assigned to a file with the SHAZAM **FILE** command or an operating system command.
	NOTE: It is important to remember to create a system file to be attached to the appropriate unit before using the **OUT**= option. Without this file the information will be lost. The use of **OUT**= will add slightly to the cost, but will substantially lower the cost of restarting the model. It is also important to run the same system on subsequent runs with the **IN**= option. The **IN**= option should *never* be run before there is anything to input. See the example in the chapter *HOW TO RUN SHAZAM*.
PITER=	Specifies the frequency with which **ITER**ations are to be Printed. The default is **PITER**=1. If **PITER**=0 is specified, no iterations are printed.
PREDICT=	Saves the **PREDICT**ed values of the dependent variable in a n by neq matrix, where n is the number of observations and neq is the number of equations.
RESID=	Saves the values of the **RESID**uals from the regression in a n by neq matrix, where n is the number of observations and neq is the number of equations.
SIGMA=	This option will save the residual covariance matrix (**SIGMA**) in the variable specified.

The following is an example of a **SYSTEM** command to estimate Klein's model I described in Theil [1971] by Three-Stage Least Squares:

```
_SYSTEM 3 WG T G TIME1 PLAG KLAG XLAG / DN
_OLS C PLAG P WGWP
_OLS I PLAG KLAG P
_OLS WP TIME1 XLAG X
THREE STAGE LEAST SQUARES--     3 EQUATIONS
    7 EXOGENOUS VARIABLES
    9 RIGHT-HAND SIDE VARIABLES IN SYSTEM
MAX ITERATIONS =  1          CONVERGENCE TOLERANCE =   0.01000
       21 OBSERVATIONS
```

```
DN OPTION IN EFFECT - DIVISOR IS N
ITERATION  0 COEFFICIENTS
   0.21623      0.17302E-01 0.81018      0.61594     -0.15779     0.15022
   0.13040      0.14667     0.43886

ITERATION  0 SIGMA
   1.0441
   0.43785       1.3832
  -0.38523       0.19261       0.47643
DET. OF SIGMA= 0.28771
ITERATION  1 SIGMA INVERSE
   2.1615
  -0.98292       1.2131
   2.1451       -1.2852        4.3530
ITERATION  1 COEFFICIENTS
   0.16314      0.12489      0.79008      0.75572     -0.19485     -0.13079E-01
   0.14967      0.18129      0.40049
ITERATION  1 SIGMA
   0.89176
   0.41132       2.0930
  -0.39361       0.40305       0.52003
LOG DETERMINANT OF SIGMA= -1.2623
SYSTEM R-SQUARE = 0.9995 ... CHI-SQUARE = 159.41  WITH 9 D.F.
VARIABLE        COEFFICIENT    ST.ERROR      T-RATIO
  PLAG          0.16314        0.10044        1.6243
  P             0.12489        0.10813        1.1550
  WGWP          0.79008        0.37938E-01   20.826
  PLAG          0.75572        0.15293        4.9415
  KLAG         -0.19485        0.32531E-01   -5.9897
  P            -0.13079E-01    0.16190       -0.80787E-01
  TIME1         0.14967        0.27935E-01    5.3579
  XLAG          0.18129        0.34159E-01    5.3073
  X             0.40049        0.31813E-01   12.589


EQUATION  1 OF  3 EQUATIONS
DEPENDENT VARIABLE = C                   21 OBSERVATIONS
R-SQUARE = 0.9801
VARIANCE OF THE ESTIMATE =  0.89176
STANDARD ERROR OF THE ESTIMATE =  0.94433
```

VARIABLE NAME	ESTIMATED COEFFICIENT	ASYMPTOTIC STANDARD ERROR	T-RATIO --------	PARTIAL CORR.	STANDARDIZED COEFFICIENT	ELASTICITY AT MEANS
PLAG	0.16314	0.10044	1.6243	0.3665	0.95785E-01	0.04948
P	0.12489	0.10813	1.1550	0.2697	0.76821E-01	0.03907
WGWP	0.79008	0.37938E-01	20.826	0.9810	0.87011	0.60697
CONSTANT	16.441	1.3018	12.630	0.9506	0.0	0.30449

```
EQUATION  2 OF  3 EQUATIONS
DEPENDENT VARIABLE = I                   21 OBSERVATIONS
R-SQUARE = 0.8258
VARIANCE OF THE ESTIMATE =   2.0930
STANDARD ERROR OF THE ESTIMATE =   1.4467
```

VARIABLE NAME	ESTIMATED COEFFICIENT	STANDARD ERROR	ASYMPTOTIC T-RATIO --------	PARTIAL CORR.	STANDARDIZED COEFFICIENT	ELASTICITY AT MEANS
PLAG	0.75572	0.15293	4.9415	0.7678	0.85704	9.7704
KLAG	-0.19485	0.32531E-01	-5.9897	-0.8237	-0.54410	-30.842
P	-0.13079E-01	0.16190	-0.80787E-01	-0.0196	-0.15540E-01	-0.17441
CONSTANT	28.178	6.7963	4.1461	0.7091	0.0	22.246

```
EQUATION  3 OF  3 EQUATIONS
DEPENDENT VARIABLE = WP                    21 OBSERVATIONS
 R-SQUARE = 0.9863
VARIANCE OF THE ESTIMATE =  0.52003
STANDARD ERROR OF THE ESTIMATE =  0.72113
```

VARIABLE NAME	ESTIMATED COEFFICIENT	STANDARD ERROR	ASYMPTOTIC T-RATIO --------	PARTIAL CORR.	STANDARDIZED COEFFICIENT	ELASTICITY AT MEANS
TIME1	0.14967	0.27935E-01	5.3579	0.7925	0.14731	0.04528
XLAG	0.18129	0.34159E-01	5.3073	0.7897	0.25647	0.28910
X	0.40049	0.31813E-01	12.589	0.9503	0.67447	0.66147
CONSTANT	0.15080	1.0160	0.14843	0.0360	0.0	0.00415

```
|_TEST P:1=P:2
TEST VALUE=  0.13797     STD. ERROR OF TEST VALUE = 0.16036
ASYMPTOTIC NORMAL STATISTIC =   0.86037777
WALD CHI-SQUARE STATISTIC =  0.74024991     WITH   1 D.F.
```

In this example a Three-Stage Least Squares procedure is done. There are 3 equations in the system and variables WG, T, G, TIME, PLAG, DLAG and XLAG are the exogenous variables. (All identities have already been substituted.) Three **OLS** commands are included to describe the three equations in the system. The **TEST** command will test the hypothesis that the coefficient on variable P in equation 1 is equal to the coefficient on variable P in equation 2.

Another example is:

```
SYSTEM 2 / RESTRICT
OLS A B C
OLS D E F
RESTRICT B:1+E:2=1
END
```

In this example a set of Seemingly Unrelated Regressions is estimated. The iteration option is not requested. The model is estimated subject to the restriction that the coefficient on variable B in equation 1 plus the coefficient on variable E in equation 2 sum to one. As the setup for equation systems is quite general, it will handle many types of linear models. Since systems estimation is rather expensive, options should be carefully specified so the system does not have to be re-estimated.

Unless the **NOCONSTANT** option is used, a system R^2 is printed at the end of the problem. This is defined as:

$$R^2 = 1 - Det(E'E)/Det(y'y)$$

where $E'E$ is the crossproduct matrix of residuals and $y'y$ is the crossproduct matrix of dependent variables. This statistic is frequently very high and should be interpreted with caution. For further information on this statistic see Berndt [1989].

A Chi-square statistic is also printed. This is equivalent to the statistic obtained when performing a likelihood ratio test to determine whether all the slope coefficients in a multiple regression model are zero. The Chi-square statistic is defined as:

$$\chi^2 = - N(LOG(1-R^2))$$

When more than one equation is estimated the value of the temporary variable $SIG2 will be the log of the Determinant of the SIGMA matrix. If there is only one equation, $SIG2 will conform to that defined for OLS estimation.

24. MAPS

"Before man reaches the moon your mail will be delivered within hours from New York to California, to England, to India or to Australia by guided missiles...We stand on the threshold of rocket mail."

Arthur E. Summerfield
U.S. Postmaster General, 1959

The **MAP** command will draw maps of any part of the world. The **MAP** command is only available on systems with the DISSPLA graphics package. Users should refer to the DISSPLA manual for more detailed information. **WARNING:** Maps (especially, world maps) require a large amount of computer time.

In general, the format of the **MAP** command is:

MAP *latvar lonvar / options*

where *latvar* and *lonvar* are variables containing data for latitudes and longitudes to be plotted. The specification of these variables is optional.

The available options are:

SHAZAM	With this option a symbol is plotted for each **SHAZAM** installation. This option is only available at the University of British Columbia. With this option, *latvar* and *lonvar* are not specified.
AREA=	Specifies the region desired. The default is **WORLD** and the choices are **ANTARCTICA, AUSTRALIA, BC, CALIFORNIA, CANADA, EUROPE, FALKLAND, NORTHAMER** and **USA**.
BEG= **END=**	Specify which observations are to be used. If these options are not used the current **SAMPLE** range is in effect.
BORDER=	Specifies which type of **BORDER** will be drawn. The default is **COAST** and the choices are: **AFRICA, ANTAR, ASIA, EURO, HERSHEY, MAPDTA, NORTHAM, PAFRICA, PASIA, PAUSTRALIA, PEUROPE, PNORTHAM, POLI, PSOUTHAM, SOUTHAM, USAH, USAL** and **USAM**.
COLOR=	Specifies the **COLOR** used for points. The choice is **BLACK** or **RED**. This option requires a plot device with colors.

HEIGHT=   Specifies the **HEIGHT** of the map. The default is 11 inches.

LATB=   Specify **LAT**itude Beginning, End and Interval.
LATE=
LATI=

LONB=   Specify the **LON**gitude Beginning, End and Interval.
LONE=
LONI=

MARK=   Specifies the symbol number to be used to **MARK** points if *latvar* and
                   lonvar or **SHAZAM** is specified. The default is 3 which corresponds to a
                   plus symbol (+). A listing of the numbers and their corresponding symbols
                   can be found in the DISSPLA manual.

OUTPUT=   Specifies the **OUTPUT** device to be used. The default is **TERMINAL** in
                   TALK mode and **PLOT** in BATCH and TERMINAL mode. If
                   OUTPUT=PLOT is used, the plot file will be written on Fortran unit 9.
                   This can then be sent to the system plotter. See your local consultant for
                   details on how to plot this file.

PROJECT=   Specifies which type of **PROJECT**ion will be used. The choices are
                   **AITOF, ALBER, AZIMU, CONFO, CORRE, CYLIN, ELLIP, EXACT,
                   GNOMO, LAMBE, MERCA, MOLLW, ORTHO, POLYC, SANSO** and
                   STERE.

TITLE=   Specifies a **TITLE** for the map. The title may be no longer than 8
                   characters.

WIDTH=   Specifies the **WIDTH** of the map. The default is 15 inches.

25. MATRIX MANIPULATION

"I am tired of all this thing called science...We have spent millions in that sort of thing for the last few years, and it is time it should be stopped."

Simon Cameron
U.S. Senator from Pennsylvania, 1861

The **MATRIX** and **COPY** commands can be used to create and manipulate matrices in SHAZAM. The **MATRIX** command will do matrix operations and create and transform matrices instead of vectors. It is similar to the **GENR** command except matrices are used. In contrast to the **GENR** command the **MATRIX** command ignores the current **SAMPLE** command. Also, **SKIPIF** commands have no effect on the **MATRIX** command.

A. *THE MATRIX COMMAND*

In general, the format of the **MATRIX** command is:

MATRIX *newmat = equation*

where *newmat* is the name of the new matrix to be created from an *equation*.

The following operators are valid on the **MATRIX** command:

-	Negation
*	Matrix Multiplication
+	Addition
-	Subtraction
,	Transpose
/	Hadamard Division
@	Kronecker Multiplication
|	Concatenation

Regular matrix rules apply on the **MATRIX** command. So, when multiplying with * the first matrix to be multiplied must have the same number of columns as the second matrix has rows. Addition (+), and subtraction (-), of matrices are done element by element, so only matrices with the same dimensions may be added to and subtracted from one another. Concatenation puts two matrices together side by side so both must have the same number of rows. Kronecker multiplication can be done with matrices of any dimension. The following examples illustrate concatenation and stacking matrices. In addition the Kronecker product of a 3 by 3 matrix, B, and a 2 by 2 matrix, A, would result in a 6 by 6 matrix:

```
|_READ A / ROWS=3 COLS=3 LIST
        3 ROWS AND              3 COLUMNS, BEGINNING AT ROW        1

...SAMPLE RANGE IS NOW SET TO:         1         3
    A
    3 BY    3 MATRIX
    1.000000        19.00000      -2.000000
    354.0000         0.0          28.00000
   -3.000000        15.00000       7.000000
|_READ B / ROWS=2 COLS=2 LIST
        2 ROWS AND              2 COLUMNS, BEGINNING AT ROW        1
    B
    2 BY    2 MATRIX
    78.00000        592.0000
    4.000000        -65.00000
|_READ C / ROWS=3 COLS=2 LIST
        3 ROWS AND              2 COLUMNS, BEGINNING AT ROW        1
    C
    3 BY    2 MATRIX
    16.00000        44.00000
   -3.000000        13.00000
    0.0             23.00000
|_* CONCATENATE A AND C SIDE BY SIDE
_MATRIX AC=A|C
_PRINT AC
    AC
    3 BY    5 MATRIX
    1.000000   19.00000    -2.000000     16.00000     44.00000
    354.0000   0.0          28.00000     -3.000000    13.00000
   -3.000000   15.00000      7.000000     0.0         23.00000
|_* STACK B AND C WITH B ON TOP
_MATRIX BC=(B'|C')'
_PRINT BC
    BC
    5 BY    2 MATRIX
    78.00000        592.0000
    4.000000        -65.00000
    16.00000        44.00000
   -3.000000        13.00000
    0.0             23.00000
|_* GET KRONECKER PRODUCT OF A AND B
_MATRIX K=A@B
_PRINT K
    K
    6 BY    6 MATRIX
    78.00000    592.0000    1482.000    11248.00    -156.0000    -1184.000
    4.000000    -65.00000   76.00000    -1235.000   -8.000000     130.0000
    27612.00    209568.0    0.0         0.0          2184.000    16576.00
    1416.000    -23010.00   0.0         0.0          112.0000    -1820.000
   -234.0000    -1776.000   1170.000    8880.000     546.0000     4144.000
   -12.00000    195.0000    60.00000    -975.0000    28.00000    -455.0000
```

Of course, any matrix can be multiplied by a constant.

The following functions are also available with the **MATRIX** command:

CHOL(*matrix*)	Cholesky's decomposition of a symmetric positive definite matrix is performed.
DET(*matrix*)	Determinant of *matrix*.
DIAG(*matrix*)	If *matrix* is n X n the **DIAG** function will create an n by 1 vector than consists of the diagonal elements of *matrix*. If *matrix* is an n X 1 vector the **DIAG** function will create an n by n matrix with zeros off the diagonal and the vector along the diagonal.
EIGVAL(*matrix*)	The eigenvalues of *matrix* are computed.
EIGVEC(*matrix*)	The eigenvector of *matrix* is computed.
EXP(*matrix*)	The exponential operator is applied to each element of *matrix*.
IDEN(*ndim*)	An identity matrix with *ndim* rows and columns is created.
IDEN(*ndim,ndiag*)	A matrix with *ndim* rows and columns is created with a diagonal of ones on the *ndiag* lower diagonal (ndiag = 1 gives an identity matrix).
INT(*matrix*)	Integer truncation of each element of the matrix is performed.
INV(*matrix*)	Inverse of *matrix*.
LAG(*matrix*,n)	Each column of *matrix* is lagged n times.
LOG(*matrix*)	The natural log of each element of *matrix* is taken.
NCDF(*matrix*)	Normal cumulative density function. The probability of each element of *matrix* is taken.
NOR(*nrow,ncol*)	A matrix of normally distributed numbers is created. The number of rows and columns is specified by *nrow,ncol*.
RANK(*matrix*)	The rank, or the number of independent rows, of *matrix* is calculated.
SAMP(*matrix,nrows*)	A new matrix with n rows is created from the old *matrix* by random sampling with replacement.
SEAS(*nob,nseas*)	A series of seasonal dummy variables is created. The number of observations and the number of seasons are specified by *nob* and *nseas*.
SIN(*matrix*)	The sine of each element of *matrix* is computed.
SQRT(*matrix*)	The square root of each element of *matrix* is computed.
SVD(*matrix*)	The Singular Value Decomposition of *matrix* is performed. The singular values are returned.
SYM(*matrix*)	Creates a symmetric matrix from a square full *matrix*.
TIME(*nob,x*)	A vector with *nob* observations is created with values equal to a time index plus *x*.
TRACE(*matrix*)	The trace, or the sum of the diagonal elements, of *matrix* is calculated.
TRI(*matrix*)	Creates a lower triangular matrix from a square full *matrix*.
UNI(*nrow,ncol*)	A matrix of random numbers between 0 and 1 is created. The number of rows and columns is specified by *nrow,ncol*.
VEC(*matrix*)	Stacks columns of a matrix into a long vector.
VEC(*matrix,nrows*)	Unstacks a vector into a matrix with *nrows*.

Calculation of the Rank of a matrix is often numerically difficult especially in the case of a near singular matrix, therefore the value returned by the RANK( ) function should be used with caution.

Although it is not a common matrix operation, SHAZAM can do multiplication and division element-by-element. These are often called Hadamard product and division (see Rao [1973, p.30]). For example, Hadamard division is done as follows:

MATRIX M = A/B

In the above example each element in the matrix A is divided by each element of the matrix B and the results of this operation are put in the matrix M. Of course, A and B must have the same dimensions unless either A or B is a constant.

It is also possible to perform Hadamard products or element-by-element multiplication. This is done in the following way:

MATRIX M = A/(1/B)

Again, A and B must have the same dimensions.

If multiplying an n x 1 vector by a matrix with n rows and any number of columns, SHAZAM will do element-by-element multiplication of the n x 1 vector times each column of the matrix so that the result will have the same number of columns as the original matrix.

In Johnston [1984, p. 178] the least squares coefficient vector β is calculated using matrices. This can be done with SHAZAM as Johnston does it, or with one matrix command. In addition we show how to extract pieces of a matrix:

```
_SAMPLE 1 5
_READ Y / BYVAR
1 VARIABLES AND        5 OBSERVATIONS STARTING AT OBS        1
? 3 1 8 3 5
_READ X / ROWS=5 COLS=3
      5 ROWS AND        3 COLUMNS, BEGINNING AT ROW        1
? 1 3 5
? 1 1 4
? 1 5 6
? 1 2 4
? 1 4 6
_MATRIX B=INV(X'X)*X'Y
_PRINT B
    B
   4.000000      2.500000      -1.500000
_* SHOW HOW TO PICK OUT ELEMENTS, AND ROWS, OR COLUMNS OF A MATRIX
_* CHANGE ROW 3 COLUMN 2 TO A 7
_MATRIX X(3,2)=7
_* GET THE SECOND COLUMN OF X
_MATRIX XTWO=X(0,2)
_PRINT XTWO / NOBYVAR
     XTWO
   3.000000
   1.000000
   7.000000
   2.000000
   4.000000
_* GET THE FOURTH ROW OF X
_MATRIX XFOUR=X(4,0)
```

```
|_PRINT XFOUR
    XFOUR
    1 BY     3 MATRIX
    1.000000         2.000000        4.000000
|_* GET ELEMENT (4,2) OF X
|_MATRIX X42=X(4,2)
|_PRINT X42
    X42
    2.000000
```

In the above output β is calculated in one step. When the transpose operator (') is used it is not necessary to use the multiplication operator (*) if multiplication between the transposed matrix and the following matrix is desired. However, without the transpose operator the multiplication operator is required.

In Johnston [1984, p. 192] there is an example of the calculation of an F-test using matrices:

```
|_SAMPLE 1 5
|_READ Y / BYVAR
    1 VARIABLES AND     5 OBSERVATIONS STARTING AT OBS        1
? 3 1 8 3 5
|_READ X / ROWS=5 COLS=3
    5 ROWS AND        3 COLUMNS, BEGINNING AT ROW        1
? 1 3 5
? 1 1 4
? 1 5 6
? 1 2 4
? 1 4 6
|_MATRIX B=INV(X'X)*X'Y
|_MATRIX EE=Y'Y-(B'(X'Y))
|_READ R / ROWS=1 COLS=3
    1 ROWS AND        3 COLUMNS, BEGINNING AT ROW        1
? 0 1 1
|_READ LR / ROWS=1 COLS=1
    1 ROWS AND        1 COLUMNS, BEGINNING AT ROW        1
? 0
|_MATRIX F=((R*B-LR)'(INV(R*(INV(X'X)*R')))*(R*B-LR))/(EE/2)
|_PRINT F
F
    1 BY     1 MATRIX
    2.666667
```

It is apparent from the SHAZAM calculation of this F-test that many calculations can be done on one **MATRIX** command. See the chapter *PROGRAMMING IN SHAZAM* for more extensive examples of the **MATRIX** command.

B. *THE COPY COMMAND*

It is also possible to partition matrices, delete rows and columns, and create matrices from vectors by using the **COPY** command. The **COPY** command is used to copy vectors or matrices into other matrices. The format of the **COPY** command is:

COPY *fromvar(s) tovar / options*

where *fromvar(s)* is either a list of vectors or a single matrix, *tovar* is the variable into which the *fromvar(s)* are to be copied and *options* is a list of desired options. The available options on the **COPY** command are:

FROW = *beg;end*   Specifies the rows of the *fromvar(s)* that are to be copied into the *tovar*. If this option is not specified the current **SAMPLE** command will be used.

FCOL = *beg;end*   Specifies the columns of the *fromvar* that are to be copied into the new variable. If the old variables are a list of vectors the **FCOL**= option need not be used as SHAZAM will automatically treat each vector as a column. Therefore, this option is only used if the old variable is a matrix.

TROW = *beg;end*   Specifies the rows of the *tovar* into which the *fromvar(s)* are to be copied. If this option is not specified the current **SAMPLE** command will be used.

TCOL = *beg;end*   Specifies the columns of the *tovar* into which the old variables are to be copied.

If no options are specified on the **COPY** command all the *fromvar(s)* will be copied into the *tovar*. It is impossible to copy from vectors and a matrix simultaneously. It is very important to specify consistent options on the **COPY** command, that is, the dimensions specified with the **COPY** options must be compatible with the dimensions of the *fromvar(s)* and *tovar*. It is also important to remember to use a semicolon (;) only to separate *beg* and *end* and no more than 8 characters are allowed.

If **SKIPIF** commands or the expanded form of the **SAMPLE** have been used the *tovar* matrix will be reduced in size. This is useful in deleting rows of a matrix to create a new matrix. For example, if A is a 15 by 5 matrix, the following commands will create a new matrix B which is 4 by 12 because rows 4,10,11 and column 3 of A have been deleted:

```
|_PRINT A
   A
  15 BY     5 MATRIX
  40.05292      1170.600      97.80000      2.528130      191.5000
  54.64859      2015.800     104.4000      24.91888      516.0000
  40.31206      2803.300     118.0000      29.34270      729.0000
  84.21099      2039.700     156.2000      27.61823      560.4000
 127.5724       2256.200     172.6000      60.35945      519.9000
 124.8797       2132.200     186.6000      50.61588      628.5000
  96.55514      1834.100     220.9000      30.70955      537.1000
```

131.1601	1588.000	287.8000	60.69605	561.2000
77.02764	1749.400	319.9000	30.00972	617.2000
46.96689	1687.200	321.3000	42.50750	626.7000
100.6597	2007.700	319.6000	58.61146	737.2000
115.7467	2208.300	346.0000	46.96287	760.5000
114.5826	1656.700	456.4000	57.87651	581.4000
119.8762	1604.400	543.4000	43.22093	662.3000
105.5699	1431.800	618.3000	22.87143	583.8000

```
_SAMPLE 1 3 5 9 12 15
_COPY A:1 A:2 A:4 A:5 B
_PRINT B
  B
 12 BY    4 MATRIX
```

40.05292	1170.600	2.528130	191.5000
54.64859	2015.800	24.91888	516.0000
40.31206	2803.300	29.34270	729.0000
127.5724	2256.200	60.35945	519.9000
124.8797	2132.200	50.61588	628.5000
96.55514	1834.100	30.70955	537.1000
131.1601	1588.000	60.69605	561.2000
77.02764	1749.400	30.00972	617.2000
115.7467	2208.300	46.96287	760.5000
114.5826	1656.700	57.87651	581.4000
119.8762	1604.400	43.22093	662.3000
105.5699	1431.800	22.87143	583.8000

26. PRICE INDEXES

"When the U.S. government stops wasting our resources by trying to maintain the price of gold, its price will sink to...$6 an ounce rather than the current $35 an ounce."

Henry Reuss
U.S. Senator from Wisconsin, 1967

SHAZAM can compute chained price indexes from a set of price and quantity data on a number of commodities. The available indexes are (i) the Laspeyres, (ii) the Paasche, (iii) the Fisher Ideal and (iv) the Divisia (Tornquist or Translog). The resulting index may then be saved as a variable to be used in subsequent calculations.

To calculate an index, it is necessary to have prices and quantities for at least two commodities. Let

$$p_{it} \quad \text{and} \quad q_{it}$$

be the price and quantity for variable i in period t where $i = 1,2,...,N$ and $t = 1,2,...,T$.

Let

$$q_t = (q_{1t}, q_{2t}, \ldots, q_{Nt})$$

and

$$p_t = (p_{1t}, p_{2t}, \ldots, p_{Nt})$$

denote the period t price and quantity vectors that are to be aggregated into scalars. The level of prices in period t relative to period t-1 for the Laspeyres, Paasche, Fisher and Divisia formulas are:

$$L^t = (p_t' q_{t-1})/(p_{t-1}' q_{t-1}), \qquad t = 2,3,\ldots,T.$$
$$P^t = (p_t' q_t)/(p_{t-1}' q_t),$$
$$F^t = (L^t P^t)^{1/2},$$

and

$$\log D^t = (.5) \sum_{i=1}^{I} (s_{it} + s_{i,t-1}) \log(p_{it}/p_{i,t-1});$$

where

$$s_{it} = (p_{it}q_{it}) / (p_t'q_t)$$

respectively. These are chain links that are used in constructing the final price index series. For example, if the Laspeyres index is chosen with the **CHAIN** option, and the base period is designated to be observation 1, the price series which is generated by the SHAZAM program is:

$$1, \ L^2, \ L^2L^3, \ldots, \ L^2L^3L^4 \ldots \ L^T.$$

If this new price series is denoted by PL, then the corresponding quantity series, QL, is computed in the following way:

$$QL^t = (p_t'q_t) / (PL^t)$$

If the Paasche, Fisher or Divisia options are chosen, the numbers L^t appearing in this paragraph are replaced by P^t, F^t or D^t respectively. These index number formulas are explained more fully in Diewert [1978].

In general, the format of the **INDEX** command is:

INDEX p_1 q_1 p_2 q_2 p_3 q_3 ... / *options*

where the p and q are names of the variables for the prices and quantities of the commodities.

As well as the **BEG** = and **END** = options as defined for **OLS**, the following options are available on the **INDEX** command:

CHAIN   This option will **CHAIN** the Laspeyres, Paasche or Fisher indexes using the method described above. The Divisia index is always chained.

EXPEND   This option indicates that the quantity variables measure **EXPEND**itures rather than quantities. SHAZAM will first divide each **EXPEND**iture variable by its respective price to get the quantities.

NOALTERN   Normally, variables are listed as described above, with p and q alternating in the list. Sometimes, it is more convenient to list all the prices followed by all the quantities. This would be the case if the prices were in one matrix and the quantities in another matrix. In this case, **NOALTERN** should be specified. The default is **ALTERN**.

NOLIST   With this option the price and quantity indexes are not printed.

BASE=   This option is used to specify the observation number to be used as the
                        BASE period for the index. The value of the index in the base period will
                        be 1.0. If the **BASE=** option is not specified SHAZAM will use the first
                        available observation as the base period. Use of **SKIPIF** commands is not
                        recommended when computing Divisia indexes since the index needs to be
                        chained.

DIVISIA=   These options specify the variable where the index will be stored for this
PAASCHE=   SHAZAM run. Note that the options beginning with the letter **Q**,
LASPEYRES=   (**QDIVISIA=**, **QPAASCHE=**, etc.) tell SHAZAM to store the the *quantity*
FISHER=   in the variable specified. Those options not preceded by **Q** tell SHAZAM to
QDIVISIA=   store the *price index* in the variable specified. The quantity is computed
QPAASCHE=   residually in this option, i.e. according to the method described above. To
QLASPEYRES=   compute quantity indexes and prices residually, interchange the role of
QFISHER=   prices and quantities in the **INDEX** command.

An example of the **INDEX** command is:

INDEX PFOOD FOOD PCLOTHES CLOTHES PHOUSE HOUSE / EXPEND BASE=23

In this example the quantity data is in expenditure form and observation 23 is to be used as the
base year.

A problem arises if there is a zero price or quantity in any year. SHAZAM handles this problem
by ignoring any commodity whenever a zero price or quantity would have to be used in a
calculation. The remaining quantities are then assumed to exhaust the set for that year. A good
reference for treatment of zero price and quantities is Diewert[1980].

Some users may wish to compute quantity indexes directly. To do this, reverse the p and q
variables on the **INDEX** command.

The following is an example of the SHAZAM output obtained from the **INDEX** command using data for price and quantity of cars for various corporations found in Newbold [1984, Ch.16]:

```
|_INDEX P1 Q1 P2 Q2 P3 Q3 P4 Q4 / QDIVISIA=QD PAASCHE=PA

BASE PERIOD IS OBSERVATION        1
PAASCHE   WILL BE STORED AS VARIABLE: PA
QDIVISIA WILL BE STORED AS VARIABLE: QD
                       PRICE INDEX              QUANTITY
   DIVISIA PAASCHE LASPEYRES FISHER  DIVISIA PAASCHE  LASPEYRES  FISHER
    1  1.000  1.000  1.000  1.000    1509.   1509.    1509.     1509.
    2  0.994  0.998  0.989  0.994    816.0   812.8    819.8     816.3
    3  0.979  0.977  0.980  0.978    733.3   735.4    732.9     734.1
    4  0.999  0.997  0.999  0.998    747.9   749.4    748.1     748.7
    5  1.045  1.044  1.045  1.044    1133.   1135.    1134.     1134.
    6  1.048  1.044  1.043  1.044    930.6   933.4    934.3     933.9
    7  1.029  1.025  1.025  1.025    637.5   639.9    639.6     639.8
    8  1.075  1.077  1.069  1.073    1213.   1211.    1219.     1215.
    9  1.110  1.106  1.106  1.106    923.6   926.6    926.9     926.8
   10  1.109  1.104  1.101  1.102    1210.   1215.    1218.     1217.
   11  1.198  1.195  1.188  1.191    1540.   1544.    1553.     1548.
   12  1.153  1.148  1.148  1.148    1178.   1184.    1184.     1184.
|_PRINT QD PA
       QD               PA
   1509.375         1.000000
   816.0446         0.9979699
   733.3490         0.9765596
   747.8928         0.9969307
   1133.374         1.043727
   930.5681         1.044271
   637.4855         1.024789
   1212.867         1.076632
   923.5981         1.106354
   1210.000         1.103586
   1540.261         1.194918
   1178.282         1.147695
```

As the above example shows, all the price indexes and quantities are computed and printed. The Divisia quantity and the Paasche price index are saved. No base period is specified on the **BASE**= option so the first observation is used.

27. PRINCIPAL COMPONENTS AND FACTOR ANALYSIS

"That's an amazing invention, but who would ever want to use one of them?"

> Rutherford B. Hayes
> U.S. President, 1876
> (after seeing the telephone)

SHAZAM has the ability to extract principal components (**PC**) from a set of data and, as an option, do a Varimax rotation for factor analysis. SHAZAM will do the analysis on either the cross-product matrix or the correlation matrix. A good reference on principal components is Jolliffe [1986]. If a listing of the actual principal components is desired, the components can be normalized four different ways. Output may include the eigenvalues, eigenvectors, components, factor matrix, and rotated factor matrix. It is possible to specify conditions under which factors are retained. Multicollinearity diagnostics including condition numbers, condition indexes, and variance proportions may also be printed. These diagnostics are discussed in Belsley, Kuh and Welsch [1980].

In general, the format of the **PC** command is:

PC *vars / options*

where *vars* is a list of the variables desired in the analysis, and *options* is a list of desired options.

The available options are:

COR This option indicates that analysis is to be done on the **COR**relation matrix. If this option is not specified, the analysis is done on the deviations from the means cross-product matrix. Since the components are sensitive to transformations, it is important that the user be sure this option is needed. If all the variables are measured in the same units, it is probably better to use the cross-product matrix. This is often the case for economists. If the variables are all measured differently, it may be more appropriate to use the correlation matrix which, in effect, normalizes all variables. See also the **SCALE** option.

LIST **LIST**s the matrix of Principal Components. If there are many observations it will be costly to list all the components.

MAX This option is equivalent to specifying the **PEVEC**, **PFM**, and **PRM** options.

PCOLLIN   This option will print the proportion of the variance of the estimate accounted for by each principal component. Multicollinearity may be a problem if a component corresponding to a high condition index contributes strongly to the variance of more than one variable. See Belsley, Kuh and Welsch [1980] for definitions.

PEVEC   This option will Print all the EigenVECtors for the retained components. If there are many variables this option could yield a lot of costly output which may have little value.

PFM   This option will Print the Factor loading Matrix for the retained factors.

PRM   This option will compute and Print the Rotated factor Matrix by a Varimax rotation. The method is described in Kaiser [1959]. This option increases costs so it should used when it is really needed. The Varimax rotation is one of the most common types of rotation.

RAW   This option indicates that analysis is to be done on the original **RAW** cross-product matrix instead of the deviations from the means cross-product matrix. If this option is not specified, the analysis is done on the deviations from the means cross-product matrix. The same warnings specified for the **COR** option apply here.

SCALE   This option indicates that analysis is to be done on a scaled cross-product matrix instead of the deviations from the means cross-product matrix. The scaled matrix transforms a RAW cross-product matrix into one where the data vectors all have unit length so that the diagonals of the cross-product matrix are all equal to 1. Note that this is *not* the same as the **COR** option. If the **SCALE** option is not specified, the analysis is done on the deviations from the means cross-product matrix. The same warnings specified for the **COR** option apply here.

EVAL=   Specifies the EigenVALues in the vector specified.

EVEC=   Saves the EigenVECtors in the matrix specified.

MAXFACT=   This option specifies the **MAX**imum number of **FACT**ors to be retained. If no value of **MINEIG** is specified **MAXFACT** will be the actual number retained. If **MAXFACT** is not specified, all will be included.

MINEIG=   This option will specify the **MIN**imum **EIG**envalue allowed to retain a component. If the **COR** option is specified, the eigenvalues will range from 0 to the number of variables in the analysis. Sometimes a convenient value is **MINEIG = 1**. This rule of thumb does not work if the analysis is done on the cross-product matrix. The default is **MINEIG = 0**.

NC=　　　　　　　　　NC is the Normalization Code which may be specified. The default is
NC=1. There does not appear to be much agreement in other computer
programs on how the components should be normalized, so SHAZAM offers
4 options. The available normalization codes are:
1.　　No normalization, variance is λ / (n-1)
2.　　Variance is 1/(n-1)(Theil's way)
3.　　Variance is λ (the BMDP way)
4.　　Variance is 1 (standard normal) (the TSP way)
where λ is the eigenvalue corresponding to the component, and n is the
number of observations.

PCINFO=　　　　　　　This option is used to save a matrix of **INFO**rmation needed for
regressions on Principal Components.

PCOMP=　　　　　　　Saves the matrix of **P**rincipal **COMP**onents in the matrix specified.

When doing regression on principal components the **PC** command is used to generate the principal
components in an **OLS** regression and then the coefficients are transformed back to correspond to
the original variables. References on Principal Components regression are in Judge, Griffiths, Hill,
Lütkepohl, and Lee [1985, Ch.22.5] and Mundlak [1981]. The following example shows the
SHAZAM output for one case in the homework example in Judge, Griffiths, Hill, Lütkepohl, and
Lee [1985, Ex.22.7, p. 932], but with only the first two principal components being used:

```
|_SAMPLE 1 20
|_READ(11) X1 X2 X3 X4 X5 Y1
   6 VARIABLES AND         20 OBSERVATIONS STARTING AT OBS          1
|_PC  X2 X3 X4 X5 / PCOMP=PC PCINFO=INFO LIST

  PRINCIPAL COMPONENTS ON     4 VARIABLES      MAXIMUM OF    4 FACTORS RETAINED
EIGENVALUES
  33.645      5.7812      0.95354      0.12366
SUM OF EIGENVALUES =   40.504
CUMULATIVE PERCENTAGE OF EIGENVALUES
0.83067      0.97340      0.99695      1.0000
VARIANCE REDUCTION BENCHMARK FUNCTION
 100.00       99.682       97.829       86.599
```

```
OB. NO.          FIRST    4 PRINCIPAL COMPONENTS       NORMALIZATION CODE = 1
                    1           2             3                  4
     1    -1.8778        0.31026      -0.15521          0.44344E-01
     2     0.15393E-01   0.72540      -0.23538E-01      0.13571
     3    -1.3298       -0.28764       0.16225          0.14582
     4     0.66189      -0.24557      -0.21644          0.27745E-01
     5    -0.83212      -1.1112       -0.29982         -0.27425E-01
     6     1.1374        0.75566      -0.23632          0.45119E-01
     7     0.70781      -0.47217       0.14150          0.17186E-02
     8     1.0430        0.32377       0.31505         -0.14265
     9     1.7218       -0.23539       0.21185         -0.71190E-02
    10    -2.2711        0.42144       0.10214E-02     -0.12579
    11    -1.5985       -0.16848       0.32797          0.61141E-01
    12     0.52248E-02   0.46462      -0.37939         -0.61193E-01
    13     0.54984      -0.14983      -0.84474E-01      0.26054E-01
```

```
14   -0.86255      -1.0520      -0.21865      -0.36310E-02
15    0.91889       0.84082     -0.11760      -0.32328E-01
16    0.43127      -0.25606      0.43964      -0.17178E-01
17    1.6980        0.13071      0.44078E-01   0.13488
18    1.8655       -0.46026     -0.96728E-01  -0.79457E-01
19    0.28293      -0.54779E-01  0.48297E-01  -0.75083E-01
20   -2.2670        0.52073      0.13650      -0.50680E-01
4 COMPONENTS STORED IN MATRIX PC
```

```
|_OLS Y1 PC:1 PC:2  / PCINFO=INFO PCOMP=PC
```

OLS ESTIMATION
       20 OBSERVATIONS   DEPENDENT VARIABLE = Y1
  R-SQUARE = 0.8913   R-SQUARE ADJUSTED = 0.8786
VARIANCE OF THE ESTIMATE = 0.91550
STANDARD ERROR OF THE ESTIMATE = 0.95682
LOG OF THE LIKELIHOOD FUNCTION = -25.8708

VARIABLE NAME	ESTIMATED COEFFICIENT	STANDARD ERROR	T-RATIO 17 DF	PARTIAL CORR.	STANDARDIZED COEFFICIENT	ELASTICITY AT MEANS
PC	1.8892	0.16496	11.453	0.9409	0.91563	0.00000
PC	-1.1455	0.39794	-2.8785	-0.5724	-0.23013	0.00000
CONSTANT	20.107	0.21395	93.979	0.9990	0.0	1.0000

ORIGINAL COEFFICIENTS TRANSFORMED BACK FROM COMPONENTS

VARIABLE NAME	ESTIMATED COEFFICIENT	STANDARD ERROR	T-RATIO 17 DF	PARTIAL CORR.	STANDARDIZED COEFFICIENT	ELASTICITY AT MEANS
X2	0.48574	0.17454	2.7830	0.5595	0.12257	0.03747
X3	1.0811	0.29365	3.6816	0.6660	0.18200	0.06803
X4	0.55642	0.16863	3.2997	0.6248	0.14715	0.04966
X5	1.7796	0.20110	8.8492	0.9064	0.61859	0.29938
CONSTANT	10.968	0.84344	13.004	0.9532	0.0	0.54546

Note that the **PCOMP=** and the **PCINFO=** options are used in both the **PC** and the **OLS** commands. In the **PC** command, it is used to store the information in the matrix INFO and the components in the matrix PC. In the **OLS** command, the information is taken from INFO and PC.

28. PROBABILITY DISTRIBUTIONS

"A severe depression like that of 1920-21 is outside the range of probability."

Harvard Economic Society
November 16, 1929

The **DISTRIB** command will compute the probability density function (PDF) and the cumulative density function (CDF) for certain distributions. This is useful if adequate statistical tables are unavailable. Since approximation formulas are often used to compute probabilities users may find that the numbers printed may not exactly match those found in statistical tables which are usually computed with far greater precision. However, the approximation formulas are usually accurate to at least two significant digits. In some cases either the PDF or CDF is difficult to compute so is not calculated.

In general, the format of the **DISTRIB** command is:

DISTRIB *vars / options*

where *vars* is a list of variables and *options* is a list of the options that are required on the specified type of distribution.

The available options are:

INVERSE	The **INVERSE** option returns critical values of the distributions instead of probabilities. SHAZAM returns the critical values X such that, in the case of a t-distribution, $Pr(t > X) =$ probability. The data must be in probabilities. This option may not be used with **TYPE = EDGE** or **TYPE = IMHOF**.
LLF	The **LLF** option computes the Log of the Likelihood Function for the data and prints it and stores it in the temporary variable \$LLF. This option may not be used with **TYPE = IMHOF**, non-central distributions, or the **INVERSE** option.
NOLIST	This option suppresses the listing of probability densities or critical values for each observation. It would normally be used only if these numbers were saved in temporary or permanent variables for later use and the listing was not required.
BEG = **END =**	Specify the **BEG**inning and **END** observations to be used for the given **DISTRIB** command. If none are specified the current **SAMPLE** range is used.

C=	Specifies the non-Centrality parameter for a non-central F-distribution. This option is only used with **TYPE=F**.
CDF=	This option saves the Cumulative Distribution Function values in the variable specified.
CRITICAL=	This option saves the **CRITICAL** values in the variable specified when the **INVERSE** option is being used.
DF=	Specifies the Degrees of Freedom. This option is used only with **TYPE=T** and **TYPE=CHI**.
DF1= **DF2=**	Specify the Degrees of Freedom for the numerator(**1**) and the denominator(**2**) respectively. This option is used only with **TYPE=F**.
EIGENVAL=	This option specifies the vector of **EIGENVAL**ues to be used with the **TYPE=IMHOF** option.
H=	This option specifies the Precision Parameter for the t-distribution. The default is **H=1** which corresponds to the most common use of the t-distribution. For examples of situations where **H≠1** see Zellner, *An Introduction To Bayesian Inference in Econometrics*, Wiley, 1971 or Chapters 4 and 7 of the *Judge Handbook*.
KURTOSIS=	Specifies the population **KURTOSIS** parameter for **TYPE=EDGE**. The coefficient of kurtosis is equal to 0 in a normal distribution.
MEAN=	Specifies the population **MEAN** value. This option is only used with **TYPE=NORMAL, TYPE=EDGE** or **TYPE=BETA**.
NEIGEN=	This option specifies the Number of **EIGEN**values to be used with **TYPE=IMHOF** if the entire vector is not required.
PDF=	This option saves the Probability Density Function for each observation in the variable specified. It may not be used with **TYPE=IMHOF**.
P= **N=**	Specify the parameters for **TYPE=BINOMIAL**.
P= **Q=**	Specify the parameters for **TYPE=BETA** or **TYPE=GAMMA**. These are not needed when **TYPE=BETA** if **MEAN=** and **VAR=** are specified.

SKEWNESS=   Specifies the population **SKEWNESS** coefficient for **TYPE=EDGE**. The coefficient of Skewness is equal to 0 in a normal distribution.

S=   Specifies the parameters for **TYPE=IG2**.
V=

TYPE=   Specifies the **TYPE** of distribution. If the type is not specified SHAZAM assumes **TYPE=NORMAL**. The other choices, described in detail later in this chapter, are **BETA, BINOMIAL, CHI, EDGE, F, GAMMA, IG2, IMHOF** and **T**.

VAR=   Specifies the population **VAR**iance. This option is only used with **TYPE=NORMAL, TYPE=EDGE** or **TYPE=BETA**.

The types of distribution available on the **TYPE=** option are:

BETA   *Beta Distribution*
When the **BETA** distribution is specified the **P=** and **Q=**, or the **MEAN=** and **VAR=** options must be used. The beta variable must be in the 0-1 interval.

BINOMIAL   *Binomial Distribution*
When the **BINOMIAL** distribution is specified the **N=** and **P=** options must be used.

CHI   *Chi-Squared Distribution*
When the **CHI** distribution is specified the **DF=** option must be used.

EDGE   *Edgeworth Approximation*
When the **EDGE** distribution is specified the **MEAN=, VAR=, SKEWNESS=,** and **KURTOSIS=** options should be used. The defaults on **EDGE** are **MEAN=0, VAR=1, SKEWNESS=0** and **KURTOSIS=0**. The Edgeworth distribution approximates many distributions. The formula for this distribution can be found in Bickel and Doksum [1977, Eq. 1.5.11, p. 33].

F   *F-Distribution*
When the **F**-distribution is specified the **DF1=** and **DF2=** options must be used.

GAMMA

Gamma Distribution
When the **GAMMA** distribution is specified the **P**= and **Q**= options must be specified. In the **GAMMA** distribution **P** is the scale parameter and **Q** is the shape parameter. The Gamma probability density function is:

$$f(x) = \frac{(x/p)^{q-1}\exp(-x/p)}{p\Gamma(q)}$$

IG2

Inverted Gamma Distribution - Type 2
When the **IG2** distribution is specified the **S**= and **V**= options must be specified. **S** is the estimate of σ and **V** is the degrees of freedom parameter. The Inverted Gamma probability density function is shown in equation 4.2.5 of Judge, Griffiths, Hill, Lütkepohl and Lee [1985]. See Chapters 4 and 7 of the *Judge Handbook* for examples of this option.

IMHOF

Imhof Distribution
This option requires the **EIGENVAL**= option. This distribution is described in Koerts and Abrahamse [1969]. The **NEIGEN**= option may also be used. See the chapter *PROGRAMMING IN SHAZAM* for an example of this option.

NORMAL

Normal Distribution
NORMAL is the default distribution. When the **NORMAL** distribution is specified, the **MEAN**= and **VAR**= options should be used. The default on **NORMAL** is **MEAN**=**0** and **VAR**=**1**.

T

Student's t-Distribution
When the **t** distribution is specified the **DF**= option must be used.

The following example (using Theil's [1971, p. 102] Textile data) shows how the **DISTRIB** command can return probabilities for t-ratios. Notice that the t-ratios are first saved from an **OLS** regression in the variable TR, and that the degrees of freedom for the **OLS** regression are available in the temporary variable $DF.

```
|_OLS CONS INCOME PRICE / TRATIO=TR

OLS ESTIMATION
      17 OBSERVATIONS        DEPENDENT VARIABLE = CONS
...NOTE..SAMPLE RANGE SET TO:    1,    17
 R-SQUARE = 0.9513     R-SQUARE ADJUSTED = 0.9443
VARIANCE OF THE ESTIMATE =     30.951
STANDARD ERROR OF THE ESTIMATE =    5.5634
MEAN OF DEPENDENT VARIABLE =    134.51
LOG OF THE LIKELIHOOD FUNCTION = -51.6471
```

VARIABLE NAME	ESTIMATED COEFFICIENT	STANDARD ERROR	T-RATIO 14 DF	PARTIAL CORR.	STANDARDIZED COEFFICIENT	ELASTICITY AT MEANS
INCOME	1.0617	0.26667	3.9813	0.7287	0.23871	0.81288
PRICE	-1.3830	0.83814E-01	-16.501	-0.9752	-0.98933	-0.78464
CONSTANT	130.71	27.094	4.8241	0.7902	0.0	0.97175

```
|_DISTRIB TR / TYPE=T DF=$DF
                 DATA        PDF         CDF         1-CDF
     TR
ROW    1      3.9813     0.18890E-01 0.99932     0.68261E-03
ROW    2     -16.501     0.11648E-02 0.71626E-10 1.0000
ROW    3      4.8241     0.13114E-01 0.99986     0.13502E-03
```

In the above example, a one-sided test of the hypothesis that the coefficient on INCOME is equal to zero would be rejected at the .00068261 level of confidence.

There are several temporary variables available from the last observation of the previous **DISTRIB** command. These are $CDF, $CRIT and $PDF. For more information on temporary variables see the chapter *MISCELLANEOUS COMMANDS AND INFORMATION*.

29. SORTING DATA

"Where a calculator on the ENIAC is equipped with 18,000 vacuum tubes and weighs 30 tons, computers in the future may have only 1,000 vacuum tubes and perhaps weigh only 1.5 tons."

Popular Mechanics
March 1949

The **SORT** command allows the user to sort data in a SHAZAM run. A variable which will be used to sort the data must be specified. When completed, all observations of the specified variables will be rearranged in ascending order according to the ranking in the sort variable.

In general, the format of the **SORT** command is:

SORT *sortvar vars / options*

where *sortvar* is the variable name of the sorting variable, *vars* is a list of the variables to be sorted and *options* is a list of desired options. Note that only the variables listed in *sortvars* and *vars* will be sorted, that only the observations for the currently defined **SAMPLE** will be sorted, and that **SKIPIF** commands are not in effect.

The available options on the **SORT** command are:

DESC   This option will cause the specified variables to be sorted in **DESC**ending, rather than ascending order.

LIST   This option will **LIST** all the sorted data. That is, it will print the sorted *vars* and the *sortvar*.

BEG=   Specify the sample range for the given **SORT** command. If these are not
END=   specified, the current **SAMPLE** range is used.

The following is an example of the **SORT** command using Theil's [1971, p. 102] Textile data. This example shows how a data file that has been typed in backward could be sorted using the **SORT** command:

```
|_SAMPLE 1 17
|_READ(11) YEAR CONSUME INCOME PRICE
   4 VARIABLES AND        17 OBSERVATIONS STARTING AT OBS 1
|_PRINT YEAR CONSUME INCOME PRICE
   YEAR            CONSUME            INCOME             PRICE
   1939.000        165.5000           103.8000           61.30000
   1938.000        149.0000           101.6000           59.50000
   1937.000        154.3000           102.4000           59.70000
   1936.000        168.0000           97.60000           52.60000
   1935.000        136.2000           96.40000           63.60000
   1934.000        140.6000           95.40000           62.50000
   1933.000        158.5000           101.7000           61.30000
   1932.000        153.6000           105.3000           65.40000
   1931.000        154.2000           109.3000           70.10000
   1930.000        136.0000           112.3000           82.80000
   1929.000        121.1000           110.8000           90.60000
   1928.000        117.6000           109.5000           89.70000
   1927.000        122.2000           104.9000           86.50000
   1926.000        111.6000           104.9000           90.60000
   1925.000        100.0000           100.0000           100.0000
   1924.000        99.00000           98.10000           100.1000
   1923.000        99.20000           96.70000           101.0000
|_SORT YEAR CONSUME INCOME PRICE
DATA HAS BEEN SORTED BY VARIABLE YEAR
|_PRINT YEAR CONSUME INCOME PRICE
   YEAR            CONSUME            INCOME             PRICE
   1923.000        99.20000           96.70000           101.0000
   1924.000        99.00000           98.10000           100.1000
   1925.000        100.0000           100.0000           100.0000
   1926.000        111.6000           104.9000           90.60000
   1927.000        122.2000           104.9000           86.50000
   1928.000        117.6000           109.5000           89.70000
   1929.000        121.1000           110.8000           90.60000
   1930.000        136.0000           112.3000           82.80000
   1931.000        154.2000           109.3000           70.10000
   1932.000        153.6000           105.3000           65.40000
   1933.000        158.5000           101.7000           61.30000
   1934.000        140.6000           95.40000           62.50000
   1935.000        136.2000           96.40000           63.60000
   1936.000        168.0000           97.60000           52.60000
   1937.000        154.3000           102.4000           59.70000
   1938.000        149.0000           101.6000           59.50000
   1939.000        165.5000           103.8000           61.30000
```

It is important to realize that once the data has been sorted it can only be unsorted back to its original state if, prior to the sort, there was a variable which was in either ascending or descending order. This type of variable may be created on a **GENR** command with the **TIME(0)** function.

30. SET AND DISPLAY

"Gone With The Wind is going to be the biggest flop in Hollywood history.
I'm just glad it'll be Clark Gable who's falling flat on his face and not Gary
Cooper."

Gary Cooper
Actor, 1938

SET commands make it possible to turn certain options on or off. In general, the format of the **SET** command to turn options on is:

SET *option*

To turn options off, the format of the **SET** command is:

SET NO*option*

where *option* is the desired option. The available options on the **SET** command are:

BATCH   **BATCH** is used in **BATCH** mode or when more extensive output is desired
or when the OUTPUT unit is assigned to a file. Most modern operating
systems can detect a batch run, so this option is rarely used. If the
operating system is not able to do this, **BATCH** is the default.

COLOR /   The **COLOR** option is used on IBM PC Compatible machines with a Color
NOCOLOR   EGA monitor to obtain a color background that changes depending on the
command in use. If you do not want color, type **SET NOCOLOR**.

DISK /   When there is insufficient memory to execute certain commands it is
NODISK   possible to allow SHAZAM to use a scratch **DISK** file to save memory.
The **DISK** option will allow this to occur, but will increase the amount of
computer time required. This option will only work on **OLS** with
METHOD=NORMAL, PLOT, PROBIT, LOGIT, TOBIT and a few
other commands. This option is automatically in effect for these
commands. To turn it off use **SET NODISK**. For higher use of the disk
at even greater cost see the **HIDISK** option.

DOECHO   Commands are normally printed for each cycle through a SHAZAM
DO-loop. To prevent these commands from being printed, **SET**
NODOECHO.

DUMP   This option **DUMP**s a lot of output which is primarily of interest to
SHAZAM consultants.

ECHO

This option causes commands to be printed in the output. In interactive mode it may be necessary to use **NOECHO** to prevent the repetition of each command, however most modern operating systems can set this automatically. The default is **ECHO** in BATCH and TERMINAL modes and **NOECHO** in TALK mode.

FRENCH

The **FRENCH** option allows all command names to be typed in **FRENCH** or **ENGLISH**. Output will still appear in English. A list of French commands is shown in the chapter *FRENCH COMMAND NAMES*.

HIDISK

The **HIDISK** option should only be used if you have raised PAR to the maximum feasible amount that your machine will allow. This option will try to conserve space by writing and reading data from disk at a very high rate. It is a rather expensive option and should only be used if you have a very large amount of data. To use the least possible memory you will need both the **DISK** and **HIDISK** options. Warning: The **HIDISK** option is still very experimental and strange things may happen if you use it. You should think of the **HIDISK** option as a *HIRISK* option. At best it only works with **OLS**, **GENR** and **PRINT** commands.

LASTCOM

This option creates a variable called **C$** which will contain the previous command typed. This variable can then be printed at any time after the **LASTCOM** option is **SET** by typing **PRINT C$**. This option is only useful in TALK mode.

LCASE

This option allows commands to be typed in either upper or lower case rather than just upper case. When this option is specified, all lower case characters will be converted to upper case before processing by SHAZAM. Note that before you use the option, input must be in upper case so you must type **SET LCASE**, not **set lcase**. After the option is set additional commands may be in lower case. Most computers automatically convert lower case to upper case so this option is rarely needed.

MAX

The **MAX** option can be **SET** to turn on the **MAX** option on each command. This eliminates the need to use the **MAX** option on every individual command if it is always desired.

NOCC

The **NOCC** option is used to turn off carriage control. When **SET CC** is in effect, some commands (like **OLS**) will still skip to a new page. The default is **SET CC**. For more information on carriage control in SHAZAM see the chapter *MISCELLANEOUS COMMANDS AND INFORMATION*.

OPTIONS

Displays the value of all command **OPTIONS** in subsequent commands. This option is primarily of interest to SHAZAM consultants.

PAUSE   The **PAUSE** option causes a pause to occur after each command is executed. This is useful when the user is working on a machine which has no pause control on its keyboard and therefore much of the output is missed as it appears on the screen. The default is **SET NOPAUSE**. On some systems the user can simply press *RETURN* on the keyboard to resume execution. However, this may not be the case on all operating systems. This option has no effect in BATCH mode.

RANFIX   When **RANFIX** is **SET** the random number generator is not set by the system clock. Thus, the same set of random numbers will be obtained in repeated jobs.

SAMPLE /   These options allow the use of the ommitted observations in the expanded
NOSAMPLE   form of the **SAMPLE** command to be turned on and off.

SCREEN /   This option works on some (but not all computers) to turn on and off the
NOSCREEN   display of the SHAZAM output on the terminal screen when the output has been redirected to a file assigned with the **FILE SCREEN** command. Due to the peculiarities of various operating systems the option may or may not work. Try it and see.

SKIP /   These options allow **SKIPIF** commands to be turned on and off. For an
NOSKIP   example of these options, see the chapter *GENERATING VARIABLES*.

TALK   **TALK** is **SET** at the beginning of an interactive session when typing commands in interactive mode. If all commands are in a file then the user is not "talking" and should use the **TERMINAL** option instead. Most modern operating systems can detect an interactive run, so it may not be necessary to **SET** this option.

TERMINAL   **TERMINAL** is used when the job is run at the terminal; the SHAZAM commands are typed into a separate file and the output is not placed in a file. Most modern operating systems can detect if this is the case, so it may not be necessary to **SET** this option.

TIMER   This option times each command and the CPU time is printed out after execution of each command.

TRACE   This option is primarily of interest to SHAZAM consultants. It prints the name of each subroutine as it is executed.

WARN /   Warning messages are normally printed for illegal operations in **GENR,**
NOWARN   **MATRIX, IF, SKIPIF** and **ENDIF** statements. These messages can be turned off with **SET NOWARN**.

WARNSKIP / **NOWARNSKIP**	A warning message is printed for every observation skipped by a **SKIPIF** command. There may be a large number of these warnings if the sample is large. These warnings can be turned off with **SET NOWARNSKIP**.
WIDE / **NOWIDE**	The **WIDE** option is used to control the line length of printed output. **WIDE** will assume that up to 120 columns are available. **NOWIDE** will try to fit all output in 80 columns. This option mainly affects the **PRINT** and **PLOT** commands. The default is **WIDE** in Batch operation and **NOWIDE** in Talk mode at a terminal.
COMLEN =	The maximum number of characters in a command line is 255 on some computers but on others the maximum length is only 80. You can see the length for your computer with the command **DISPLAY COMLEN**. At times you may want to attempt to either increase or reduce **COMLEN**. For example: if a file of SHAZAM commands is assigned to Unit 5 with the MTS operating system then the default is the maximum length line in the file. However, if the file assigned to Unit 5 is a concatenation, SHAZAM will not be able to compute the maximum length of a line correctly and this option may be needed. This option could also be used to prevent SHAZAM from reading commands beyond a certain column. For example, for a deck with sequence numbers in columns 73-80, **COMLEN =** 72 would be appropriate. **COMLEN** should never be specified at a value of greater than 255 under any circumstance. Note that on all computers, commands can be continued onto additional lines if the continuation symbol (&) is used at the end of a line. The use of continuation lines allows a total command length on all computers of 1024 characters.
MAXCOL =	When using the colon (:) function to specify a row of a matrix or a number in a vector, the default maximum number is 1000. If a larger number is required a **SET** command such as **SET MAXCOL = 1500** should be used.
OUTUNIT =	The **OUTUNIT =** option is **SET** when the SHAZAM output for the run is to be put into more than one file. In this case, the output files are assigned to appropriate units and addressed with the **OUTUNIT =** option. Of course, if one of the files is originally assigned to Unit 6, SHAZAM automatically outputs into this file and continues until another file is specified on a **SET OUTUNIT =** command. This option is rarely used.
RANSEED =	If you wish to initialize the random number generator with a particular integer number use the **SET RANSEED = xxx** option where xxx is a positive integer. This can be used to obtain the same set of random numbers in different runs. This option should be used before any random numbers are generated in the run. **SET RANSEED = 0** is the same as **SET RANFIX**.

The **DISPLAY** command displays the current value of any option that has been specified with the **SET** command. The format of the **DISPLAY** command is:

DISPLAY *option*

where *option* is the option or a list of the options previously set on a **SET** command.

An additional option available on the **DISPLAY** command, but is not available on the **SET** command, is **CPUTIME**.

CPUTIME   This option prints the total computing time used from the beginning of the run up to the current command.

In addition to the **DISPLAY** command the **DUMP** command described in the chapter *MISCELLANEOUS COMMANDS AND INFORMATION* is useful for SHAZAM consultants who wish to see the value of COMMON blocks and other variables.

31. MISCELLANEOUS COMMANDS AND INFORMATION

"If God had wanted a Panama Canal, he would have put one here."

King Philip II of Spain
1552

This is a very important chapter that all user should read. There are various SHAZAM commands available that do not require separate chapters, but are very useful.

1. Users can manipulate carriage control in SHAZAM on most machines. For example, by inserting the number one (1) before a command the user can ensure that the output for that command will be printed on a new page. Similarly, a zero (0) inserted before a command tells the printer to skip a line before printing output. Consider, for example, the following commands:

SAMPLE 1 10
READ A B
1PRINT A B

The **SAMPLE** and the **READ** commands will appear on the first page of the output and the results of the **PRINT** command will appear on the following page. Some commands (like OLS) automatically start a new page.

NOTE: Carriage control can be turned on or off for commands that automatically start a new page by using the **SET CC** or **SET NOCC** commands. The default is **SET CC**. For more information on **SET CC** see the chapter *SET AND DISPLAY*.

2. The **CHECKOUT** command prints information about the machine being used. This information is primarily of interest to SHAZAM consultants. The format of the **CHECKOUT** command is:

CHECKOUT

3. Comment lines are permitted in SHAZAM. The first column of the line must have an asterisk (*), but the rest of the line may contain anything the user desires. Thus, a comment line might look like the following:

* ORDINARY LEAST SQUARES REGRESSION USING TEXTILE DATA

This comment line will appear in the output for the run and can be used to identify which regressions were run. Comment lines may not be placed inside data to be read.

4. The **COMPRESS** command is used to retrieve the space of deleted variables. (See **DELETE**.) Since there is a limited amount of memory available in a SHAZAM run, and

since deleting variables does not automatically free previously occupied space, the **COMPRESS** command is invaluable for runs with large numbers of variables where some have been deleted. However, the **COMPRESS** command can be expensive to use. The format of the **COMPRESS** command is:

COMPRESS

5.   Continuation lines are permitted in SHAZAM. An ampersand (&) is used at the end of the line to be continued. For example, if a long and complicated equation were to be given on a **GENR** command, it could be continued onto the following line in this way:

GENR Y = LOG(X) + P**16*T/(X-2/P)*203 &
-6042

SHAZAM will remove the & from the equation and put the two pieces together. The continued line need not start in the first column. Any space typed before the ampersand will be retained in the equation. The maximum length of a command including continuation lines is 1024 characters.

6.   The **DELETE** command is used to delete variables. The format of the **DELETE** command is:

DELETE *vars*

where *vars* is a list of variables to be deleted. You can **DELETE** all *vars* with:

DELETE / ALL

7.   The **DEMO** command is used to teach beginners the basic commands in SHAZAM. To see a SHAZAM **DEMO**nstration type **DEMO** and follow the instructions displayed at the terminal. The DEMO can be restarted at any time with: **DEMO START**.

8.   The **DIM** command dimensions a vector or matrix before any data is defined. This is useful if the data for a given variable or matrix comes from several sources. In this case, **COPY** commands are useful for filling the previously dimensioned vector or matrix. The format of the **DIM** command is:

DIM *var size var size ...*

where *var* is the name of the vector or matrix to be dimensioned, and *size* is either one or two numbers separated by a space to indicate the size of the *var* to be dimensioned. If only one number is given, SHAZAM assumes the *var* is a vector. If two numbers are given, SHAZAM assumes that the *var* specified is a matrix and that the first number given specifies the rows of the matrix, and the second number specifies the columns. More than one vector or matrix can be dimensioned with a single **DIM** command, as shown above. In the example below, the vector V is dimensioned to 12 rows (or observations).

DIM V 12

Similarly, if a matrix M were to be dimensioned to 4 rows and 5 columns, the following **DIM** command would be appropriate (matrices may have a maximum of 2 dimensions):

DIM M 4 5

9. **DO**-loops perform repeat operations. The format of the **DO**-loop is best shown by the following examples:

DO # = 1,10
GENR LVAR# = LOG(VAR#)
PLOT LVAR# VAR#
ENDO

This example will create 10 new variables and 10 plots of the log of each variable against that variable. (It is assumed that the variables VAR1, VAR2,...VAR10 have previously been defined.) If a character other than the # character is desired, any of the ? % $! symbols can be used. It is also possible to increment the **DO**-loop by any integer. For example, **DO # = 1,9,2** would set # to the numbers: 1,3,5,7,9. For more examples of **DO**-loops see the chapter *PROGRAMMING IN SHAZAM*. NOTE: An **ENDO** command *must* be used at the end of the **DO**-loop commands. The value of the **DO**-loop index is contained in the temporary variable $DO. **DO**-loops can be nested up to 2 levels, the second level should use a different character than # and the value of the second loop is contained in the temporary variable $DO2.

DO # = 2,3
DO % = 1,3
GENR X#% = X%*#
ENDO
ENDO

This example takes the variables X1, X2 and X3 and multiplies them by 2 to get X21, X22, X23 and then by 3 to get X31, X32, X33.

10. The **DUMP** command prints out information that is primarily of interest to SHAZAM consultants. The format of the **DUMP** command is:

DUMP *options*

where *options* is a list of desired options.

There are many options available on the **DUMP** command, although most of these options are only useful for those who have a source listing of SHAZAM. **DUMP DATA** prints a chart of all the current variables, their addresses, increment, type, their number of observations and their second dimension. **DUMP VNAME** lists all the current variable names. **DUMP KADD** prints the first address of each variable. The following common block options are also available for SHAZAM consultants: **ADDCOM, DATCOM, FCOM, GENCOM, INPCOM, IOCOM, LODCOM, MACOM, NLCOM, OCOM, OLSCOM, OPTCOM, OSCOM, RANCOM, SCNCOM, SYSCOM, TEMCOM, VCOM, VLCOM, VPLCOM, VTCOM, VTECOM** and **VTICOM**. Finally, any range of data in the SHAZAM workspace can be dumped by typing the first and last word desired. For example, the command **DUMP 30 50** would print words 30 through 50 of SHAZAM memory. This would normally be used in conjunction with the information obtained from the **DUMP DATA** command.

11. The **FILE** command is used to assign units to files. This is used *before* any **READ** or **WRITE** command. The format of the **FILE** command is:

FILE *unit filename*

For example:

FILE 11 MYDATAFILE

If the file is UNFORMATTED (as is the case for the **OUT=** option in **SYSTEM** and **NL** problems or the **BINARY** option on a **WRITE** command) a decimal point (.) should be placed next to the unit number. For example:

FILE 12. MYDUMPFILE

The **FILE** command is not available on some systems. In this case files must be assigned with System Control Commands. IBM OS/VS/VM/CMS/TSO are systems that do not permit the **FILE** command.

In addition, the **FILE** command can be used to assign special units, these are:

FILE OUTPUT *filename*	Puts the output in the assigned *filename*. This should be the first **FILE** command.
FILE SCREEN *filename*	Displays the output on the screen and puts the output in a file simultaneously.
FILE INPUT *filename*	If all the commands are in a file, this command is used.
FILE CLOSE *filename*	Closes the specified *filename*.
FILE LIST *filename*	Lists the specified file on the screen.
FILE PRINT *filename*	Prints the file specified on a printer (Macintosh only).

12. Help on various SHAZAM commands and options is available on the **HELP** command. The format of the **HELP** command is:

HELP *command*

where *command* is any SHAZAM command name.

13. The **MENU** command is useful when you are running SHAZAM interactively and you need a list of available commands. At any point in time some commands may not be valid. These are indicated by an * in the menu list.

14. The **NAMES** command will print out the **NAMES** of all the variables that have been read or generated in a particular SHAZAM run. It is mainly used in TALK mode to see which variables are currently defined. The format of the **NAMES** command is:

NAMES

or

NAMES LIST

which will print a table of names, the type of variable and the size of the variable.

15. The **PAR** command sets the **PAR** value. The **PAR** value specifies the amount of memory (in batches of 1024 bytes) that is needed. The format of the **PAR** command is:

PAR *number*

where *number* specifies the amount of memory that is needed. On several operating systems (MTS, IBM, UNIVAC) the PAR is easier to set with a system command than with the **PAR** command. Some operating systems do not allow the use of the **PAR** command. In this case the local SHAZAM consultant should be consulted to arrange an increase in memory. The **PAR** command can not be used on the IBM-PC or Macintosh.

16. The **PAUSE** command can be used anywhere in a SHAZAM run to cause a display on the screen to pause after the chosen commands. This command might be used, for example, on a machine that has no scroll key on the keyboard. Strategically placed **PAUSE** commands make it possible to view the output from commands as they are executed even when there is no scroll control. Users who wish to **PAUSE** after every command may **SET PAUSE**. This command has no effect in BATCH mode.

17. The **RENAME** command is used to rename variables that already exist in the current run. The format of the **RENAME** command is:

RENAME *oldname newname*

where *oldname* is the name of the variable whose name is to be changed, and *newname* is the new name to be given to that variable.

18. The **REWIND** command is used to rewind any unit, usually the **WRITE** unit. **REWIND** is also available as an option on the **WRITE** command. After a **REWIND** command, anything written to the specified unit will overlay what was already there. The format of the **REWIND** command is:

REWIND *unit*

where *unit* is the unit assigned to the **WRITE** file.

19. Normally, SHAZAM allows at least 300 variables. This can be changed with the **SIZE** command on most (but not all) systems. The format of the **SIZE** command is:

SIZE *maximum*

For example:

SIZE 500

The **SIZE** command should be placed at the beginning of the command file. This command can *not* be used on the IBM-PC or Macintosh.

20. The **STOP** command is used to indicate that the SHAZAM run is finished. If no **STOP** command is included SHAZAM will read to the end of the command file.

21. Temporary variables are statistics that have been computed from previous commands. They contain current values and are redefined each time a new estimation is performed. For example, the temporary variables which are available following the **TEST** command are:

$CHI, $DF1, $DF2, $F, $STES, $T and $VAL.

The available variables from the previous **DISTRIB** command are:

$CDF, $CRIT, $LLF, $PDF.

The available variables from the previous **AUTO**, **BOX**, **GLS**, **MLE**, **OLS**, **POOL**, or **2SLS** regression commands are:

$ANF, $DF, $DW, $K, $LLF, $N, $R2, $R2OP, $RAW, $RHO, $SIG2, $SSE, $SSR, $SST, $ZANF, $ZDF, $ZSSR.

The current values of each index from the **DO** command is in:

$DO, $DO2

Temporary variables are useful where a variable for the adjusted R^2, as defined in Judge et al [1988, p.845], is needed. This variable could be calculated in the following way:

GEN1 AR2 = 1-($N-1)/($N-$K)*(1-$R2)

22. The **TIME** command specifies the beginning year and frequency for a time series so that an alternate form of the **SAMPLE** command can be used. The format is:

TIME *beg freq var*

For example:

TIME 1981 12
SAMPLE 1982.3 1984.10

This sets the **SAMPLE** from March of 1982 to October of 1984 for monthly data. The date can also be saved in a variable by specifying a variable name in *var* if a **SAMPLE** range for *var* has previously been defined. However, this variable should only be used for labelling output and not in calculations as it often has no useful numerical meaning.

If yearly data is used a decimal point must be included. For example, for Theil's, [1971, p.102] Textile data you could use:

SAMPLE 1 17
TIME 1923 1 YEAR
SAMPLE 1930.0 1939.0

A **SAMPLE** command without a decimal point is interpreted to be the observation number.

23. The **TITLE** command prints the specified title at the top of selected pages of output. The **TITLE** may be changed at any time, and as many times as desired. The format of the **TITLE** command is:

TITLE *title*

where *title* is any title the user requires.

24. To suppress the output from **ARIMA, AUTO, BOX, DISTRIB, FC, GLS, INST, LOGIT, MLE, NL, OLS, PC, POOL, PROBIT, ROBUST, STAT, SYSTEM, TEST, TOBIT, 2SLS** and other commands a question mark (?) may be placed in the first column of the line on which the command is typed. To suppress the output from an **OLS** command, use:

?OLS A B C / RSTAT

This is useful when a particular statistic is needed (say the Durbin-Watson statistic) for a subsequent test, but no other output is needed. In this case the Durbin-Watson statistic would have been stored in the temporary variable $DW, and can easily be retrieved when required.

To suppress the printing of the command itself, but not the output an equal sign (=) may be placed in the first column of the line on which the command is typed. For example, to suppress the **OLS** command, type:

=OLS A B C

To suppress both the command and the output from that command an equal sign and a question mark are placed in the first and second columns of the line on which the command is typed. To suppress both an **OLS** command and its output, use:

=?OLS A B C

32. PROGRAMMING IN SHAZAM

"Everything that can be invented has been invented."

Charles H. Duell
U.S. Patent Office, 1899

SHAZAM provides many features to aid users who wish to write their own algorithms or procedures. This chapter outlines some of these features by giving examples which illustrate programming methods.

A. DO-*LOOPS*

DO-loops provide repeat operations. The format of the DO-loop is best shown by the following example:

```
READ(11) VAR1-VAR10
DO # = 1,10
GENR LVAR# = LOG(VAR#)
PLOT LVAR# VAR#
ENDO
```

This example will create 10 new variables and 10 plots of the log of each variable against each original variable. (It is assumed that the variables VAR1, VAR2,...VAR10 are in a file.) The # character, or any of % ? $! may be used with the DO command. Note that an ENDO command *must* be used to end the list of commands contained in the DO-loop. The DO-loop facility provides a numeric character substitution for the # symbol. This example also shows how a series of variables with the same initial letters (in this case, VAR) can be easily specified. Warning: Some operating systems do not permit the use of the # symbol and another one must be used. For example, on CMS operating systems the # sometimes indicates the end of a line.

The next example shows how a second level DO-loop can be used to run a total of 6 regressions. In this case the dependent variables VAR1, VAR2, and VAR3, are each run with VAR4 and then run with VAR5 as independent variables. Note that when a second level is used the first ENDO closes the DO $=4,5$ loop and the second ENDO closes the DO $\#=1,3$ loop.

```
SAMPLE 1 10
READ(11) VAR1-VAR5
DO #=1,3
DO $=4,5
OLS VAR# VAR$
ENDO
ENDO
```

B. *SPLICING INDEX NUMBER SERIES*

Suppose you have 2 overlapping price indexes where the base year has changed from $1971 = 100$ to $1976 = 100$ and you want to create a new Spliced Index with $1976 = 100$. You can use the overlapping year, 1976, to adjust the 1971 data as follows:

```
_*   Example of splicing Index Numbers from:
_*      Newbold, Statistics for Business and Economics, p. 682.
_*   First READ the data for the 1971 and 1976 based indexes.
_SAMPLE 1 10
_READ YEAR  P71 P76 / LIST
   3 VARIABLES AND       10 OBSERVATIONS STARTING AT OBS        1
   1971.000       100.0000      0.0
   1972.000        92.20000     0.0
   1973.000       131.2000      0.0
   1974.000       212.0000      0.0
   1975.000       243.0000      0.0
   1976.000       198.5000       100.0000
   1977.000        0.0           94.00000
   1978.000        0.0           86.70000
   1979.000        0.0           94.90000
   1980.000        0.0          107.0000
_SAMPLE 6 10
_* Copy the last 5 years of P76 into the SPLICE index.
_GENR SPLICE=P76
_SAMPLE 1 5
_* Compute the first 5 years of P71 using 1976 base.
_GENR SPLICE=P71*P76:6/P71:6
_SAMPLE 1 10
_* Now PRINT and PLOT all 10 years of the SPLICED INDEX.
_PRINT YEAR SPLICE
       YEAR            SPLICE
   1971.000        50.37783
   1972.000        46.44836
   1973.000        66.09572
   1974.000       106.8010
   1975.000       122.4181
   1976.000       100.0000
   1977.000        94.00000
   1978.000        86.70000
   1979.000        94.90000
   1980.000       107.0000
```

```
|_PLOT SPLICE YEAR
        10 OBSERVATIONS
                     *=SPLICE
   122.42    |                              *
   118.42    |
   114.42    |
   110.42    |
   106.42    |                   *                              *
   102.43    |
   98.428    |                        *
   94.429    |                                        *
   90.431    |                                 *
   86.432    |                                    *
   82.434    |
   78.436    |
   74.437    |
   70.439    |
   66.440    |
   62.442    |         *
   58.444    |
   54.445    |
   50.447    |
   46.448    |*    *
            _____

             1971.000  1973.250  1975.500  1977.750  1980.000

                                 YEAR
```

C. *COMPUTING THE POWER OF A TEST*

DO-loops can be useful in computing the power of tests. Consider the output from the following example in which the power function is computed and plotted using SHAZAM for the **TEST** that the coefficient on **INCOME** is equal to 1 in an OLS regression.

```
_SAMPLE 1 17
_READ(11) YEAR CONSUME INCOME PRICE
_* Convert data to base 10 logs since that is what Theil uses.
_GENR CONSUME=LOG(CONSUME)/2.3026
_GENR INCOME=LOG(INCOME)/2.3026
_GENR PRICE=LOG(PRICE)/2.3026
_* Run OLS save coefficients, assume these are true coefficients.
_OLS CONSUME INCOME PRICE / COEF=BETA
OLS ESTIMATION
      17 OBSERVATIONS     DEPENDENT VARIABLE = CONSUME
 R-SQUARE = 0.9744     R-SQUARE ADJUSTED = 0.9707
VARIANCE OF THE ESTIMATE =  0.18340E-03
STANDARD ERROR OF THE ESTIMATE =  0.13542E-01
LOG OF THE LIKELIHOOD FUNCTION =  50.6612
```

VARIABLE NAME	ESTIMATED COEFFICIENT	STANDARD ERROR	T-RATIO 14 DF	PARTIAL CORR.	STANDARDIZED COEFFICIENT	ELASTICITY AT MEANS
INCOME	1.1432	0.15600	7.3279	0.8906	0.32163	1.0839
PRICE	-0.82884	0.36111E-01	-22.952	-0.9870	-1.0074	-0.73137
CONSTANT	1.3739	0.30609	4.4886	0.7681	0.0	0.64742

```
_* Dimension room for 11 values of Power Function.
_DIM  P 11 B 11
_SAMPLE 1 1
_* Assume true SIGMA**2 is the OLS SIGMA**2.
_GEN1 SIG2=$SIG2
..NOTE..CURRENT VALUE OF $SIG2=  0.18340E-03
_* Next find the alpha critical value (Type I error).
_GEN1 ALPHA=.05
_DISTRIB ALPHA/ TYPE=F DF1=1 DF2=14 INVERSE
               PROBABILITY     CRITICAL VALUE
   ALPHA
 ROW     1     0.50000E-01  4.6000
|_GEN1 CR=$CRIT
..NOTE..CURRENT VALUE OF $CRIT=   4.6000
_* Turn off the DO-LOOP ECHOing of commands.
_SET NODOECHO
_DO #=1,11
_* Let BETA:1(INCOME) vary between .5 and 1.5, other BETAS unchanged.
_GEN1 BETA:1=.4+.1*#
_* Store the hypothesized value of BETA:1(INCOME) in vector B.
_GEN1 B:#=BETA:1
_SAMPLE 1 17
_* Now substitute in the "true" BETAS in OLS.
_* The next OLS is simply to compute information with given BETA
_* and SIG2 so the TEST command can be used. Since the OLS output
_* itself is useless it is suppressed by using ? before the OLS.
|_?OLS CONSUME INCOME PRICE / INCOEF=BETA INSIG2=SIG2
```

```
_* Compute the non-centrality parameter.
_* It is the same as the chi-square statistic for TEST and is
_* in $CHI.
_* Suppress the TEST output with "?".
_?TEST INCOME=1
_SAMPLE 1 1
_* Also, suppress the DISTRIB output with "?".
_?DISTRIB CR / TYPE=F DF1=$DF1 DF2=$DF2 C=$CHI
_* P is now the Power (the probability of rejecting the null if
_* the alternative is true).
_?GENR P:#=1-$CDF
_ENDO
****** EXECUTION BEGINNING FOR DO LOOP
****** EXECUTION FINISHED FOR DO LOOP
_SAMPLE 1 11
_* Now print the Power for INCOME coefficient varying between .5 and 1.5
_PRINT B P
      B              P
  0.5000000      0.8459275
  0.6000000      0.6648547
  0.7000000      0.4330394
  0.8000000      0.2230297
  0.9000000      0.9189934E-01
  1.000000       0.5000252E-01
  1.100000       0.9189934E-01
  1.200000       0.2230297
  1.300000       0.4330394
  1.400000       0.6648547
  1.500000       0.8459275
_PLOT P B
       11 OBSERVATIONS
                    *=P
                  M=MULTIPLE POINT
  0.84593       |*                              *
  0.80404       |
  0.76215       |
  0.72026       |
  0.67836       |
  0.63647       |      *                    *
  0.59458       |
  0.55269       |
  0.51080       |
  0.46891       |
  0.42702       |          *              *
  0.38513       |
  0.34324       |
  0.30135       |
  0.25946       |
  0.21757       |            *          *
  0.17567       |
  0.13378       |
  0.91893E-01   |              *      *
  0.50003E-01   |                *
                 _____
              0.500      0.750      1.000      1.250     1.500
                                  B
```

Initially it is assumed that the coefficients from the first **OLS** regression are the true coefficients and the critical value is calculated on the basis of the "true" coefficient for INCOME. Next, a **DO**-loop is set up in which 11 hypothetical coefficients are generated and 11 power values (P) are generated in conjunction with the hypothetical coefficients. Notice that the variables for the hypothetical coefficients and the power values are **DIM**ensioned before the **DO**-loop to be vectors of 11 observations so that their values will be saved as they are calculated in the **DO**-loop. Several commands are used to generate P within the **DO**-loop. The **OLS** command is used in order to allow the subsequent **TEST** command since **TEST** commands must directly follow a regression command. The **TEST** command results in the calculation of the chi-square statistic which is stored in the temporary variable $CHI and used in the **DISTRIB** command which follows. The **DISTRIB** command calculates the CDF which is stored in the temporary variable $CDF (Cumulative Distribution Function) and is used in the final command of the **DO**-loop to compute the power value for the particular hypothetical coefficient. Finally, the power values are plotted against the coefficient values.

The values of the power in the variable P are the probabilities of rejecting the null hypothesis when the alternative is true. The hypothetical values of the INCOME coefficient are the alternatives. Thus, we would hope that the probability of rejecting the null hypothesis (that the coefficient on INCOME is 1) would increase as the alternative (B) moves away from 1. This turns out to be the case as can be seen from the plotted power function. Of course, the ideal power function is one in which the probability of rejecting the null hypothesis when it is true is extremely low and in which the probabilities increase rapidly as the alternatives (the true values) move away from the null value.

A good reference on the non-central F-distribution and power functions can be found in Graybill [1976, Ch.4.3].

D. *RIDGE REGRESSION*

DO-loops can also be used to plot a Ridge Trace for Ridge Regressions. See Watson and White [1976] for further explanation of Ridge Regression. The following output computes a Ridge Trace for Theil's Textile data:

```
|_READ(11) YEAR CONSUME INCOME PRICE
...SAMPLE RANGE IS NOW SET TO:              1         17
 _* Make room for 10 different sets of coefficients.
 _DIM BETA 3 10   K 10
 _* Let Ridge k go from .1 to .9, turn off warning messages.
 _SET NOWARN
 _DO #=1,9
 _ GENR K:#=.#
 _* Suppress printing of OLS output by using "?".
 _?OLS CONSUME INCOME PRICE / RIDGE=.# COEF=BETA:#
 |_ENDO
******* EXECUTION BEGINNING FOR DO LOOP
#_ GENR K:1=.1
#_?OLS CONSUME INCOME PRICE / RIDGE=.1 COEF=BETA:1
#_ENDO
#_ GENR K:2=.2
#_?OLS CONSUME INCOME PRICE / RIDGE=.2 COEF=BETA:2
#_ENDO
#_ GENR K:3=.3
#_?OLS CONSUME INCOME PRICE / RIDGE=.3 COEF=BETA:3
#_ENDO
#_ GENR K:4=.4
#_?OLS CONSUME INCOME PRICE / RIDGE=.4 COEF=BETA:4
#_ENDO
#_ GENR K:5=.5
#_?OLS CONSUME INCOME PRICE / RIDGE=.5 COEF=BETA:5
#_ENDO
#_ GENR K:6=.6
#_?OLS CONSUME INCOME PRICE / RIDGE=.6 COEF=BETA:6
#_ENDO
#_ GENR K:7=.7
#_?OLS CONSUME INCOME PRICE / RIDGE=.7 COEF=BETA:7
#_ENDO
#_ GENR K:8=.8
#_?OLS CONSUME INCOME PRICE / RIDGE=.8 COEF=BETA:8
#_ENDO
#_ GENR K:9=.9
#_?OLS CONSUME INCOME PRICE / RIDGE=.9 COEF=BETA:9
#_ENDO
******* EXECUTION FINISHED FOR DO LOOP
 _* Now put OLS coefs in the 10th column, ridge k=0.
 _GENR K:10=0
 _?OLS CONSUME INCOME PRICE / COEF=BETA:10
 _* Now transpose the beta matrix to make it easier to plot.
 _MATRIX BETA=BETA'
 _PRINT K BETA
K
  0.10       0.20       0.30       0.40       0.50       0.60       0.70       0.80
  0.90       0.0
```

```
BETA
     10 BY        3 MATRIX
     0.8957645      -1.248780         137.5545
     0.7689530      -1.138775         142.2192
     0.6695782      -1.046880         145.4404
     0.5900597      -0.9689098        147.6794
     0.5252973      -0.9018889        149.2343
     0.4717498      -0.8436397        150.3036
     0.4268921      -0.7925306        151.0229
     0.3888814      -0.7473141        151.4868
     0.3563458      -0.7070192        151.7624
     1.061710       -1.382985         130.7066
_SAMPLE 1 10
_* Now plot the INCOME(BETA:1) and PRICE(BETA:2) coefs against k.
_* This gives the Ridge Trace for these coefficients in the
_* PLOT INCOME=* AND CONSUME=+.
_PLOT BETA:1 BETA:2  K / NOWIDE
     10 OBSERVATIONS
                        *=BETA
                        +=BETA
     1.0617          |*
     0.93304         |
     0.80437         |          *
     0.67571         |             *
     0.54704         |                *    *
     0.41837         |                       *   *   *
     0.28970         |                                 *     *
     0.16103         |
     0.32364E-01     |
    -0.96304E-01     |
    -0.22497         |
    -0.35364         |
    -0.48231         |
    -0.61098         |
    -0.73964         |                                       +
    -0.86831         |                          +   +   +
    -0.99698         |                 +    +
    -1.1256          |              +
    -1.2543          |        +    +
    -1.3830          |+

              0.0         0.225    0.450    0.675    0.900
                                    K
```

In the above program, the Textile data is read in. Next, two variables, BETA and K are dimensioned to be a 3x10 matrix and a vector of 10 observations, respectively. BETA will be used in the subsequent **DO**-loop to store the values of the coefficients for each Ridge Regression. K will be used in the subsequent **DO**-loop to increment the value of K used in the Ridge Regressions. In this way, the Ridge k goes from .1 to .9 in increments of .1. Notice the **SET NOWARN** command turns off the printing of any warning message that may occur, thus minimizing the amount of output generated. Notice also the question mark (?) that is typed before the **OLS** commands to suppress the output. Since **OLS** is a special case of Ridge Regression where K=0, an additional **OLS** regression is run without the **RIDGE** option. In all, 10 regressions are run and the intercept and the coefficients on each of INCOME and PRICE for each of these regressions are saved in the variable BETA. BETA is then transposed to facilitate the plotting of the coefficients of each INCOME and PRICE against K. In the plot INCOME is * and PRICE is +. This plot is what is often referred to as the Ridge Trace.

E. *AN EXACT DURBIN-WATSON TEST*

The following SHAZAM run will compute (the hard way) an exact Durbin-Watson Test for Theil's [1971, p.102] Textile data. The easy way is to use the **EXACTDW** option on the **OLS** command.

As is shown in Judge, Griffiths, Hill, Lütkepohl and Lee [1985, p.322 Eq. 8.4.5] the Durbin-Watson Test is based on the statistic:

$$d = \sum_{t=2}^{T} (\epsilon_t - \epsilon_{t-1})^2 \Big/ \sum_{t=1}^{T} \epsilon_t^2$$

where ϵ_t is an element of $\epsilon = y - X\beta$.

Also shown in this same reference is that this formula can be simplified to:

$$d = \epsilon MAM\epsilon / \epsilon'M\epsilon$$

where $M = I - X(X'X)^{-1}X'$ and A is a matrix with 2 on the main diagonal (except in the extreme corners where there is a 1), the upper and lower off diagonals have the value -1, and 0 is everywhere else.

The following SHAZAM commands will compute ϵ and then A and M to be used in the final **DISTRIB** command to get the exact Durbin-Watson probability.

```
|_READ(11) YEAR CONSUME INCOME PRICE
...SAMPLE RANGE IS NOW SET TO:          1         17
|_* Create X.
_GENR ONE=1
_COPY INCOME PRICE ONE X
_* Compute M.
_MATRIX M=IDEN(17)-X*INV(X'X)*X'
_* Generate the "A" matrix.
_* The Diagonal has 2 everywhere except 1 in the corners.
_GENR D=1
_SAMPLE 2 16
_GENR D=2
_SAMPLE 1 17
_* Put 1 on the off-diagonals.
_MATRIX A=IDEN(17,2)
_* Turn off diagonal to -1 and add the diagonal.
_MATRIX A=-(A+A')+DIAG(D)
_* Compute the eigenvalues of "MA".
_MATRIX MA=M*A
_MATRIX E=EIGVAL(MA)
_* Run OLS just to get the DW statistic from $DW when RSTAT is used.
_OLS CONSUME INCOME PRICE / RSTAT
```

```
OLS ESTIMATION
       17 OBSERVATIONS     DEPENDENT VARIABLE = CONSUME
  R-SQUARE = 0.9513     R-SQUARE ADJUSTED = 0.9443
VARIANCE OF THE ESTIMATE =    30.951
STANDARD ERROR OF THE ESTIMATE =    5.5634
LOG OF THE LIKELIHOOD FUNCTION = -51.6471
VARIABLE ESTIMATED    STANDARD    T-RATIO   PARTIAL STANDARDIZED ELASTICITY
  NAME   COEFFICIENT   ERROR        14 DF    CORR.   COEFFICIENT  AT MEANS


INCOME     1.0617      0.26667      3.9813   0.7287  0.23871      0.81288
PRICE     -1.3830      0.83814E-01 -16.501  -0.9752 -0.98933     -0.78464
CONSTANT  130.71       27.094       4.8241   0.7902  0.0          0.97175


DURBIN-WATSON = 2.0185    VON NEUMAN RATIO = 2.1447    RHO = -0.18239
RESIDUAL SUM =  0.96212E-12  RESIDUAL VARIANCE =    30.951
SUM OF ABSOLUTE ERRORS=   72.787
R-SQUARE BETWEEN OBSERVED AND PREDICTED = 0.9513
|_* Sort the Eigenvalues so largest is first.
|_SORT E / DESCEND
DATA HAS BEEN SORTED BY VARIABLE E
|_* Use the DISTRIB command to compute the exact DW probability.
|_DISTRIB $DW / EIGENVAL=E TYPE=IMHOF NEIGEN=14
                 DATA          CDF        1-CDF
  $DW
  ROW     1      2.0185        0.30127      0.69873
```

These SHAZAM commands reproduce the method used by SHAZAM and discussed in Judge, Griffiths, Hill, Lütkepohl and Lee [1985, p.323]. First, A and M are generated in matrix form. The generation of M is straightforward; the independent variables, INCOME and PRICE, and a column of ones for the intercept, are copied into a matrix, X, with a **COPY** command and M is then generated with a **MATRIX** command. The generation of A, however, takes several steps. First, to create the diagonal of twos with ones in the extreme corners, a vector of twos is generated with a **GENR** command and this vector is then modified to have ones in the first and last rows (which will later become the extreme corners of the A matrix) with the use of two **IF** commands. The A matrix is then generated as an identity matrix with the ones starting on the second row. The A matrix is then transformed again to its final form with another **MATRIX** command. This is done by adding A and A' and multiplying the result by -1 (thus creating the upper and lower off-diagonals of -1) and adding D to be the diagonal of the A matrix. Next, the eigenvalue of the product of M and A is computed. The Durbin-Watson statistic from the **OLS** regression is automatically stored during the **OLS** run in a temporary variable called $DW. This variable is then used with the **DISTRIB** command to compute the exact Durbin-Watson Test. The **TYPE=IMHOF, EIGENVAL=** and **NEIGEN=** options must be used for correct results. Note that all of this could be done with one command by specifying the **EXACTDW** option on the **OLS** command. In this example we find that **DW=2.0185**. If the null hypothesis (of no autocorrelation) is true, then the probability of observing a DW statistic of 2.0185 or less is 0.30127. This implies that we cannot reject the null hypothesis.

F. *ITERATIVE COCHRANE-ORCUTT ESTIMATION*

The easy way to do Iterative Cochrane-Orcutt estimation of the first-order Autoregressive model is to use the **AUTO** command. However, the example below shows how the method can also be programmed in SHAZAM. The final results are compared to the SHAZAM **AUTO** command:

```
_* Program to perform Iterative Cochrane-Orcutt estimation of AR(1) Model.
_READ (11) CONSUME INCOME PRICE
...SAMPLE RANGE IS NOW SET TO:          1         17
_* Initialize RHO to first estimate OLS.
_GEN1 RHO=0
_* Initialize LASTRHO to a high number.
_GEN1 LASTRHO=999
_* Turn off useless output in DO-loop.
_SET NODOECHO NOWARN
_* Try up to 20 iterations.
_DO #=1,20
_* Transform all but first observation including CONSTANT.
_SAMPLE 2 17
_GENR C=CONSUME-RHO*LAG(CONSUME)
_GENR I=INCOME-RHO*LAG(INCOME)
_GENR P=PRICE-RHO*LAG(PRICE)
_GENR CONS=1-RHO
_* Transform first observation.
_SAMPLE 1 1
_GENR C=SQRT(1-RHO**2)*CONSUME
_GENR I=SQRT(1-RHO**2)*INCOME
_GENR P=SQRT(1-RHO**2)*PRICE
_GENR CONS=SQRT(1-RHO**2)
_* Run OLS on transformed data, suppress OLS output with "?".
_SAMPLE 1 17
_* Check for convergence, if so jump out of loop.
_ENDIF(ABS(RHO-LASTRHO).LT.0.01)
_?OLS C I P CONS / NOCONSTANT  COEF=BETA
_* Take OLS coefficients and get RHO using original data.
_?FC CONSUME INCOME PRICE / COEF=BETA
_* Save RHO to check for convergence next time.
_GEN1 LASTRHO=RHO
_PRINT $DO $SSE $RHO
_* Put latest value of $RHO into RHO.
_GEN1 RHO=$RHO
_ENDO
****** EXECUTION BEGINNING FOR DO LOOP  # =  1
    $DO       1.000000
    $SSE      433.3130
    $RHO      -0.1823932
    $DO       2.000000
    $SSE      419.9997
    $RHO      -0.1947947
    $DO       3.000000
    $SSE      419.8044
    $RHO      -0.1953525
...ENDIF IS TRUE AT OBSERVATION          1
...DO LOOP ENDED AT  #=      4
```

```
|_* Print final results.
|_OLS C I P CONS / NOCONSTANT NOANOVA
```

OLS ESTIMATION
            17 OBSERVATIONS   DEPENDENT VARIABLE = C

 R-SQUARE = 0.9709   R-SQUARE ADJUSTED = 0.9668
VARIANCE OF THE ESTIMATE =   29.986
STANDARD ERROR OF THE ESTIMATE =   5.4759
LOG OF THE LIKELIHOOD FUNCTION = -51.3777
RAW MOMENT R-SQUARE = 1.0000

VARIABLE NAME	ESTIMATED COEFFICIENT	STANDARD ERROR	T-RATIO 14 DF	PARTIAL CORR.	STANDARDIZED COEFFICIENT	ELASTICITY AT MEANS
I	1.0650	0.22819	4.6670	0.7802	0.32371	0.81699
P	-1.3751	0.71053E-01	-19.353	-0.9818	-0.86151	-0.78297
CONS	129.62	23.048	5.6240	0.8326	0.22468	0.96562

```
|_* Compare to SHAZAM AUTO command.
|_AUTO CONSUME INCOME PRICE /  CONV=.01 NOANOVA
```

DEPENDENT VARIABLE = CONSUME
..NOTE..R-SQUARE,ANOVA,RESIDUALS DONE ON ORIGINAL VARS

LEAST SQUARES ESTIMATION   17 OBSERVATIONS
BY COCHRANE-ORCUTT TYPE PROCEDURE WITH CONVERGENCE = 0.01000

ITERATION	RHO	LOG L.F.	SSE
1	0.0	-51.6471	433.31
2	-0.18239	-51.3987	420.00
3	-0.19479	-51.3972	419.80
4	-0.19535	-51.3972	419.80

 LOG L.F. =   -51.3972   AT RHO =   -0.19535

	ESTIMATE	ASYMPTOTIC VARIANCE	ASYMPTOTIC ST.ERROR	ASYMPTOTIC T-RATIO
RHO	-0.19535	0.05658	0.23786	-0.82128

 R-SQUARE = 0.9528   R-SQUARE ADJUSTED = 0.9461
VARIANCE OF THE ESTIMATE =   29.986
STANDARD ERROR OF THE ESTIMATE =   5.4759
LOG OF THE LIKELIHOOD FUNCTION = -51.3972

VARIABLE NAME	ESTIMATED COEFFICIENT	STANDARD ERROR	T-RATIO 14 DF	PARTIAL CORR.	STANDARDIZED COEFFICIENT	ELASTICITY AT MEANS
INCOME	1.0650	0.22819	4.6670	0.7802	0.23944	0.81539
PRICE	-1.3751	0.71053E-01	-19.353	-0.9818	-0.98369	-0.78016
CONSTANT	129.62	23.048	5.6240	0.8326	0.0	0.96370

Note that the output from the programmed procedure matches that of the **AUTO** command except for certain statistics like R-SQUARE, LOG OF THE LIKELIHOOD FUNCTION, STANDARDIZED COEFFICIENT and ELASTICITY AT MEAN which are not properly computed with an OLS algorithm. The **AUTO** output has the correct values of these statistics.

G. *NONLINEAR LEAST SQUARES BY THE RANK ONE CORRECTION METHOD*

The next example illustrates how to write a SHAZAM program to do least squares by the rank one correction (ROC) method described in Judge, Griffiths, Hill, Lütkepohl and Lee [1985, p.959]. This method merely minimizes the sum of squared residuals and thus produces the same results as the OLS run. The following commands assume use of the data from Table B.2 on page 956 of the above reference.

```
READ(11) Y X1 X2 X3
COPY X1 X2 X3 X
MATRIX YY=Y'Y
MATRIX XX=X'X
MATRIX XY=X'Y
MATRIX H=2*XX
MATRIX HINV=INV(H)
MATRIX P=IDEN(3)
DIM B 3
GENR B:1=1
GENR B:2=1
GENR B:3=1
MATRIX S=YY-2*B'XY+B'XX*B
MATRIX G=-2*XY+2*XX*B
* Print starting value info.
PRINT S G
PRINT B YY XX XY H HINV
* Program to do least squares by rank one correction (ROC) method.
* Allow up to 10 iterations.
DO #1,10
* First compute the gradient.
MATRIX GLAST=G
* Now get next round betas.
MATRIX BLAST=B
MATRIX B=B-P*G
MATRIX G=-2*XY+2*XX*B
* Now compute S.
MATRIX S=YY-2*B'XY+B'XX*B
MATRIX ETA=(B-BLAST)-P*(G-GLAST)
MATRIX M=(ETA*ETA')/(ETA'(G-GLAST))
MATRIX P=P+M
PRINT B S G P M
MATRIX GG=G'G
* Now check for convergence.
ENDIF(GG.LT.0.0000001)
ENDO
* End of loop.
MATRIX VB=2*(S/20)*P
PRINT VB
MATRIX SE=SQRT(DIAG(VB))
MATRIX T=B/SE
PRINT B SE T
* Now compare to regular OLS.
OLS Y X / ANOVA DN PCOV NOCONSTANT
```

As can be seen in the above example, the ROC method involves computing the gradient at each iteration to see if it is close to zero and thus minimized. To do this, first S is computed, which is the objective function to be minimized. G, the gradient, is then computed from S. Next, a **DO**-loop is initiated to perform the necessary computations until convergence, i.e. until $G'G$ is close to zero. The starting value for B (beta) is one, but this value is transformed on each iteration, thus transforming the values for G and P. P is the inverse of the Hessian and is transformed on each iteration by M, a correction matrix. When convergence occurs, or when the **DO**-loop is performed 10 times, the current values of S and P are used to compute the variance of beta and ultimately to compute a t-ratio. In the commands above, a **PRINT** command is used to print out the final values of beta, the standard error and the t-ratio. These results can then be compared to the **OLS** results which will be generated by the final **OLS** command. The results should be the same.

H. *MONTE CARLO EXPERIMENTS*

The next example shows how to perform a Monte Carlo experiment to check the accuracy of OLS estimation. This, of course, is a waste of money since it is well known that OLS is unbiased.

```
_* MONTE CARLO EXPERIMENT to see if OLS is unbiased in samples of 30.
_* Generate 500 samples with true model Y=3+2*X+e where e is
_* normally distributed with std. dev = 1.
_DIM B 2 500 SE 2 500 S2 500
_* Above DIMENSIONS room to hold 500 estimates.
_SAMPLE 1 30
_* Create an X varying between 10 and 20.
_GENR X=UNI(10,20)
_PRINT X
X
```

13.19578	19.32915	15.80001	13.70389	14.95253
13.24376	14.55565	14.18657	13.40778	19.57403
11.60804	12.77102	13.10780	13.74533	18.72050
18.22053	13.86238	11.80604	13.69497	12.88897
12.67599	16.93879	13.29933	18.43116	17.51485
12.33888	11.46806	12.56810	17.28497	17.33486

```
_* Suppress useless output.
_SET NODOECHO NOWARN
_* OLS sample size is 30.
_SAMPLE 1 30
_* DO this 500 times.
_DO #=1,500
_* Generate Y given X and e.
_GENR Y=3+2*X+NOR(1)
_* Run regression, suppress useless output with "?".
_?OLS Y X /  COEF=B:# STDERR=SE:#
_* Save sigma-squared in S2.
_GEN1 S2:#=$SIG2
_ENDO
****** EXECUTION BEGINNING FOR DO LOOP
****** EXECUTION FINISHED FOR DO LOOP
_* Transpose B and SE to put it the way STAT likes it.
_MATRIX B=B'
_MATRIX SE=SE'
_* Print out the results.
_SAMPLE 1 500
_STAT B SE S2
```

NAME	N	MEAN	ST. DEV	VARIANCE	MINIMUM	MAXIMUM
...NOTE...TREATING COLUMNS OF B			AS VARIABLES			
B	500	2.0011	0.76493E-01	0.58512E-02	1.8042	2.2163
B	500	2.9932	1.1346	1.2874	-0.89018E-01	5.8360
...NOTE...TREATING COLUMNS OF SE			AS VARIABLES			
SE	500	0.74272E-01	0.97621E-02	0.95299E-04	0.46592E-01	0.10846
SE	500	1.1098	0.14587	0.21278E-01	0.69620	1.6207
S2	500	1.0072	0.26359	0.69481E-01	0.38965	2.1117

```
_* We see that on average B is close to the true parameters 3 and 2
_* and the Std. Dev. of B is close to the average estimated OLS STD. ERROR
_* Also S2 appears close to true value of 1.
```

I. *BOOTSTRAPPING REGRESSION COEFFICIENTS*

The next example shows how to estimate the standard errors of a regression by using the Efron [1979] Bootstrapping Method. This is illustrated on an OLS regression. Note that the Bootstrap Method is a very expensive and inaccurate way of getting OLS standard errors, but might be useful on other kinds of models.

```
_* Program to get OLS standard errors by Bootstrapping.
_* Warning: This is a very expensive run.
_READ(11) YEAR CONSUME INCOME PRICE
...SAMPLE RANGE IS NOW SET TO:          1        17
_* Run the original regression, save residuals and coefficients.
_OLS CONSUME INCOME PRICE / RESID=E COEF=B
OLS ESTIMATION
      17 OBSERVATIONS      DEPENDENT VARIABLE = CONSUME
 R-SQUARE = 0.9513       R-SQUARE ADJUSTED = 0.9443
VARIANCE OF THE ESTIMATE =    30.951
STANDARD ERROR OF THE ESTIMATE =    5.5634
LOG OF THE LIKELIHOOD FUNCTION = -51.6471
```

VARIABLE NAME	ESTIMATED COEFFICIENT	STANDARD ERROR	T-RATIO 14 DF	PARTIAL CORR.	STANDARDIZED COEFFICIENT	ELASTICITY AT MEANS
INCOME	1.0617	0.26667	3.9813	0.7287	0.23871	0.81288
PRICE	-1.3830	0.83814E-01	-16.501	-0.9752	-0.98933	-0.78464
CONSTANT	130.71	27.094	4.8241	0.7902	0.0	0.97175

```
_* The regression has 3 coefficients.
_* Create space to hold 1000 vectors of bootstrapped coefficients.
_DIM BETA 3 1000
_* Turn off DO-loop printing or you will get lots of output.
_SET NODOECHO
_DO #=1,1000
_* Draw a random sample of errors with replacement.
_* Do this for 1000 replications.
_GENR NEWE=SAMP(E)*SQRT(17/(17-3))
_* Generate new dependent variable by using NEWE.
_GENR Y=B:3+B:1*INCOME+B:2*PRICE+NEWE
_* Suppress printing of OLS output for each of 1000 samples.
_?OLS Y INCOME PRICE / COEF=BETA:#
_ENDO
****** EXECUTION BEGINNING FOR DO LOOP
****** EXECUTION FINISHED FOR DO LOOP
_* Transpose the BETA matrix for use in STAT and PLOT commands.
_* This is needed to get the numbers in column order.
_MATRIX BETA=BETA'
_* Set the sample size to number of replications.
_SAMPLE 1 1000
```

```
|_* Get the statistics on the replications.
|_STAT BETA
NAME        N     MEAN        ST. DEV       VARIANCE      MINIMUM      MAXIMUM
...NOTE...TREATING COLUMNS OF BETA     AS VARIABLES
BETA       1000   1.0548      0.24526       0.60154E-01   0.34391      1.8545
BETA       1000  -1.3852      0.73804E-01   0.54470E-02  -1.6322      -1.1814
BETA       1000   131.63      24.989        624.45        47.948       203.44

|_* Look at the frequency distribution for the INCOME coefficient.
|_PLOT BETA:1  / HISTO

        1000 OBSERVATIONS
HISTOGRAM - BETA
  PCT.      N
 0.049     49   I                              X     X
 0.047     47   I                           X  X     X
 0.045     45   I                           X  X     X
 0.043     43   I                           X  X  X  X
 0.041     41   I                           X  X  X  X
 0.039     39   I                           X  X XX  X
 0.037     37   I                     X    X  X  XXXX
 0.035     35   I                     X    X  X  XXXX   X
 0.033     33   I                   XXX  X  X  XXXX    X
 0.031     31   I                   XXXXX X  XXXX   XX
 0.029     29   I                   XXXXX XXXXXX XXXX
 0.027     27   I                   XXXXX XXXXXXXXXXX
 0.025     25   I                 XXXXXXXXXXXXXXXXXXX
,0.023     23   I             X XXXXXXXXXXXXXXXXXXXXX
 0.021     21   I            XX XXXXXXXXXXXXXXXXXXXXX X
 0.019     19   I            XX XXXXXXXXXXXXXXXXXXXXX X
 0.017     17   I            XXXXXXXXXXXXXXXXXXXXXXXX X
 0.015     15   I          XXXXXXXXXXXXXXXXXXXXXXXXXX XXX
 0.013     13   I          XXXXXXXXXXXXXXXXXXXXXXXXXXXXX
 0.011     11   I        X XXXXXXXXXXXXXXXXXXXXXXXXXXXXXX   X
 0.009      9   I        XXXXXXXXXXXXXXXXXXXXXXXXXXXXXXXX   X
 0.007      7   I        XXXXXXXXXXXXXXXXXXXXXXXXXXXXXXXX   X
 0.005      5   I      XXXXXXXXXXXXXXXXXXXXXXXXXXXXXXXXXXX XXX
 0.003      3   IX     XXXXXXXXXXXXXXXXXXXXXXXXXXXXXXXXXXXXXXX XX  X
 0.001      1   IXXX XXXXXXXXXXXXXXXXXXXXXXXXXXXXXXXXXXXXXXXXXXXXXXXX X
                I---------I---------I---------I---------I---------I---------I
                0.319     0.564     0.810     1.05      1.30      1.55      1.79
```

J. *HETEROSKEDASTIC CONSISTENT COVARIANCE MATRICES*

The easy way to get White's [1980] Heteroskedastic Consistent Covariance matrix is to use the **HETCOV** option on **OLS**. However, this example shows how to program it and some variations discussed in Mackinnon and White [1985]. The example also shows how to use the estimator proposed by Cragg [1983].

```
|_READ(11) YEAR CONSUME INCOME PRICE
...SAMPLE RANGE IS NOW SET TO:            1        17
|_* first run OLS, save residuals
|_OLS CONSUME INCOME PRICE / RESID=U STDERR=OSE

OLS ESTIMATION
        17 OBSERVATIONS     DEPENDENT VARIABLE = CONSUME

 R-SQUARE = 0.9513     R-SQUARE ADJUSTED = 0.9443
 VARIANCE OF THE ESTIMATE =     30.951
 STANDARD ERROR OF THE ESTIMATE =   5.5634
 LOG OF THE LIKELIHOOD FUNCTION = -51.6471

VARIABLE    ESTIMATED   STANDARD  T-RATIO   PARTIAL STANDARDIZED ELASTICITY
  NAME      COEFFICIENT   ERROR    14 DF     CORR.  COEFFICIENT AT MEANS

INCOME    1.0617      0.26667       3.9813  0.7287   0.23871      0.81288
PRICE    -1.3830      0.83814E-01 -16.501  -0.9752  -0.98933     -0.78464
CONSTANT  130.71      27.094        4.8241  0.7902   0.0          0.97175
|_* Next square the residuals and copy the independent variables
|_* into the X matrix.
|_GENR U2=U**2
|_GENR ONE=1
|_COPY INCOME PRICE ONE X
|_* Now HC is White's(1980) covariance matrix for heteroskedasticity.
|_MATRIX HC=INV(X'X)*X'DIAG(U2)*X*INV(X'X)
|_* Now get the corrected standard errors and print them out.
|_MATRIX HSE=SQRT(DIAG(HC))
|_PRINT OSE
OSE
  0.2666740     0.8381426E-01   27.09429
|_PRINT HSE
HSE
  0.2172196     0.7422455E-01   23.66507
|_* Note that the corrected standard errors are smaller.
|_* Now get HC1, the Hinkley method of estimation.
|_MATRIX HC1=($N/$DF)*HC
..NOTE..CURRENT VALUE OF $N   =    17.000
..NOTE..CURRENT VALUE OF $DF  =    14.000
|_MATRIX KTT=DIAG(X*INV(X'X)*X')
|_MATRIX SIG2=U2/(1-KTT)
|_* HC2 is the Horn and Duncan estimate.
|_MATRIX HC2=INV(X'X)*X'DIAG(SIG2)*X*INV(X'X)
|_MATRIX USTAR=U/(1-KTT)
|_MATRIX OM=DIAG(USTAR**2)
|_* HC3 is the MacKinnon and White(1985) Jackknife estimate.
|_MATRIX HC3=(($N-1)/$N)*INV(X'X)*(X'OM*X-(1/$N)*(X'USTAR*USTAR'X))*INV(X'X)
```

```
|_* Now print out the 4 different covariance matrix estimates.
|_PRINT HC HC1 HC2 HC3
HC
    3 BY      3 MATRIX
  0.4718433E-01  0.2076371E-03  -4.957136
  0.2076371E-03  0.5509284E-02  -0.4802344
 -4.957136       -0.4802344      560.0357
HC1
    3 BY      3 MATRIX
  0.5729526E-01  0.2521307E-03  -6.019380
  0.2521307E-03  0.6689845E-02  -0.5831418
 -6.019380       -0.5831418      680.0433
HC2
    3 BY      3 MATRIX
  0.6044015E-01 -0.5570915E-03  -6.295172
 -0.5570915E-03  0.6942529E-02  -0.5138845
 -6.295172       -0.5138845      704.1588
HC3
    3 BY      3 MATRIX
  0.7333148E-01 -0.1782186E-02  -7.563165
 -0.1782186E-02  0.8325627E-02  -0.4927166
 -7.563165       -0.4927166      836.8303
|_* Now do the Cragg (1983) estimator using X**2 as auxiliary variables.
|_GENR INCOME2=INCOME**2
|_GENR PRICE2=PRICE**2
|_COPY INCOME PRICE ONE INCOME2 PRICE2 Q
|_* The coefficient vector BA is Cragg's equation (13), p. 753.
|_MATRIX BA=INV(X'Q*INV(Q'DIAG(U2)*Q)*Q'X)*X'Q*INV(Q'DIAG(U2)*Q)*Q'CONSUME
|_* The covariance matrix VBA is Cragg's equation (14), p. 754.
|_MATRIX VBA=INV(X'Q*INV(Q'DIAG(U2)*Q)*Q'X)
|_* Note that BA and VBA have many similar terms. It would have
|_* been cheaper to compute them separately first.
|_PRINT BA VBA
BA
  0.9725258      -1.367748      138.8088
VBA
    3 BY      3 MATRIX
  0.3068722E-01  0.1126381E-02  -3.324788
  0.1126381E-02  0.5418412E-02  -0.5683495
 -3.324788       -0.5683495      398.3224
```

K. *HAUSMAN SPECIFICATION TEST*

This example shows how to use Hausman's [1978] Specification Test in an Errors in Variables model following the example in his article. The model is a regression of consumption on income where it is suspected that income is measured with error. The investment variable is used as an Instrumental Variable:

```
_* Hausman Specification Test on errors in variables.
_* Use data from Judge[1982], p. 545 on INVESTMENT, CONSUME, INCOME
_* OLS and Instrumental Variables Estimators will be used.
_SAMPLE 1 20
_READ I C Y / LIST
   3 VARIABLES AND       20 OBSERVATIONS STARTING AT OBS        1
   2.000000       15.30000       21.79000
   2.000000       19.91000       21.93000
   2.200000       20.94000       19.94000
   2.200000       19.66000       21.16000
   2.400000       21.32000       22.21000
   2.400000       18.33000       20.78000
   2.600000       19.59000       22.83000
   2.600000       21.30000       23.09000
   2.800000       20.93000       24.80000
   2.800000       21.64000       23.86000
   3.000000       21.90000       24.24000
   3.000000       20.50000       25.69000
   3.200000       22.83000       24.81000
   3.200000       23.49000       24.38000
   3.400000       24.20000       27.06000
   3.400000       23.05000       26.32000
   3.600000       24.01000       28.81000
   3.600000       25.83000       27.86000
   3.800000       25.15000       29.52000
   3.800000       25.06000       28.67000
_* First estimate using the efficient estimator (OLS) under the nulL.
_OLS C Y / COEF=B0 COV=V0 PCOV
OLS ESTIMATION
      20 OBSERVATIONS      DEPENDENT VARIABLE = C
 R-SQUARE = 0.6524      R-SQUARE ADJUSTED = 0.6331
VARIANCE OF THE ESTIMATE =    2.4174
STANDARD ERROR OF THE ESTIMATE =    1.5548
LOG OF THE LIKELIHOOD FUNCTION = -36.1521
```

VARIABLE NAME	ESTIMATED COEFFICIENT	STANDARD ERROR	T-RATIO 18 DF	PARTIAL CORR.	STANDARDIZED COEFFICIENT	ELASTICITY AT MEANS
Y	0.72785	0.12522	5.8126	0.8077	0.80772	0.81957
CONSTANT	3.9237	3.0860	1.2715	0.2871	0.0	0.18043

```
VARIANCE-COVARIANCE MATRIX OF COEFFICIENTS
Y         0.15680E-01
CONSTANT -0.38397         9.5233
              Y              CONSTANT
_* Next estimate using the consistent estimator(IV) under both the
_* null and the alternative hypotheses in SHAZAM the 2SLS command is
_* used for Instrumental Variable Estimation.
```

PROGRAMMING IN SHAZAM

```
|_2SLS C Y (I) / COEF=B1 COV=V1 PCOV
 TWO STAGE LEAST SQUARES - DEPENDENT VARIABLE = C
  1 EXOGENOUS VARIABLES
        20 OBSERVATIONS

  R-SQUARE = 0.6370     R-SQUARE ADJUSTED = 0.6168
 VARIANCE OF THE ESTIMATE =    2.5246
 STANDARD ERROR OF THE ESTIMATE =    1.5889
 VARIABLE    ESTIMATED    STANDARD    T-RATIO    PARTIAL STANDARDIZED ELASTICITY
   NAME     COEFFICIENT    ERROR      18 DF       CORR.  COEFFICIENT AT MEANS

 Y           0.83970     0.13505     6.2177      0.8260  0.93184     0.94552
 CONSTANT    1.1848      3.3261      0.35621     0.0837  0.0         0.05488

 VARIANCE-COVARIANCE MATRIX OF COEFFICIENTS
 Y          0.18239E-01
 CONSTANT  -0.44662         11.063
                Y                CONSTANT
|_* Now form the Hausman Specification Test statistic.
|_SAMPLE 1 2
|_GENR Q=B1-B0
|_MATRIX VQ=V1-V0
|_MATRIX M=Q'INV(VQ)*Q
|_* The statistic M is distributed Chi-square(1) under the null hypothesis.
|_* If it is greater than 3.84 we can reject the null hypothesis.
|_PRINT M
M
    4.889505
```

L. *NON-NESTED MODEL TESTING*

This example shows how to apply the Non-Nested Cox and J-Tests described in Judge [1985, pp. 883-884] to two linear models. Using Theil's Textile data we will test the two regressions CONSUME on INCOME and CONSUME on PRICE. The test procedures will first test H1 (INCOME is the proper variable) and then H2 (PRICE is the proper variable). The output below indicates that the INCOME model is not rejected, but the PRICE model is rejected (It should be noted that we have strong theoretical reasons to believe that both INCOME and PRICE belong in the regression in this example.)

```
_SAMPLE 1 17
_READ(11) YEAR CONSUME INCOME PRICE
   4 VARIABLES AND         17 OBSERVATIONS STARTING AT OBS        1
_* Non-nested Cox Test, H1: Consume on income, H2: Consume on price.
_*  See BIG JUDGE pp. 883-884.
_OLS CONSUME INCOME / COEF=B1 DN PREDICT=Y1HAT
```

OLS ESTIMATION
      17 OBSERVATIONS   DEPENDENT VARIABLE = CONSUME
...NOTE..SAMPLE RANGE SET TO: 1,   17

 R-SQUARE = 0.0038   R-SQUARE ADJUSTED =-0.0626
VARIANCE OF THE ESTIMATE =   521.19
STANDARD ERROR OF THE ESTIMATE =   22.830
LOG OF THE LIKELIHOOD FUNCTION = -77.2990

	ASYMPTOTIC				
VARIABLE NAME	ESTIMATED COEFFICIENT	STANDARD ERROR	T-RATIO -------	PARTIAL CORR.	STANDARDIZED COEFFICIENT	ELASTICITY AT MEANS
INCOME	0.27473	1.0767	0.25517	0.0657	0.61769E-01	0.21035
CONSTANT	106.21	111.02	0.95673	0.2398	0.0	0.78965

```
| GEN1 S1=$SIG2
..NOTE..CURRENT VALUE OF $SIG2=    521.19
|_OLS CONSUME PRICE / COEF=B2 DN PREDICT=Y2HAT
```

OLS ESTIMATION
      17 OBSERVATIONS   DEPENDENT VARIABLE = CONSUME
...NOTE..SAMPLE RANGE SET TO: 1,   17

 R-SQUARE = 0.8961   R-SQUARE ADJUSTED = 0.8892
VARIANCE OF THE ESTIMATE =   54.348
STANDARD ERROR OF THE ESTIMATE =   7.3721
LOG OF THE LIKELIHOOD FUNCTION = -58.0829

	ASYMPTOTIC				
VARIABLE NAME	ESTIMATED COEFFICIENT	STANDARD ERROR	T-RATIO -------	PARTIAL CORR.	STANDARDIZED COEFFICIENT	ELASTICITY AT MEANS
PRICE	-1.3233	0.1093	-12.110	-0.9525	-0.94664	-0.7508
CONSTANT	235.49	8.5283	27.613	0.9903	0.0	1.7508

```
| GEN1 S2=$SIG2
..NOTE..CURRENT VALUE OF $SIG2=    54.348
|_* Create the X and Z matrices, X for H1, Z for H2.
|_GENR ONE=1
```

```
_COPY INCOME ONE X
_COPY PRICE ONE Z
_* Create the M matrices, M1 for H1, M2 for H2.
_MATRIX M2=IDEN(17)-Z*INV(Z'Z)*Z'
_MATRIX M1=IDEN(17)-X*INV(X'X)*X'
_* Test H1: The hypothesis that income is the true model.
_* The test statistic H1 is asymptotically normally distributed.
_MATRIX S21=S1+1/$N*(B1'X'M2*X*B1)
..NOTE..CURRENT VALUE OF $N   =   17.000
_MATRIX C12=$N/2*LOG(S2/S21)
..NOTE..CURRENT VALUE OF $N   =   17.000
_MATRIX VC12=(S1/S21**2)*(B1'X'M2*M1*M2*X*B1)
_MATRIX H1=C12/SQRT(VC12)
_PRINT C12 VC12 H1
   C12
 -19.24761
   VC12
 0.2001174E-02
   H1
 -430.2633
_* Now test H2: The hypothesis that price is the true model.
_* The test statistic H2 is asymptotically normally distributed.
_MATRIX S12=S2+1/$N*(B2'Z'M1*Z*B2)
..NOTE..CURRENT VALUE OF $N   =   17.000
_MATRIX C21=$N/2*LOG(S1/S12)
..NOTE..CURRENT VALUE OF $N   =   17.000
_MATRIX VC21=(S2/S12**2)*(B2'Z'M1*M2*M1*Z*B2)
_MATRIX H2=C21/SQRT(VC21)
_PRINT C21 VC21 H2
   C21
 0.2147064
   VC21
 0.5193263E-01
   H2
 0.9421603


_* Now try the Davidson-MacKinnon J Test.
_* To test H1, see if coef on Y2HAT is zero.
_OLS CONSUME INCOME Y2HAT

OLS ESTIMATION
     17 OBSERVATIONS     DEPENDENT VARIABLE = CONSUME
...NOTE..SAMPLE RANGE SET TO:    1,    17

 R-SQUARE = 0.9513     R-SQUARE ADJUSTED = 0.9443
VARIANCE OF THE ESTIMATE =    30.951
STANDARD ERROR OF THE ESTIMATE =    5.5634
LOG OF THE LIKELIHOOD FUNCTION = -51.6471
```

VARIABLE NAME	ESTIMATED COEFFICIENT	STANDARD ERROR	T-RATIO 14 DF	PARTIAL CORR.	STANDARDIZED COEFFICIENT	ELASTICITY AT MEANS
INCOME	1.0617	0.26667	3.9813	0.7287	0.23871	0.81288
Y2HAT	1.0451	0.63337E-01	16.501	0.9752	0.98933	1.0451
CONSTANT	-115.40	30.204	-3.8208	-0.7145	0.0	-0.85798

```
_* To test H2, see if coef on Y1HAT is zero.
_OLS CONSUME PRICE Y1HAT

REQUIRED MEMORY IS PAR=     8 CURRENT PAR=    40
OLS ESTIMATION
      17 OBSERVATIONS     DEPENDENT VARIABLE = CONSUME
...NOTE..SAMPLE RANGE SET TO:    1,   17

 R-SQUARE = 0.9513     R-SQUARE ADJUSTED = 0.9443
VARIANCE OF THE ESTIMATE =    30.951
STANDARD ERROR OF THE ESTIMATE =    5.5634
LOG OF THE LIKELIHOOD FUNCTION = -51.6471
```

VARIABLE NAME	ESTIMATED COEFFICIENT	STANDARD ERROR	T-RATIO 14 DF	PARTIAL CORR.	STANDARDIZED COEFFICIENT	ELASTICITY AT MEANS
PRICE	-1.3830	0.83814E-01	-16.501	-0.9752	-0.98933	-0.78464
Y1HAT	3.8645	0.97066	3.9813	0.7287	0.23871	3.8645
CONSTANT	-279.75	129.58	-2.1590	-0.4998	0.0	-2.0799

M. *SOLVING SIMULTANEOUS EQUATIONS*

This example was prepared by James Chalfant and Jeff Perloff of the University of California - Berkeley to show how to solve algebraic simultaneous equations. Note that this is a different problem than estimating the parameters of a simultaneous equation econometric model. There are many potential applications for this method. For example, Gallant [1987, Ch. 1] uses a similar procedure to obtain starting values for a nonlinear estimation.

Suppose you want to solve the following equation for X where a,b, and c are known parameters:

$$aX^2 + bX + c = 0$$

First, write it in implicit form:

$$0 = aX^2 + bX + c$$

Next, let Y be the left-hand-side variable and W be an arbitrary multiplier (for example: W=1). Then the equation can be written as:

$$Y = W(a(X^2) + bX + c)$$

Tell SHAZAM that there is only one observation with Y=0 and W=1 and use the NL and EQ commands as in the following output:

```
_  SAMPLE 1 1
_  GEN1 Y=0
_  GEN1 W=1
_  NL 1 / NCOEF=1  RSTAT
_  EQ Y=W*(1*(X*X) - 4*X + 4)
_  COEF X 1
    2 VARIABLES IN  1 EQUATIONS WITH  1 COEFFICIENTS
        1 OBSERVATIONS

COEFFICIENT STARTING VALUES
X          1.0000
        100 MAXIMUM ITERATIONS, CONVERGENCE = 0.000010

  QUASI-NEWTON METHOD USING BFGS UPDATE FORMULA

INITIAL STATISTICS :

TIME =    0.005 SEC.   ITER. NO.     1 FUNCTION EVALUATIONS     1
LOG-LIKELIHOOD FUNCTION=    -1.418939

COEFFICIENTS
   1.000000
GRADIENT
  -2.000000
...ERROR...DETERMINANT OF SIGMA NOT POSITIVE =  0.0
```

```
FINAL STATISTICS :

TIME =    0.009 SEC.    ITER. NO.      2 FUNCTION EVALUATIONS      19
LOG-LIKELIHOOD FUNCTION=   0.5000000E+20

COEFFICIENTS
   2.000000
GRADIENT
  0.0

MAXIMUM LIKELIHOOD ESTIMATE OF SIGMA-SQUARED =  0.0
GTRANSPOSE*INVERSE(H)*G (LM) STATISTIC   -  =  0.0

        COEFFICIENT    ST. ERROR    T-RATIO

X          2.0000      0.70711      2.8284

DURBIN-WATSON = 0.0      VON NEUMAN RATIO = 0.0       RHO =  0.0
RESIDUAL SUM =  0.0         RESIDUAL VARIANCE =  0.0
SUM OF ABSOLUTE ERRORS=  0.0
R-SQUARE BETWEEN OBSERVED AND PREDICTED = 0.0
|_ END
```

The solution of the equation is near $X=2$. Note that the RSTAT option produces some irrelevant summary statistics. The RESIDUAL SUM tells how far your answer is from the solution of the equation. Note that you should ignore the warning messages about the inability of SHAZAM to compute SIGMA in this case (since there is only one observation).

If you have more than one equation, you can generalize this technique. For example, suppose you want to solve two equations with X1 and X2. The implicit form in SHAZAM notation is:

```
0 = X1**2 + b*X1*X2 + c
0 = X2**2 + d*X1*X2 + e
```

The following output shows the solution. Note that the variables W1 and W2 are used to identify the two equations.

```
|_ *  Now claim that you have 2 observations and 1 equation:
|_ SAMPLE 1 2
|_ * Read in 2 observations on left hand side and weights
|_ * defined as follows:
|_ *    Z      W1      W2
|_ *    0      1       0
|_ *    0      0       1
|_ READ Z W1 W2 / LIST
   3 VARIABLES AND         2 OBSERVATIONS STARTING AT OBS       1
      Z                 W1                 W2
  0.0              1.000000        0.0
  0.0              0.0             1.000000
|_ * Note that we are using W1 and W2 as arbitrary weights.  That is, we are
|_ * writing the two equations by first examining Equation 1 (when W1 = 1 and
```

```
|_ *  W2 = 0) and then Equation 2 (when W1 = 0 and W2 = 1):
|_ * Be warned that since there should be a perfect fit and the NL
|_ * routine is not set up for this type of problem you should
|_ * expect some nonsense results for GRADIENTS, STANDARD ERRORS,
|_ *  T-RATIOS and SIGMA
|_ * Sometimes the NUMERIC option gives better results.
|_ NL 1 / NCOEF=2  RSTAT
|_ EQ Z=W1*(X1**2 + 3*X1*X2 - 22) + W2*(X2**2 + 2*X1*X2 - 21)
|_ COEF X1 1 X2 1
   3 VARIABLES IN  1 EQUATIONS WITH  2 COEFFICIENTS
         2 OBSERVATIONS

COEFFICIENT STARTING VALUES
X1       1.0000       X2         1.0000
       100 MAXIMUM ITERATIONS, CONVERGENCE = 0.000010

INITIAL STATISTICS :

TIME =        0.007 SEC.   ITER. NO.      0   FUNCT. EVALUATIONS    1
LOG-LIKELIHOOD FUNCTION=   -8.618621
COEFFICIENTS
   1.000000        1.000000
GRADIENT
 -0.3888889      -0.3888889

FINAL STATISTICS :

TIME =        0.020 SEC.   ITER. NO.      6   FUNCT. EVALUATIONS   45
LOG-LIKELIHOOD FUNCTION=    9.087325
COEFFICIENTS
   1.999557        3.000509
GRADIENT
  -3114.110       1217.794


MAXIMUM LIKELIHOOD ESTIMATE OF SIGMA-SQUARED =  0.66214E-05
GTRANSPOSE*INVERSE(H)*G (LM) STATISTIC  -  =   68.902



        COEFFICIENT   ST. ERROR   T-RATIO

X1       1.9996      0.24552E-02  814.43
X2       3.0005      0.72016E-02  416.65

DURBIN-WATSON = 1.9942    VON NEUMAN RATIO = 3.9884    RHO = -0.89761
RESIDUAL SUM = 0.27729E-03 RESIDUAL VARIANCE =  0.66214E-05
SUM OF ABSOLUTE ERRORS= 0.51389E-02
R-SQUARE BETWEEN OBSERVED AND PREDICTED = 0.0
|_ * Remember that there may be multiple answers,
|_ * so you many need to experiment with different starting values.
```

The solution to the equations is near $X1 = 2$ and $X2 = 3$.

N. *LIMITED INFORMATION MAXIMUM LIKELIHOOD*

This example was proposed by Ray Byron of Australian National University. SHAZAM easily computes Two-Stage Least Squares estimation of a single equation in a simultaneous equation model with the 2SLS command as described in the chapter *TWO-STAGE LEAST SQUARES AND SYSTEMS OF EQUATIONS.* An alternative estimation method is Limited Information Maximum Likelihood (LIML) which can easily be computed with a set of MATRIX commands as shown below for the Consumption equation of Klein's Model I. The method shown can be also be used to compute k-Class estimates by selecting a desired value of k. The results from the LIML estimation can be compared to the 2SLS results. See Amemiya[1985, Section 7.3.2] for further information on the LIML model and the notation used in this example.

```
_* LIML estimation of equation 1 in Klein's Model I
_SAMPLE 1 21
_* EXOGENOUS VARIABLES
_* ONE    CONSTANT
_* PLAG   PROFITS LAGGED ONE PERIOD
_* KLAG   STOCK OF CAPITAL AT END OF PREVIOUS PERIOD
_* XLAG   PRIVATE PRODUCT LAGGED ONE PERIOD
_* TIME1 TIME TREND
_* WG     GOVERNMENT WAGE BILL
_* T      INDIRECT TAXES
_* G      GOVERNMENT EXPENDITURES
_* ENDOGENOUS VARIABLES
_* C      CONSUMPTION
_* I      INVESTMENT
_* WP     PRIVATE WAGE BILL
_* P      PROFITS
_* WGWP   WAGES
_* PP     PRIVATE PRODUCT
_* First equation of Klein Model is C= f( ONE, PLAG, P, WGWP)
_GENR ONE=1
_* Define X as all exogenous variables in system
_COPY ONE PLAG KLAG XLAG TIME1 WG T G X
_* Define X1 as right-hand-side exogenous variables
_COPY ONE PLAG X1
_* Compute the M matrices for X and X1
_MATRIX M=IDEN(21)-X*INV(X'X)*X'
_MATRIX M1=IDEN(21)-X1*INV(X1'X1)*X1'
_* Define Y1 as all right-hand-side endogenous variables
_COPY P WGWP Y1
_* Define Y as all endogenous variables in equation
_COPY C P WGWP Y
_* Define Z as all right-hand-side variables, exogenous first
_MATRIX Z= X1 | Y1
_* Compute W and W1
_MATRIX W=Y'M*Y
_MATRIX W1=Y'M1*Y
_* Get the eigenvalues from the W1 and INV(W) matrix computations
_MATRIX LAMBDA=EIGVAL(W1*INV(W))
_PRINT LAMBDA
   LAMBDA
 186.1614        7.617559        1.498746
```

```
|_* Get the minimum eigenvalue and use it for k
|_STAT LAMBDA / MIN=K
NAME         N    MEAN      ST. DEV      VARIANCE      MINIMUM      MAXIMUM
LAMBDA       3    65.093    104.89       11003.        1.4987       186.16
|_PRINT K
    K
   1.498746
|_* Note that k-class estimation can be done by choosing
|_* a different value of k
|_MATRIX ALPHA=INV(Z'(IDEN(21)-K*M)*Z) * Z'(IDEN(21)-K*M)*C
|_* Now print the LIML coefficients
|_* The order is: CONSTANT PLAG P WGWP
|_PRINT ALPHA
   ALPHA
   17.14765       0.3960273      -0.2225131       0.8225587
|_* Get the residuals and variance
|_MATRIX E=C-Z*ALPHA
|_* Print SIGMA**2 using 17 Degrees of freedom
|_MATRIX SIG2=E'E/(21-4)
|_PRINT SIG2
    SIG2
   2.404952
|_* Get the Covariance matrix
|_MATRIX V=SIG2*INV(Z'(IDEN(21)-K*M)*Z)
|_PRINT V
    V
    4 BY      4 MATRIX
   4.183554        0.2948809E-01 -0.8698058E-01 -0.7431826E-01
   0.2940000D 01   0.3722705E-01 -0.3598255E-01 -0.7560770E-03
  -0.8698058E-01  -0.3598255E-01  0.5027916E-01 -0.4170617E-02
  -0.7431826E-01  -0.7560770E-03 -0.4170617E-02  0.3788332E-02
|_* Get the standard errors
|_MATRIX SE=SQRT(DIAG(V))
|_PRINT SE
    SE
   2.045374        0.1929431      0.2242301      0.6154943E-01
```

33. **SUMMARY OF COMMANDS**

"The Sun never sets on the SHAZAM empire."

Kenneth J. White
1980

The following is a list of all the available SHAZAM commands and their available options. The underlined letters of each command and option are the acceptable abbreviations.

ARIMA *var*

ALL, DN, LOG, NOCONSTANT, NOWIDE, PITER, PLOTAC, PLOTDATA, PLOTFORC, PLOTPAC, PLOTRES, START, WIDE, BEG=, END=, COEF=, FBEG=, FEND=, ITER=, NAR=, NDIFF=, NLAG=, NLAGP=, NMA=, NSAR=, NSDIFF=, NSMA=, NSPAN=, PREDICT=, RESID=.

AUTO *depvar indeps*

ANOVA, DLAG, DN, DROP, DUMP, GF, GS, LINLOG, LIST, LOGLIN, LOGLOG, MAX, MISS, ML, NOCONSTANT, NOWIDE, PAGAN, PCOR, PCOV, RESTRICT, RSTAT, WIDE, BEG=, END=, COEF=, CONV=, COV=, GAP=, ITER=, NMISS=, ORDER=, PREDICT=, RESID=, RHO=, SRHO=, STDERR=, TRATIO=.

BAYES *options*

NOANTITHET, NORMAL, NSAMP=, OUTUNIT=.

BOX *depvar indeps*

ACCUR, ALL, ANOVA, AUTO, DLAG, DN, DUMP, FULL, GF, LIST, MAX, NOCONSTANT, PCOR, PCOV, RESTRICT, RSTAT, TIDWELL, UT, BEG=, END=, COEF=, COV=, LAMBDA=, LAME=, LAMI=, LAMS=, PREDICT=, RESID=, RHO=.

CHECKOUT

No options.

COEF *names values*

No options.

COMPRESS

No options.

CONFID *coef1 coef2*

EGA, GOAWAY, GRAPHICS, HERCULES, HOLD, NOBLANK, NOFPLOT, NOMID, NORMAL, NOTPLOT, NOWIDE, PAUSE, PRINT, SYMBOL, TOSHIBA, WIDE, COEF1=, COEF2=, COVAR12=, DF=, FCRIT=, MODE=, POINTS=, TCRIT=, VAR1=, VAR2=, XMAX=, XMIN=, YMAX=, YMIN=.

COPY *fromvar(s) tovar*

FCOL=, FROW=, TCOL=, TROW=.

DELETE *vars*   ALL.

DEMO   START.

DIAGNOS *options*   ACF, BACKWARD, BOOTLIST, CHOWTEST, HET, JACKKNIFE,
                         LIST, MAX, NORECEST, NORECRESID, NOWIDE, RECEST,
                         RECRESID, RECUR, RESET, WIDE, BOOTSAMP=, BOOTUNIT=,
                         GQOBS=, MHET=, RECUNIT=, SIGLEVEL=.

DIM *var size*   No options.

DISPLAY *option*   CPUTIME, other options same as for the SET command.

DISTRIB *vars*   INVERSE, LLF, NOLIST, BEG=, END=, C=, CDF=, CRITICAL=,
                         DF=, DF1=, DF2=, EIGENVAL=, H=, KURTOSIS=, MEAN=,
                         NEIGEN=, PDF=, P= N=, P= Q=, SKEWNESS=, S=, V=, TYPE=,
                         VAR=.

DO *#=beg,end,inc*   No options.

DUMP *option*   ADDCOM, DATA, DATCOM, FCOM, GENCOM, INPCOM, IOCOM,
                         KADD, LODCOM, MACOM, NLCOM, OCOM, OLSCOM, OPTCOM,
                         OSCOM, RANCOM, SCNCOM, SYSCOM, TEMCOM, VCOM, VLCOM,
                         VNAME, VPLCOM, VTCOM, VTECOM, VTICOM.

END   No options.

ENDIF *(equation)*   No options.

ENDO   No options.

EQ *equation*   No options.

FC *depvar indeps*   AFCSE, ALL, BLUP, IBLUP, DYNAMIC, GF, LIST, MAX,
                         NOCONSTANT, RESTRICT, UPPER, BEG=, END=, COEF=,
                         CSNUM=, ESTEND=, FCSE=, LAMBDA=, LIMIT=, MODEL=, NC=,
                         ORDER=, POOLSE=, PREDICT=, RESID=, RHO=, SRHO=.

FILE *unit filename*   Unit can be from 11-49 or the keywords: INPUT, LIST,
                         OUTPUT, PRINT (Macintosh only) or SCREEN.

FORMAT *statement*   No options.

GENR *newvar=equation*   No options.

GEN1 *equation*   No options.

GLS *depvars indeps*   ANOVA, BLUP, DLAG, DN, DUMP, FULLMAT, GF, LIST, MAX, NOCONSTANT, NOMULSIGSQ, PCOR, PCOV, RSTAT, UT, BEG=, END=, COEF=, COR=, COV=, OMEGA=, OMINV=, PMATRIX=, PREDICT=, RESID=, STDERR=, TRATIO=.

HELP *command*   ARIMA, AUTO, BAYES, BOX, CHECKOUT, COEF, COMPRESS, CONFID, COPY, DELETE, DEMO, DIAGNOS, DIMENSION, DISPLAY, DISTRIB, DO, DUMP, END, ENDIF, ENDO, EQ, FC, FILE, FORMAT, GENR, GEN1, GLS, HELP, IF, INDEX, INST, LAMBDA, LOGIT, MAP, MATRIX, MENU, MLE, NAMES, NL, OLS, PAR, PAUSE, PC, PLOT, POOL, PRINT, PROBIT, READ, RENAME, RESTORE, RESTRICT, REWIND, ROBUST, SAMPLE, SET, SIZE, SKIPIF, SORT, STAT, STOP, SYSTEM, TEST, TIME, TITLE, TOBIT, WRITE, 2SLS.

IF *(expression)*   No options.

INDEX *p1 q1...pn qn*   ALTERN, CHAIN, EXPEND, NOALTERN, NOLIST, BASE=, BEG=, END=, DIVISIA=, FISHER=, LASPEYRES=, PAASCHE=, QDIVISIA=, QFISHER=, QLASPEYRES=, QPAASCHE=.

INST *dep ind (inst)*   DUMP, GF, LIST, MAX, NOCONSTANT, PCOR, PCOV, RESTRICT, RSTAT, BEG=, END=, COEF=, COV=, PREDICT=, RESID=.

LAMBDA *var=value*   No options.

LOGIT *depvar indeps*   DUMP, LIST, MAX, NOCONSTANT, NONORM, PCOR, PCOV, RSTAT, BEG=, END=, COEF=, CONV=, COV=, IMR=, INDEX=, ITER=, PITER=, PREDICT=, WEIGHT=.

MAP *latvar lonvar*   SHAZAM, AREA=, BEG=, END=, BORDER=, COLOR=, HEIGHT=, LATB=, LATE=, LATI=, LONB=, LONE=, LONI=, MARK=, OUTPUT=, PROJECT=, TITLE=, WIDTH=.

MATRIX *newmat=equation*   No options.

MENU   No options.

MLE *depvar indeps*

ANOVA, DUMP, GF, LIST, LM, MAX, NOCONSTANT, NONORM, PCOR, PCOV, RSTAT, BEG=, END=, COEF=, CONV=, COR=, COV=, IN=, OUT=, ITER=, METHOD=, PREDICT=, PITER=, RESID=, STDERR=, TRATIO=, TYPE=, WEIGHT=.

NAMES *options*

LIST

NL *neq*

ACROSS, AUTO, DRHO, DUMP, EVAL, GENRVAR, LIST, LOGDEN, NUMCOV, NUMERIC, OPGCOV, PCOR, PCOV, RSTAT, SAME, BEG=, END=, COEF=, CONV=, COR=, COV=, IN=, OUT=, ITER=, METHOD=, NCOEF=, ORDER=, PITER=, START=, STDERR=, STEPSIZE=, TRATIO=.

OLS *depvar indeps*

ANOVA, DFBETAS, DLAG, DN, DUMP, EXACTDW, GF, HETCOV, INFLUENCE, LINLOG, LIST, LM, LOGLIN, LOGLOG, MAX, NOCONSTANT, NOMULSIGSQ, NONORM, PCOR, PCOV, PLUSH, REPLICATE, RESTRICT, RSTAT, UT, BEG=, END=, COEF=, COV=, FE=, FX=, HATDIAG=, IDVAR=, INCOEF=, INCOVAR=, INSIG2=, METHOD=, PCINFO=, PCOMP=, PE=, PX=, PREDICT=, RESID=, RIDGE=, STDERR=, TRATIO=, WEIGHT=.

PAR *number*

No options.

PAUSE

No options.

PC *vars*

COR, LIST, MAX, PCOLLIN, PEVEC, PFM, PRM, RAW, SCALE, EVAL=, EVEC=, MAXFACT=, MINEIG=, NC=, PCINFO=, PCOMP=.

PLOT *depvars indep*

ALTERNATE, EGA, GOAWAY, GRAPHICS, HERCULES, HISTO, HOLD, LINE, LINEONLY, NOBLANK, NOPRETTY, NOSAME, NOWIDE, PAUSE, PRINT, RANGE, SAME, TIME, TOSHIBA, WIDE, BEG=, END=, GROUPS=, SYMBOL=, XMAX=, XMIN=, YMAX=, YMIN=.

POOL *depvar indeps*

ANOVA, CORCOEF, DLAG, DUMP, FULL, GF, LIST, MAX, MULSIGSQ, NOCONSTANT, PCOR, PCOV, RSTAT, SAME, UT, BEG=, END=, COEF=, COV=, NC=, PREDICT=, RESID=, RHO=, STDERR=, TRATIO=.

PRINT *vars*

BYVAR, FORMAT, NEWLINE, NEWPAGE, NEWSHEET, NONAMES, NOWIDE, WIDE, BEG=, END=.

PROBIT *depv indeps*

DUMP, LIST, MAX, NOCONSTANT, NONORM, PCOR, PCOV, RSTAT, BEG=, END=, COEF=, CONV=, COV=, IMR=, INDEX=, ITER=, PITER=, PREDICT=, WEIGHT=.

READ *(unit) vars*

BINARY, BYVAR, CLOSE, EOF, FORMAT, LIST, REWIND, BEG=, END=, COLS=, ROWS=, SKIPLINES=.

RENAME *old new*

No options.

RESTORE *vars*

CITIBASE, UNIT=.

RESTRICT *equation*

No options.

REWIND *unit*

No options.

ROBUST *depvar indeps*

FIVEQUAN, GASTWIRT, LAE, LINLOG, LIST, LOGLIN, LOGLOG, MAX, PCOR, PCOV, RSTAT, TUKEY, UNCOR, BEG=, END=, COEF=, CONV, COV=, DIFF=, ITER=, MULTIT=, PREDICT=, RESID=, STDERR=, THETA=, THETAB=, THETAE=, THETAI=, TRATIO=, TRIM=.

SAMPLE *beg end beg end*

No options.

SET *option*

BATCH, COLOR, DISK, DOECHO, DUMP, ECHO, FRENCH, HIDISK, LASTCOM, LCASE, MAX, NOCC, NOCOLOR, NODISK, NOSKIP, NOSAMPLE, NOSCREEN, NOWARN, NOWARNSKIP, NOWIDE, OPTIONS, PAUSE, RANFIX, SCREEN, SKIP, SAMPLE, TALK, TERMINAL, TIMER, TRACE, WARN, WARNSKIP, WIDE, COMLEN=, MAXCOL=, OUTUNIT=, RANSEED=.

SIZE *maximum*

No options.

SKIPIF*(expression)*

No options.

SORT *sortvar vars*

DESC, LIST, BEG=, END=.

STAT *vars*

ALL, ANOVA, BARTLETT, DN, MATRIX, MAX, PCOR, PCOV, PCP, PCPDEV, PFREQ, PMEDIAN, PRANKCOR, BEG=, END=, COR=, COV=, CP=, CPDEV=, MAXIM=, MEAN=, MINIM=, RANKCOR=, STDEV=, SUMS=, VAR=, WEIGHT=.

STOP

No options.

SYSTEM *neq exogs*   DN, DUMP, FULL, GF, LIST, MAX, NOCONSTANT, PCOR, PCOV,
                              PINVEV, PSIGMA, RESTRICT, RSTAT, COEF=, COEFMAT=,
                              CONV=, COV=, IN=, OUT=, ITER=, PITER=, PREDICT=,
                              RESID=, SIGMA=.

TEST *equation*   No options.

TIME *beg freq var*   No options.

TITLE *title*   No options.

TOBIT *depvar indeps*   DUMP, LIST, MAX, NOCONSTANT, NONORM, PCOR, PCOV,
                              UPPER, BEG=, END=, COEF=, CONV=, COV=, INDEX=, ITER=,
                              LIMIT=, PITER=, PREDICT=, WEIGHT=.

WRITE*(unit) vars*   BINARY, BYVAR, CLOSE, FORMAT, NAMES, NONAMES, REWIND,
                              WIDE, BEG=, END=.

2SLS *depvar rhsvars (exogs)* DUMP, GF, LIST, MAX, NOCONSTANT, PCOR, PCOV, RESTRICT,
                              RSTAT, BEG=, END=, COEF=, COV=, PREDICT=, RESID=.

34. FRENCH COMMAND NAMES

*"I tell you Wellington is a bad general, the English are bad soldiers; we will
settle the matter by lunch time."*

Napolean Bonaparte
Waterloo, June 18, 1815

The following is a complete list of the French equivalents to the English SHAZAM commands. To
use French commands the **SET FRENCH** command must be used. This will allow either English
or French commands. To return to English only, type: **OUVRE NOFRANCAIS.**

ARIMA	ARIMA
AUTO	AUTO
BAYES	BAYES
BOX	BOX
CHECKOUT	VERIFIE
COMPRESS	COMPRIME
CONFID	INTCONF
COEF	COEF
COPY	COPIE
DELETE	SUPPRIME
DEMO	DEMO
DIAGNOS	DIAGNOS
DIM	DIM
DISPLAY	VISUEL
DISTRIB	DISTRIB
DO	FAIS
DUMP	DEVERSE
END	FIN
ENDIF	FINSI
ENDO	FFIN
EQ	EQ
FCAST	PREVOIS
FILE	FICHIER
FORMAT	FORMAT
GENR	GENR
GEN1	GEN1
GLOBAL	MONDIAL
GLS	MCG
GOTO	VA
HELP	AIDE
IF	SI
INDEX	INDEX
INST	INST
LAG	RETARD
LIST	LISTE
LOGIT	LOGLA
MAP	CARTE
MATRIX	MATRICE
MLE	EMV
NAMES	NOMS
NLIN	NLIN
OLS	MCO

PAR	PAR
PAUSE	PAUSE
PCOMP	COMPR
PROBIT	PROBLA
PC	CP
PLOT	TRACE
POOL	MELE
PRINT	IMPRIME
READ	LIS
RENAME	RENOMME
RESTORE	RETABLIS
RESTRICT	RESTR
REWIND	REBOBINE
ROBUST	ROBUSTE
SAMPLE	PRENDS
SAVE	GARDE
SET	OUVRE
SIZE	NOMBRE
SKIPIF	SAUTESI
SORT	CLASSE
STAT	STAT
STOP	ARRETE
SYSTEM	SYSTEME
TEST	TESTE
TIME	CHRONO
TITLE	TITRE
TOBIT	TOBLA
USER	USAGER
WRITE	ECRIS
2SLS	2MC

35. NEW FEATURES IN SHAZAM

"I've changed a lot in the past year."

Margaret Trudeau
1979

There are many differences between SHAZAM Versions. This appendix itemizes a few of these differences. SHAZAM is a continuously expanding program with many new capabilities in econometrics. Always use the latest version available, older versions may not contain the new features.

A. *VERSION 5.0*

Before Version 5.0 was released in 1985, SHAZAM was completely rewritten to make it a modern and flexible package. Users of Versions 1.0-4.6 found that they had entered a new world of econometric computing. A matrix programming language had been added and all procedures had been rewritten to provide the flexibility that economists require. Versions prior to Version 5.0 are called **OLD-OLD SHAZAM** and should no longer be used by anyone except Econometric Historians.

B. *VERSION 5.1*

The following are some of the major changes and additions to Version 5.1 of SHAZAM:

COMMAND	*NEW AVAILABLE OPTIONS*
DISTRIB	**LLF, S=**, and **V=**
GENR	**MOD(X,Y)**
MLE	**LM**
OLS	**DFBETAS, INFLUENCE, REPLICATE, HATDIAG=**, and **UT=**
PROBIT / LOGIT	**NONORM**
SET	**NOWIDE, WIDE**, and **RANSEED=**
STAT	**WEIGHT=**
TOBIT	**NONORM**

C. *VERSION 6.0*

A large number of changes were made to SHAZAM between Versions 5.1 and 6.0. Version 6.0 SHAZAM is capable of computing Box-Jenkins Models (ARIMA) Time-Series models, Bayesian Inequality Restrictions, Confidence Intervals and Ellipses, and Robust Regressions. It can also perform a variety of Regression Diagnostic Tests including many Heteroskedasticity Tests, Recursive Residuals, CUSUM tests and Specification Error Tests as well as Jackknife and Bootstrap estimates. Furthermore, many new options were developed for existing commands. The following are some of the major new commands and options found in Version 6.0 of SHAZAM:

COMMAND	*NEW AVAILABLE OPTIONS*
ARIMA	New Command:
	Identification Phase:
	ALL, NOWIDE, PLOTAC, PLOTDATA, PLOTPAC, WIDE, BEG= END=, NDIFF=, NLAG=, NLAGP=, NSDIFF=, and NSPAN=
	Estimation Phase:
	DN, NOCONSTANT, PITER, PLOTRES, START, BEG= END=, COEF=, ITER=, NAR=, NDIFF=, NMA=, NSAR=, NSDIFF=, NSMA=, NSPAN=, and PREDICT=
	Forecasting Phase:
	LOG, NOCONSTANT, PLOTFORC, COEF=, FBEG= FEND=, NAR=, NDIFF=, NMA=, NSAR=, NSDIFF=, NSMA=, NSPAN=, PREDICT=, and RESID=
AUTO	**NOWIDE, PAGAN,** and **WIDE**
BAYES	New Command:
	NOANTHITHET, NORMAL, NSAMP=, and **OUTUNIT=**
CONFID	New Command:
	EGA, GRAPHICS, HERCULES, HOLD, NOBLANK, NOWIDE, SYMBOL, TOSHIBA, and **WIDE**
DIAGNOS	New Command:
	ACF, BACKWARD, CHOWTEST, HET, JACKKNIFE, LIST, MAX, NOWIDE, RECEST, RECRESID, RECUR, RESET, WIDE, GQOBS=, RECUNIT=, and **SIGLEVEL=**
DISTRIB	**LLF, H=, P= N=, S= V=,** and **TYPE=BINOMIAL**
FC	**FCSE=**
MATRIX	Concatenation (**|**), **SYM**(*matrix*), **TRI**(*matrix*), **VEC**(*matrix*), and **VEC**(*matrix,nrows*)

MENU	Gives the list of available commands in SHAZAM while in interactive mode.
NL	**LOGDEN, NUMCOV, START=, STDERR=, STEPSIZE=,** and **TRATIO=**
OLS	**GF** and **INCOVAR=**
PLOT	**ALTERNATE, EGA, GRAPHICS, HERCULES,** and **TOSHIBA**
POOL	**MULSIGSQ, CORCOEF=,** and **RHO=**
PC	**PCOLLIN, RAW,** and **SCALE**
PROBIT / LOGIT	**IMR=** and **WEIGHT=**
ROBUST	New command:
	FIVEQUAN, GASTWIRT, LAE, LINLOG, LIST, LOGLIN, LOGLOG, MAX, PCOR, PCOV, RSTAT, TUKEY, UNCOR, BEG= END=, COEF=, CONV=, COV=, DIFF=, ITER=, MULTIT=, RESID=, STDERR=, THETA=, THETAB=, THETAE=, THETAI=, TRATIO= and **TRIM=**
SAMPLE	Formerly called **SMPL**
SYSTEM	**COEF=, COEFMATS=, COV=, PITER=,** and **SIGMA=**
TOBIT	**NONORM**
2SLS	**COV=**

D. *VERSION 6.1*

Further additions were made after Version 6.0 to make SHAZAM Version 6.1 a more powerful program than ever before. The Macintosh version of SHAZAM now supports the Macintosh interface and graphics, and many other substantial changes have been made. Some of the major new options are:

COMMAND	*NEW AVAILABLE OPTIONS*
AUTO	**DLAG**
BOX	**DLAG**
CONFID	**GOAWAY, PAUSE, PRINT,** and Macintosh **GRAPHICS**
DIAGNOS	**BOOTLIST, NORECEST, NORECRESID, BOOTSAMP=,** and **MHET=**
DISPLAY	**CPUTIME, SCREEN,** and **WARNSKIP**

DLAG	Command is no longer needed. Distributed lags are now specified on **AUTO, BOX, GLS, OLS**, and **POOL** commands directly. The command is redesigned to make Almon Lag estimation even easier.
FC	**AFCSE, CSNUM=, ESTEND=, LIMIT=**, and **POOLSE=**.
FILE	Available for many machines: **CLOSE, INPUT, LIST, OUTPUT**, and **SCREEN** Available for the Macintosh only: **PRINT**
GLS	**DLAG**
MATRIX	More flexible definition of matrix multiplication added.
NL	**GENRVAR** and **OPGCOV**
OLS	**DLAG**
PLOT	**GOAWAY, PAUSE, PRINT**, and Macintosh **GRAPHICS**
POOL	**DLAG, MULSIGSQ**, and **PCOV**
READ	**CLOSE** and **SKIPLINES=**
SET	**NOSCREEN, NOWARNSKIP**, and **WARNSKIP**
STAT	**SUMS=**
WRITE	**CLOSE**

36. REFERENCES

A. BOOKS

Amemiya, T., *Advanced Econometrics*, Harvard University Press, 1985.

Belsley, D., Kuh, E., and Welsh, R., *Regression Diagnostics*, Wiley, 1980.

Berndt, E.R., *The Practice Of Econometric*, Addison-Wesley, 1989, forthcoming.

Bickel, P., and Doksum, K., *Mathematical Statistics: Basic Ideas and Selected Topics*, Holden-Day, 1977.

Box, G.E.P., and Jenkins, G.M., *Time Series Analysis: Forecasting and Control*, Holden-Day, 1976.

Cerf, C., and Navasky, V. *The Experts Speak: The Definitive Compendium of Authoritative Misinformation*, Pantheon Books, 1984.

Chow, G., *Econometrics*, McGraw-Hill, 1983.

Dhrymes, P., *Econometrics*, Harper and Row, 1970.

Dhrymes, P., *Distributed Lags: Problems of Estimation and Formulation*, Holden-Day, 1971.

Fomby, T., IIill, R., and Johnson, S., *Advanced Econometric Methods*, Springer-Verlag, 1984.

Gallant, A.R., *Nonlinear Statistical Models*, Wiley, 1987.

Srivastava, V.K., and Giles, D.E.A., *Seemingly Unrelated Regression Equations Models*, Dekker, 1987.

Goldberger, A.S., *Econometric Theory*, Wiley, 1964.

Goldfeld, S., and Quandt, R., *Nonlinear Methods in Econometrics*, North-Holland, 1972.

Graybill, F., *Theory and Application of the Linear Model*, Duxbury Press, 1976.

Griliches, Z., and Intriligator, M., *Handbook of Econometrics*, North-Holland, 1983.

Gujarati, D., *Basic Econometrics*, McGraw-Hill, Second Edition, 1987.

Hanushek, E., and Jackson, J., *Statistical Methods for Social Scientists*, Academic Press, 1977.

Harvey, A., *The Econometric Analysis of Time Series*, Halsted Press, 1981.

Hensher, D.A., and Johnson, L.W., *Applied Discrete Choice Modeling*, Wiley, 1981.

Intriligator, M., *Econometric Models, Techniques and Applications*, Prentice-Hall, 1978.

Johnston, J., *Econometric Methods*, McGraw-Hill, 1984

Jolliffe, I.T., *Principal Component Analysis*, Springer-Verlag, 1986.

Judge, G., Hill, R., Griffiths, W., Lütkepohl, H., and Lee, T., *Introduction to the Theory and Practice of Econometrics*, Wiley, Second Edition, 1988.

Judge, G., Griffiths, W., Hill, R., Lütkepohl, H., and Lee, T., *The Theory and Practice of Econometrics*, Wiley, Second Edition, 1985.

Kennedy, P., *A Guide to Econometrics*, MIT Press, 1985.

Klein, L., *Textbook of Econometrics*, Prentice-Hall, 1974.

Kmenta, J., *Elements of Econometrics*, Second Edition, Macmillan, 1986.

Koerts, J., and Abrahamse, A.P.J., *On the Theory and Application of the General Linear Model*, Rotterdam University Press, 1969.

Maddala, G.S., *Econometrics*, McGraw-Hill, 1977.

Maddala, G.S., *Introduction to Econometrics*, Macmillan, 1988.

Maddala, G.S., *Limited Dependent and Qualitative Variables in Econometrics*, Cambridge University Press, 1983.

Murphy, J., *Introductory Econometrics*, Irwin, 1973.

Nelson, C., *Applied Time Series Analysis*, Holden-Day, 1973.

Newbold, P., *Statistics for Business and Economics*, Prentice-Hall, 1984.

Pindyck, R., and Rubinfeld, D., *Econometric Models and Economic Forecasts*, McGraw-Hill, 1981.

Rao, C.R., *Linear Statistical Inference and its Applications*, Wiley, 1973.

Smillie, K.R., *An Introduction to Regression and Correlation*, Ryerson Press, 1966.

Theil, H., *Principles of Econometrics*, Wiley, 1971.

Theil, H., *Applied Economic Forecasting*, North-Holland, 1966.

Wallace, T., and Silver, J., *Econometrics: An Introduction*, Addison-Wesley, 1988.

Wells, D., *The Penguin Dictionary of Curious and Interesting Numbers*, Penguin Books, 1986.

White, H., *Asymptotic Theory for Econometricians*, Academic Press, 1984.

White, K.J. and Bui, L.T.M., *Basic Econometrics: A Computer Handbook Using SHAZAM*, McGraw-Hill, 1988. ISBN 0-07-834463-8, *Gujarati Handbook*.

White, K.J. and Bui, L.T.M., *The Practice of Econometrics: A Computer Handbook Using SHAZAM*, forthcoming, for use with Berndt, E.R., *The Practice of Econometrics*.

White, K.J. and Courchene, M.P.A., *Introduction to Econometrics: A Computer Handbook Using SHAZAM*, forthcoming, for use with Maddala, G.S., *Introduction to Econometrics*.

White, K.J., Haun, S.A., and Gow, D.J., *Introduction to the Theory and Practice of Econometrics: A Computer Handbook Using SHAZAM and SAS*, John Wiley And Sons, 1988. ISBN 0-471-85946-X, *Judge Handbook*.

White, K.J., Haun, S.A., Horsman, N.G., and Wong, S.D., *SHAZAM User's Reference Manual*, McGraw-Hill, 1988. ISBN 0-07-069781-7.

Zarembka, P., *Frontiers of Econometrics*, Academic Press, 1974.

Zellner, A., *An Introduction to Baryesian Inference in Econometrics*, John Wiley and Sons, 1971.

B. OTHER PUBLICATIONS

Almon, S., "Distributed Lag Between Capital Appropriations and Expenditures," *Econometrica*, Vol. 33, January 1965, p.178-196.

Amemiya, T., "Qualitative Response Models: A Survey," *Journal of Economic Literature*, Vol. XIX, December 1981, p.1483-1536.

Amemiya, T., "Nonlinear Regression Models," Chapter 6, *Handbook of Econometrics*, 1983.

Baillie, R., "The Asymptotic Mean Squared Error of Multistep Prediction from the Regression Model with Autoregressive Errors," *Journal of the American Statistical Association*, 1979, pp.179-184.

Beach, C., and MacKinnon, J., "A Maximum Likelihood Procedure for Regression with Autocorrelated Errors," *Econometrica*, January 1978, pp.51-58.

Belsley, D., "On the Computation of the Nonlinear Full-Information Maximum-Likelihood Estimation," *Journal of Econometrics*, October 1980, p. 203-278.

Box, G.E.P., and Cox, D.R., "An Analysis of Transformations," *Journal of the Royal Statistical Society*, 1964.

Box, G.E.P., and Tidwell, P., "Transformation of the Independent Variables," *Technometrics*, 1962.

Bofinger, E., "Estimation of a Density Function using Order Statistics", *Australian Journal of Statistics*, Vol. 17, 1975, pp. 1-7.

Breusch, T.S. and Pagan, A.R., "A Simple Test For Heteroscedasticity And Random Coefficient Variation", *Econometrica*, Vol. 47, 1979, pp. 1287-94.

Buse, A., "Goodness of Fit in Generalized Least Squares Estimation," *American Statistician*, Vol. 27, 1973, pp. 106-108.

Businger, P., Golub, G.H., "Linear Least Squares Solutions by Householder Transformations," *Numerische Mathematik*, Vol. 7, 1965, pp. 269-276.

Cameron, T.A. and White, K.J., "Generalized Gamma Family Regression Models for Long-distance Telephone Call Durations" in A. de Fontenay, M. Shugard, and D. Sibley (eds.) *Telecommunications Demand Modelling*, Amsterdam: North Holland, 1988.

Cameron, T.A. and White, K.J., "The Demand for Computer Services: A Disaggregate Decision Model," *Managerial and Decision Economics*, March 1986, pp. 37-41.

Cassing, S.A., and White, K.J., "An Analysis of the Eigenvector Condition in the Durbin-Watson Test," *Australian Journal of Statistics*, March 1983, pp. 17-22.

Chalfant J., and White, K.J., "Estimation of Demand Systems with Concavity and Monotonicity Constraints," *University of British Columbia Discussion Paper*, 1988.

Cragg, J.G., "More Efficient Estimation in the Presence of Heteroscedasticity of Unknown Form," *Econometrica*, May 1983, pp.751-763.

Deegan, J., and White, K., "An Analysis of Nonpartisan Election Media Expenditure Decisions Using Limited Dependent Variable Methods," *Social Science Research*, June 1976, pp.127-135.

Diewert, W.E., "Superlative Index Numbers and Consistency in Aggregation," *Econometrica*, July 1978, pp.883-900.

Diewert, W.E., "Aggregation Problems in the Measurement of Capital," *The Measurement of Capital*, Dan Usher(ed.), NBER, University of Chicage Press, 1980, pp. 433-528.

Durbin, J., "Testing for Serial Correlation in Systems of Simultaneous Regression Equations," *Biometrika*, Vol. 44, 1957, pp. 370-377.

Efron, B., "Bootstrap Methods: Another Look at the Jackknife," *Annals of Statistics*, 7, 1-26, 1979.

Farebrother, R.W., "Gram-Schmidt Regression," *Applied Statistics*, Vol.23, No. 3, 1974, pp. 470-476.

Freedman, D.A. and Peters, S.C., "Bootstrapping a Regression Equation: Some Empirical Results," *Journal of the American Statistical Association*, Vol 79, 1984, pp.97-106.

Geweke, J., "Exact Inference in the Inequality Constrained Normal Linear Regression Model," *Journal of Applied Econometrics*, 1986.

Geweke, J., "Antithetic Acceleration of Monte Carlo Integration In Bayesian Inference," *Journal of Econometrics*, Volume 38, No. 1/2, 1988, pp. 72-89.

Godfrey, L.G., McAleer, M., and McKenzie, C.R., "Variable Addition and Lagrange Multipler Tests for Linear and Logarithmic Regression Models", *Review of Economics and Statistics*, 1988.

Goldberger, A.S., "Best Linear Unbiased Prediction in the Linear Regression Model," *Journal of the American Statistical Association*, 1962.

Golub, G.H., and Styan, G.P.H., "Numerical Computations for Univariate Linear Models," *Journal of Statistical Computation and Simulation*, Vol. 2, 1973, pp. 253-274.

Gregory, A. and Veall, M., "On Formulating Wald Tests of Nonlinear Restrictions," *Econometrica*, Vol. 53, 1985, pp. 1465-1468.

Hausman, J.A., "Specification Tests in Econometrics," *Econometrica*, Vol.46, No.6, November 1978, pp.1251-1271.

Heckman, J.J., "Sample Bias as a Specification Error", *Econometrica*, Vol.47, No.1, January 1979, pp.153-161.

Hildreth, C., and Lu, J.Y., "Demand Relations with Autocorrelated Disturbances," *Technical Bulletin 276*, Michigan State University Agricultural Experiment Station, May 1960.

Jarque, C.M., and Bera, A.K., "Efficient Tests of Normality, Homoscedasticity and Serial Independence of Regression Residuals," *Economics Letters*, Vol. 6, 1980, pp. 255-259.

Imhof, J.P., "Computing the Distribution of Quadratic Forms in Normal Variables," *Biometrika*, Vol.48, 1961, pp. 419-426.

Kaiser, H.F., "Computer Program for Varimax Rotation in Factor Analysis," *Educational and Psychological Measurement*, Vol. XIX, 1959, pp.413-420.

Kiefer, N.M., "Economic Duration Data and Hazard FUnctions," *Journal of Economic Literature*, Vol. XXVI, June 1988, pp.646-679.

Kelejian, H., and Purcha, I., "Independent or Uncorrelated Disturbances in Linear Regression: An Illustration of the Difference", *Economics Letters*, Volume 19, No. 1, 1985, pp. 35-38.

Koenker, R., and Bassett, G., "Regression Quantiles", *Econometrica*, Volume 46, 1978, p.33-50.

Koenker, R., and D'Orey, V., "Computing Regression Quantiles", *Applied Statistics*, 1987.

Lafontaine, F., and White, K.J., "Obtaining Any Wald Statistic You Want," *Economics Letters*, Volume 21, No. 1, 1986, pp. 35-40.

McKelvey, R.D., and Zavoina, W., "A Statistical Model for the Analysis of Ordinal Level Dependent Variables," *Journal of Mathematical Sociology*, Vol. 4, 1975, pp. 103-120.

MacKinnon, J.G., and White, H., "Some Heteroskedasticity Consistent Covariance Matrix Estimators with Improved Finite Sample Properties," *Journal of Econometrics*, Vol. 29, September 1985, pp. 305-325.

Magee, L., "The Behaviour of a Modified Box-Cox Regression Model When Some Values of the Dependent Variable are Close to Zero," *Review of Economics and Statistics*, Vol. 70, 1988, pp. 362-366.

Mundlak, Y., "On the Concept of Non-Significant Functions and its Implications for Regression Analysis," *Journal of Econometrics*, Vol. 16, 1981, pp. 139-150.

Pagan, A.R., "A Generalized Approach to the Treatment of Autocorrelation," *Australian Economic Papers*, Vol. 13, 1974, pp. 267-280.

Pagan, A.R. and Hall, A.D., "Diagnostic Tests As Residual Analysis", *Econometric Reviews*, Vol. 2, 1983, pp. 159-218.

Pagan, A.R. and Nichols, D.F., "Estimating Predictions, Prediction Errors and their Standard Deviations Using Constructed Variables", *Journal of Econometrics*, Vol. 24, 1984, pp. 293-310.

Pan, Jie-Jian, "Distribution of Noncircular Serial Correlation Coefficients," *Selected Translations in Mathematical Statistics and Probability*, (Printed for the Institute of Mathematical Statistics by the American Mathematical Society), Vol. 7, 1968, pp. 281-291.

Poirier, D.J., "The Effect of the First Observation in Regression Models with First-order Autoregressive Disturbances," *Applied Statistics*, Vol. 27, No. 1, 1978, pp.67-68.

Ramsey, J.B., "Tests for Specification Errors in Classical Linear Least Squares Regression Analysis," *Journal of the Royal Statistical Society*, Ser. B, Pt. 2, 1969, pp.350-371.

Richardson, S.M., and White, K., "The Power of Tests for Autocorrelation with Missing Observations," *Econometrica*, May 1979, pp. 785-788.

Salkever, S., "The Use of Dummy Variables to Compute Predictions, Prediction Errors, and Confidence Intervals," *Journal of Econometrics*, Vol. 4, No. 4, November 1976, pp. 393-397.

Savin, N.E., "Conflict Among Testing Procedures in a Linear Regression Model With Autoregressive Disturbances," *Econometrica*, Vol. 44, No. 6, November 1976, pp. 1303-1315.

Savin, N.E., "Friedman-Meiselman Revisited: A Study in Autocorrelation," *Economic Inquiry*, Vol.16(1) 1978, pp.37-52.

Savin, N.E., and White, K.J., "Estimation and Testing for Functional Form and Autocorrelation: A Simultaneous Approach," *Journal of Econometrics*, Vol. 8, No. 1, August 1978, pp. 1-12.

Savin, N.E., and White, K.J., "The Durbin-Watson Test for Autocorrelation with Extreme Sample Sizes or Many Regressors," *Econometrica*, November 1977, pp. 1989-1996.

Savin, N.E., and White, K.J., "Testing for Autocorrelation With Missing Observations," *Econometrica*, January 1978, pp. 59-68.

Schmidt, P., "Estimation of a Distributed Lag Model With Second Order Autoregressive Disturbances: A Monte Carlo Experiment," *International Economic Review*, October 1971, pp.372-380.

Siddiqui, M. "Distribution of Quantiles in Samples from a Bivariate Population", *Journal of Research National Bureau of Standards Sect B. 64*, 1960, pp.145-150.

Tobin, J., "Estimation of Relationships for Limited Dependent Variables," *Econometrica*, 1958, pp. 24-36.

Vinod, H., "Generalization of the Durbin-Watson Statistic for Higher Order Autoregressive Processes," *Communications In Statistics*, Vol. 2, March 1973, pp. 115-144.

Watson, D.E., and White, K.J., "Forecasting the Demand for Money Under Changing Term Structure of Interest Rates: An Application of Ridge Regression," *Southern Economic Journal*, October 1976, Vol. 43, No. 2, pp. 1096-1105.

White, H., "A Heteroskedasticy-Consistent Covariance Matrix Estimator and a Direct Test for Heteroskedasticity," *Econometrica*, Vol. 48, 1980, pp.817-838.

White, H., "Using Least Squares to Approximate Unknown Regression Functions," *International Economic Review*, February 1980.

White, K.J., "Estimation of the Liquidity Trap With a Generalized Functional Form," *Econometrica*, January 1972, pp. 193-199.

White, K.J., "Consumer Choice and Use of Bank Credit Cards: A Model and Cross-Section Results," *Journal of Consumer Research*, June 1975, pp. 10-18.

White, K.J., "A General Computer Program for Econometric Methods - SHAZAM," *Econometrica*, January 1978, pp. 239-240.

White, K.J., "Applications in Econometrics: Problems, Programs, and Procedures," *Proceedings of the Third Annual Conference of the SAS Users Group International*, January 1978.

White, K.J., "SHAZAM: A General Computer Program for Econometric Methods (Version 5)," *American Statistician*, February 1987, Vol. 41, No.1, p. 80.

White, K.J., "SHAZAM: A Comprehensive Computer Program For Regression Models (Version 6)," *Computational Statistics & Data Analysis*, December 1988.

Zellner, A., "An Efficient Method of Estimating Seemingly Unrelated Regressions and Tests for Aggregation Bias," *Journal of the American Statistical Association*, Vol. 57, 1962, pp. 348-368.

Zellner, A., and Theil, H., "Three-stage Least Squares: Simultaneous Estimation of Simultaneous Equations," *Econometrica*, Vol. 30, pp. 54-78.

37. HOW TO RUN SHAZAM

"Every regression matters."

Angela Redish
1986

A. *HOW TO RUN* SHAZAM *ON MTS OPERATING SYSTEMS*

SHAZAM is available in the file *SHAZAM at the University of British Columbia. Other MTS installations may use a different filename. SHAZAM commands may be up to 255 characters long and may be typed in upper or lower case.

EXAMPLE 1

To run SHAZAM when your data is not in a separate file use:

$RUN *SHAZAM
SAMPLE *beg end*
READ *vars / options*
(data goes here)
(other commands go here)
STOP

EXAMPLE 2

If your data is in a separate file, it should enter SHAZAM on units 11-49:

$RUN *SHAZAM 11 = *datafilename*
SAMPLE *beg end*
READ(11) *vars / options*
(other commands go here)
STOP

EXAMPLE 3

You could have all your SHAZAM commands and data together in one file which should be read from unit 5 as follows:

$RUN *SHAZAM 5 = *myfile*

EXAMPLE 4

You could have all commands in one file and data in another, as follows:

$RUN *SHAZAM 5 = *commandfile* **11** = *datafile*

EXAMPLE 5

Sometimes you will want to use the **WRITE** command to write data into a file. In this case you must assign units 11-49 to the filename. Be sure to **$CREATE** the file first:

$CREATE *writefilename*
$RUN *SHAZAM 16 = *writefilename*
SAMPLE *beg end*
.
.
.
WRITE(16) *vars / options*
(other commands go here)
STOP

EXAMPLE 6

Frequently, users want to be relieved of counting the number of observations in their data and wish they did not have to specify this number on the **SAMPLE** command. It is possible to have SHAZAM do the counting for you if you do not specify the number of observations on the **SAMPLE** command and your data is in a separate file:

$RUN *SHAZAM 11 = *datafile*
READ(11) *vars*
(other commands)

The use of this feature saves a lot of trouble. SHAZAM will just read the whole file unless a **SAMPLE** command specifies the number of observations to be read. Note that if you use the **BYVAR** option on the **READ** command then you are not allowed to have SHAZAM do your counting as the correct number of observations must be specified on a **SAMPLE** command.

EXAMPLE 7

If you use **READ** commands to read from several files, the run might look like this:

$RUN *SHAZAM 11 = *data1* **12** = *data2* **13** = *data3*
SAMPLE *beg end*
READ(11) *vars*
READ(12) *vars*

READ(13) *vars*
(other commands)
STOP

EXAMPLE 8

If you use the **OUT=** and **IN=** options in a **SYSTEM** or **NL** problem, the first run would look something like this:

$CREATE *restartfile*
$RUN *SHAZAM *unit*=restartfile
SAMPLE *beg end*
.
.
.
SYSTEM 3 / DN ITER= 10 OUT= *unit*
OLS *depvar indeps*
OLS *depvar indeps*
OLS *depvar indeps*
STOP

where *unit* is any MTS unit number from 11 to 49.

In the next run, to restart where you left off, you should eliminate the **$CREATE** command and add the **IN=** option. The **SYSTEM** command might read as follows:

SYSTEM DN ITER= 20 OUT= *unit* **IN=** *unit*

In this case, the model will continue at the point it left off in the first run and update the file on the specified unit (i.e. the contents of the file assigned to a unit) up to iteration 20. Do not attempt to use the **IN=** option before you have anything to **IN**put.

In a **SYSTEM**, the file can be quite large in large models, so you should be certain that you have ample file space left in your computer account.

EXAMPLE 9

To run SHAZAM and use the **MAP** command, type:

$RUN *SHAZAM(2)
MAP / *options*
STOP

The **MAP** command is only available on systems with the DISSPLA graphics package.

RUNNING OUT OF MEMORY

When SHAZAM is unable to run a problem because of insufficient memory, you will usually get a message telling you how to set the PAR= value. The PAR= value specifies the amount of memory (in batches of 1024 bytes) that is needed. If you need to specify the PAR= value, it should be the *last* item on the **$RUN** command. For example, if you run SHAZAM and get the message:

RUN AGAIN WITH PAR=284

you should then use:

$RUN *SHAZAM PAR=284

If you also need to assign a unit be sure to put the PAR= value last, or the units won't get assigned. The default is PAR=40. Since you pay for memory, you will not want to set the PAR= value higher than is necessary. For small problems, the default (40) is sufficient. Details on the **PAR** command can be found in the chapter *MISCELLANEOUS COMMANDS AND INFORMATION*.

SUBMITTING A BATCH JOB FROM A TERMINAL

It is possible to save computer funds by submitting a batch job to run SHAZAM. To do this you would normally have all your commands in a file as in Examples 3 and 4. You may then submit a batch job from your terminal using the *BATCH program. This program requires that you type a **$SIGNON** command with a * instead of your CCID. You should then enter your SHAZAM **$RUN** command and when this is finished type **$SIGNOFF**. For example:

$RUN *BATCH
$SIGNON * *options*
$RUN *SHAZAM 5=*commandfile* 11=*datafile*
$SIGNOFF

The **$SIGNOFF** command above is for the *BATCH program. It will not cause your terminal session to end. The command and data files must be permanent files unless they are created in the Batch job. The *BATCH program will submit your job and it will print out on the system printer. There are many options you can put on the **$SIGNON** command to increase time and print limits, set low priority to save more money, and route or deliver your output. Three commonly used options are P= and T= and PRIO=L. The P= option sets the page limit. The default in batch mode is 20 pages. The T= option sets the time limit. If you exceed the time limit you can reset it to a higher value. The PRIO=L option will run your job at low priority at very low cost.

You will find that large amounts of money can be saved by submitting Batch jobs, especially low priority Batch jobs.

SUMMARY OF INPUT-OUTPUT UNITS

1-3	Internal use. Not available to the user.
5	SHAZAM commands and input data stream; defaults to *SOURCE*.
6	Output unit; defaults to *SINK*. If unit 6 is assigned to a file it will be EMPTIED by SHAZAM before each use.
8-10	Internal use. Not available to the user.
11-49	Available to user.
50-99	Internal use. Not available to the user.

B. *HOW TO RUN* SHAZAM *ON IBM OS/VS/MVS/TSO*

This section tells how to run SHAZAM under IBM OS/VS/MVS/TSO operating systems. SHAZAM commands may be up to 80 columns. SHAZAM will check if line numbers are in columns 73-80 , and, if so, will only scan commands to column 72. This check is performed by testing whether "00" is in columns 73-74 of the first command. Exact JCL may differ at different installations. Do not use the SHAZAM **FILE** command to assign files. Note that these instructions may differ for each installation.

EXAMPLE 1

To run SHAZAM when your data is not in a separate file, use:

```
//    EXEC SHAZAM
//SYSIN DD *
SAMPLE beg end
READ vars
.
.
.
STOP
//
```

EXAMPLE 2

If your data is in a separate file, for example, unit 11, it should enter SHAZAM as follows:

```
//    EXEC SHAZAM
//FT11F001 DD DSN=userid.dataname.data,DISP=SHR
//SYSIN DD *
SAMPLE beg end
READ(11) vars
.
.
.
STOP
//
```

EXAMPLE 3

You could have all your SHAZAM commands and data together in one file which should be read from SYSIN as follows:

```
//    EXEC SHAZAM
//SYSIN DD DSN=userid.myfile.data,DISP=SHR
//
```

EXAMPLE 4

You could have all commands in one file and data in another file as follows:

```
//      EXEC SHAZAM
//FT11F001 DD DSN=userid.dataname.data,DISP=SHR
//SYSIN DD DSN=userid.myfile.data,DISP=SHR
//
```

EXAMPLE 5

Sometimes you will request output with the **WRITE** command and will need to assign a file to receive the output. For example, if unit 16 is used:

```
//      EXEC SHAZAM
//FT16F001 DD DSN=userid.write.data,DISP=(NEW,CATLG),UNIT=SYSDA,
// DCB=(RECFM=FB,LRECL=130,BLKSIZE=5320),SPACE=(TRK,(5,5),RLSE)
//SYSIN DD *
SAMPLE beg end
READ vars
WRITE(16) vars
.
.
.
STOP
//
```

If you want your **WRITE** output to be punched out on cards then use:

```
//FT16F001 DD SYSOUT=B
```

EXAMPLE 6

Frequently, users want to be relieved of counting the number of observations in their data and wish they did not have to specify this number on the **SAMPLE** command. It is possible to have SHAZAM do the counting for you if you do not specify the number of observations on the **SAMPLE** command and your data is in a separate file:

```
//      EXEC SHAZAM
//FT11F001 DD DSN=userid.dataname.data,DISP=SHR
//SYSIN DD *
READ(11) A B C D E
.
.
.
STOP
//
```

The use of this feature saves a lot of trouble. SHAZAM will just read the whole file unless the **SAMPLE** command specifies the number of observations to be read. Note that if you use the **BYVAR** option on the **READ** command, you are not allowed to have SHAZAM do your counting as the correct number of observations must be specified on the **SAMPLE** command.

EXAMPLE 7

If you use the **OUT=** and **IN=** options in a **SYSTEM** or **NL** problem, the first run will look something like this:


```
//     EXEC SHAZAM
//FT17F001 DD DSN= userid.save.data,DISP= (NEW,CATLG),UNIT= SYSDA,
// DCB= (RECFM= VBS,LRECL= 1000,BLKSIZE= 8008),SPACE= (TRK,(5,5),RLSE)
//SYSIN DD *
.
.
.
SYSTEM 3 / DN ITER= 10 OUT= 17
OLS depvar indeps
OLS depvar indeps
OLS depvar indeps
END
STOP
//
```

This would save the estimates on unit 17. In the next run, to restart where you left off, you should use **DISP=SHR** instead of **DISP=(NEW,CATLG)** and rerun the model and add the **IN=** option, so the **SYSTEM** command might read:

SYSTEM 3 / DN ITER= 20 OUT= 17 IN= 17

In this case the model will continue at the point it left off in the first run and update the file on unit 17 until iteration 20. Do not attempt to use the **IN=** option before you have anything to INput. In a **SYSTEM** the file can be quite large in large models so you should be certain that you can afford to pay disk storage charges. In an **NL** problem the file will be quite small. Units 11-49 are available for use.

EXAMPLE 8

If you use **READ** commands to read from several files, the setup might look like this:


```
//     EXEC SHAZAM
//FT11F001 DD DSN= userid.data1.data,DISP= SHR
//FT12F001 DD DSN= userid.data2.data,DISP= SHR
//FT13F001 DD DSN= userid.data3.data,DISP= SHR
//SYSIN DD *
SAMPLE beg end
READ(11) vars
```

READ(12) *vars*
READ(13) *vars*
(other commands)
STOP
//

If any //**FT** command is included it should be placed before the //**SYSIN** statement. The //**SYSIN** statement is always the last **DD** statement.

RUNNING OUT OF MEMORY

Whenever SHAZAM is unable to run a problem because of insufficient memory you will get a message telling you how to set the PAR= and REGION= values. These parameters are needed for internal storage and for the whole program respectively. The PAR= and REGION= parameters are specified on the EXEC card. For example, if you run SHAZAM and get this message:

RUN AGAIN WITH AT LEAST PAR=292 OR REGION=496K

you should then use:

//   **EXEC SHAZAM,REGION=496K**

Some VS1 systems will require that you *always* use PAR= and not REGION=:

//   **EXEC SHAZAM,PAR=292**

In most cases it is not necessary to include the PAR= value since it will be determined automatically from the REGION. If you are using files with large block sizes you may need to increase the REGION while keeping PAR constant in order to leave room for the input buffers. This problem may arise if the program bombs with an 80A or 804 error message. Since you pay for memory you will not want to set the REGION higher than is necessary. For most problems you will not have to worry about either of these. The REGION is at least 200 greater than PAR. Some installations may require REGION or PAR values much higher than the suggested values. Note further that the REGION size is followed by a K where the PAR is not. Do *not* use the SHAZAM **PAR** command to raise the PAR value. On the IBM operating system it will not work; you may only raise it on the EXEC statement.

SHAZAM *AT A TERMINAL WITH TSO*

Once you LOGON, and TSO answers with READY, you may either allocate files or begin execution of SHAZAM. If your data is in a file you should type:

ALLOC FI(FT11F001) DA(*my.data***) SHR**

This command is the TSO equivalent of the //FT11F001 JCL statement.

If you need to allocate files for other uses (for example, unit 16), and the file does not already exist, type:

ALLOC FI(FT16F001) DA(*more.data***) DISP(NEW)**

If the file already exists, type:

ALLOC FI(FT16F001) DA(*more.data***) SHR**

The command ALLOC FI( ) DA( ), with the brackets filled according to the task you wish to accomplish, is the TSO equivalents of the //FT JCL statement.

After all files are allocated, run SHAZAM by typing:

SHAZAM

or if all your SHAZAM commands are in a file, type:

SHAZAM IN(*myfile.data***)**

If you wish to have your output go into a file instead of to the screen, type:

SHAZAM IN(*myfile.data***) OUT(***myout.data***)**

This statement will begin execution of the program. With a little care you can easily run SHAZAM interactively at a terminal. The procedure is exactly the same as in batch except some of the usual output will be deleted unless specifically requested. At a terminal, it is almost always useful to have your data in a file. This is not necessary if you want to input your data directly. However direct data input is not recommended since an error would require that you start again.

At a terminal, keep output to a minimum. If you are in the middle of a subproblem procedure and you want to stop execution simply press ATTN or BREAK. SHAZAM will then stop execution. Unfortunately, you will then be kicked out of the program and will have to start all over again. TSO is not yet smart enough to recover from an attention interrupt.

A nicer way to end a terminal session is to type **STOP** and SHAZAM will stop.

If you need more memory when running at a terminal you should attempt to LOGON with a higher region by using the appropriate option on the LOGON command.

One final warning is probably appropriate here. Beginners should probably not attempt to use SHAZAM under TSO until they have mastered TSO. Users will find that everything they do under TSO costs substantially more than in Batch. **TSO** is not always smart enough to know the difference between **TALK** mode and **TERMINAL** mode in **SHAZAM**. Therefore, when running in interactive **TALK** mode, it would be wise to type **SET TALK** as your first command. See the chapter **SET AND DISPLAY** for more details.

C. *HOW TO RUN* SHAZAM *ON IBM VM/CMS*

This section tells how to run SHAZAM under IBM VM/CMS operating systems. SHAZAM commands may be up to 80 columns long. SHAZAM will check if line numbers are in columns 73-80, and, if so, will only scan commands to column 72. This check is performed by testing whether "00" is in columns 73-74 of the first command. Do not use the SHAZAM **FILE** command to assign files. Do not use the character '#' in **DO**-loops as this often signifies the end of a line on CMS. Instead, you may use the characters $,!,%, or some other strange character. SHAZAM will not run in a 1 Meg machine so you should arrange to have at least 2 Meg of memory. Note that these instructions may differ for each installation. In the examples below CMS commands are typed in lower case to distinguish them from SHAZAM commands.

EXAMPLE 1

To run SHAZAM when your data is not in a separate file, use:

shazam
SAMPLE *beg end*
READ *vars*
.
.
.
STOP

EXAMPLE 2

If your data is in a separate file, for example unit 11, it should enter SHAZAM as follows:

filedef 11 disk *datafilename filetype*
shazam
SAMPLE *beg end*
READ(11) *vars*
.
.
.
(other commands)
STOP

EXAMPLE 3

You could have all your SHAZAM commands and data together in one file which should be read as shown below. The filetype of your command file must have filetype: SHAZAM.

shazam *myfile*

If you wish to have your output go in a file you would type:

shazam *myfile myoutput*

Your listing from the above run will be in the file *myoutput* with a filetype of: LISTING.

EXAMPLE 4

You could have all commands in one file and data in another file as follows:

filedef 11 disk *datafilename filetype*
shazam *commandfile*

EXAMPLE 5

Sometimes you will request output with the **WRITE** command and will need to assign a file to receive the output. For example, if unit 16 is used:

filedef 16 disk *writefile filetype* **a(lrecl 130 recfm fb blksize 5200)**
shazam
SAMPLE *beg end*
READ *vars*
WRITE(16) *vars*
.
.
.
STOP

EXAMPLE 6

Frequently, users want to be relieved of counting the number of observations in their data and wish they did not have to specify this number on the **SAMPLE** command. It is possible to have SHAZAM do the counting for you if you do not specify the number of observations on the **SAMPLE** command and your data is in a separate file:

filedef 11 disk *datafilename filetype*
shazam
READ(11) A B C D E
.
.
.
STOP

The use of this feature saves a lot of trouble. SHAZAM will just read the whole file unless the **SAMPLE** command specifies the number of observations to be read. Note that if you use the

BYVAR option on the **READ** command you are not allowed to have SHAZAM do your counting because the correct number of observations must be specified on the **SAMPLE** command.

EXAMPLE 7

If you use the **OUT=** and **IN=** options in a **SYSTEM** or **NL** problem, the first run will look something like this:

filedef 17 disk *resfile filetype* **a(lrecl 1000 recfm vbs blksize 8008**
shazam
.
.
.
SYSTEM 3 / DN ITER= 10 OUT= 17
OLS *depvar indeps*
OLS *depvar indeps*
OLS *depvar indeps*
END
STOP

This will save the estimates on unit 17. In the next run, to restart where you left off, you should rerun the model and add the **IN=** option, so the **SYSTEM** command might read:

SYSTEM 3 / DN ITER= 20 OUT= 17 IN= 17

In this case the model will continue at the point it left off in in the first run and update the file on unit 17 until iteration20. Do not attempt to use the **IN=** option before you have anything to **IN**put. In a **SYSTEM** the file can be quite large in large models so you should be certain that you can afford to pay disk storage charges. In an **NL** problem the file will be quite small.

EXAMPLE 8

If you use **READ** commands to read from several files, the setup might look like this:

filedef 11 disk *data1 filetype*
filedef 12 disk *data1 filetype*
filedef 13 disk *data1 filetype*
SAMPLE *beg end*
READ(11) *vars*
READ(12) *vars*
READ(13) *vars*
(other commands)
STOP

If you need more memory use the appropriate CMS command to provide more memory. See your local SHAZAM consultant for details. It is necessary that you run SHAZAM in a 2 Meg or larger machine.

D. *HOW TO RUN* SHAZAM *ON CDC UNDER NOS*

This section illustrates how to use SHAZAM on the Control Data Cyber 170 under NOS operating system. In the examples below CDC commands are typed in lower case to distinguish them from SHAZAM commands, although, in practice, all commands are typed in upper case. SHAZAM commands may be up to 80 columns long. WARNING: The instructions in this section may differ for each installation.

EXAMPLE 1

To run SHAZAM when your data is not in a separate file use:

> **attach,shazam/un = lib**
> **shazam.**
> **/eor**
> **SAMPLE** *beg end*
> **READ** *vars*
> (other commands)
> **STOP**

EXAMPLE 2

If your data is in a separate file (called mydat), it may enter SHAZAM on unit 11 as follows:

> **attach,shazam/un = lib**
> **get,tape11 = mydat.**
> **shazam.**
> **/eor**
> **SAMPLE** *beg end*
> **READ(11)** *vars*
> (Data is read from file: mydat)
> (other commands)
> **/eor**

EXAMPLE 3

You could have all your SHAZAM commands and data together in one file (called myshaz) which should be read from the standard input unit as follows:

> **attach,shazam/un = lib**
> **get,myshaz.**
> **shazam,myshaz.**
> **/eor**

EXAMPLE 4

You could have all commands in one file (mycmds) and data in another file (mydat), as follows:

```
attach,shazam/un=lib
get,tape11=mydat.
get,mycmds.
shazam.
/eor
```

EXAMPLE 5

Sometimes you will want to request **WRITE** output using some SHAZAM option and will want it placed in a file. In this case you must assign unit 16 to the filename:

```
attach,shazam/un=lib
shazam.
save,tape16=myjunk.
/eor
SAMPLE beg end
READ vars
WRITE(16) vars / options
.
(other commands)
STOP
/eor
```

EXAMPLE 6

If you use the **OUT=** and **IN=** options in a **SYSTEM** or **NL** problem, the first run will look something like this:

```
attach,shazam/un=lib
shazam.
save,tape17=sdump.
/eor
SAMPLE beg end
READ vars
(other commands)
SYSTEM 3 / DN ITER=10 OUT=17
OLS depvar indeps
OLS depvar indeps
OLS depvar indeps
END
STOP
/eor
```

In the next run, to restart where you left off, you should use the following control cards and add the **IN=** option:

```
attach,shazam/un = lib
get,tape17 = sdump.
shazam.
save,tape17 = sdump2.
/eor
SAMPLE beg end
READ vars
(other commands)
SYSTEM 3 / DN ITER = 20 IN = 17 OUT = 17
OLS depvar indeps
OLS depvar indeps
OLS depvar indeps
END
STOP
/eor
```

In this case, the model will continue at the point it left off in the first run and update the file on tape17 until iteration 20. Do not attempt to use the **IN=** option before you have anything to INput.

In a **SYSTEM**, the file can be quite large in large models. Be certain that the resulting disk files will not exceed your permanent file limits and that you can afford to pay the disk storage charges. In an **NL** problem the file will be quite small.

EXAMPLE 7

If you use **READ** commands to read from several files, the setup might look like this:

```
attach,shazam/un = lib
get,tape11 = dat1.
get,tape12 = dat2.
get,tape13 = dat3.
shazam.
/eor
SAMPLE beg end
READ(11) vars
READ(12) vars
READ(13) vars
(other commands)
STOP
/eor
```

EXAMPLE 8

When SHAZAM is unable to run a problem because of insufficient memory, you will usually get a message telling you how to set the **PAR** value. The **PAR** value specifies the amount of memory (in batches of 1024 bytes) that is needed. If you need to specify the **PAR** value, it should be done with the **PAR** command. For example, if you run SHAZAM and get the message:

RUN AGAIN WITH PAR=64

you should then use:

> **attach,shazam/un = lib**
> **shazam.**
> **/eor**
> **PAR 64**
> **SAMPLE** *beg end*
> **READ** *vars*
> (other commands)
> **STOP**

If used, the **PAR** command must be the first command in the SHAZAM run. The **PAR** command determines the maximum amount of memory available for internal SHAZAM workspace. The current default value of **PAR** is 20 which, for example, would quite easily handle a run with 20 variables and 50 observations. For most problems you will not have to worry about use of the **PAR** command.

USING SHAZAM *INTERACTIVELY AT A TERMINAL*

Users are referred to Control Data manuals such as the *NOS Time-Sharing Reference Manual* and the *Test Editor Manual* for instructions on how to logon, create files interactively, save permanent files and run Pseudo-Batch jobs. With a little care, you can easily run SHAZAM interactively at a terminal. The procedure is exactly the same as in batch except some of the usual output will be deleted unless specifically requested. First, you will probably need to assign files:

If your data is in a permanent file (mydat), type:

get,tape11 = mydat.

If you are using a file created in a previous SHAZAM run, for example unit 12, type:

get,tape12 = file.

To make SHAZAM available to your program, type:

get,shazam/un = lib

After all files are allocated you run SHAZAM by typing:

shazam.

This statement will begin execution of the program. The prompt is now: ?. The first command to be entered when prompted will usually be **SET TALK**. This will tell SHAZAM that you are at an interactive terminal. The next command will usually be **SAMPLE**. At a terminal, it is almost always useful to have your data in a file. This is not necessary if you want to input your data directly. However, direct data input is not recommended since an error would require that you start over.

At a terminal, keep output to a minimum. If you are in the middle of a subproblem procedure and you want to stop execution, simply hit the ATTN or BREAK key. SHAZAM will then interrupt execution. To resume SHAZAM, press RETURN. Unfortunately, once a SHAZAM command (for example, **OLS**) has begun execution, the only way to terminate execution of that option is to terminate SHAZAM completely.

To terminate SHAZAM completely, type CNTRL T (hold down the CNTRL key while typing T) then RETURN.

A nicer way to end a terminal session is to type **STOP**. To end the Terminal Session type BYE in response to the System Prompt: /.

E. *HOW TO RUN* SHAZAM *ON CDC UNDER NOS/VE*

This section illustrates how to use SHAZAM on the Control Data Cyber 180 under the NOS/VE operating system. SHAZAM commands may be up to 80 columns long. In the examples below CDS NOS/VE commands are displayed in lower case to distinguish them from SHAZAM commands. WARNING: The instructions in this section may differ for each installation.

EXAMPLE 1

To run SHAZAM when your data is not in a separate file use:

shazam
SAMPLE *beg end*
READ *vars*
(data goes here)
(other commands)
STOP

EXAMPLE 2

If your data is in a separate file (called mydat), it should enter SHAZAM on unit 11 as follows:

attf mydat tape11
shazam
SAMPLE *beg end*
READ(11) *vars*
(other commands)
STOP

EXAMPLE 3

You could have all your SHAZAM commands and data together in one file (called myshaz) which should be read as follows:

attf myshaz
shazam myshaz

You could have the output from the run placed into a file with:

attf myshaz
cref myoutput
shazam myshaz myoutput

EXAMPLE 4

You could have all commands in one file (mycmds) and data in another file (mydat), as follows:

attf mydat tape11
attf mycmds tape5
shazam mycmds

EXAMPLE 5

Sometimes you may want to use the **WRITE** command to write a file. In this case, you must assign a file to a unit:

cref mywrite tape16
shazam
SAMPLE *beg end*
READ *vars*
WRITE (16) vars
(other commands)
STOP

EXAMPLE 6

Users frequently wish to be relieved of counting the number of observations in their data; they do not want to have to put this number on the **SAMPLE** command. You can have SHAZAM do the counting for you by omitting the **SAMPLE** command and by placing your data in a separate file. When the data is in a separate file and there is no **SAMPLE** command in effect SHAZAM reads to the end of the data file referenced by a **READ** command:

attf mydat tape11
shazam
READ(11) *vars*
(other commands)
STOP

The use of this feature eliminates a lot of work. Note that if you are using the **BYVAR** option to read your data you are not allowed to have SHAZAM do your counting as the correct number of observations must be specified on the **SAMPLE** command.

EXAMPLE 7

If you use the **OUT=** and **IN=** options in a **SYSTEM** or **NL** problem, the first run will look something like this:

cref sdump tape17
attf sdump tape17
shazam
SAMPLE *beg end*
READ *vars*
(other commands)
SYSTEM 3 / DN ITER= 10 OUT= 17
OLS *depvar indeps*
OLS *depvar indeps*
OLS *depvar indeps*
END
STOP

In the next run the **SYSTEM** command is replaced with:

SYSTEM 3 / DN ITER= 20 OUT= 17 IN= 17

The model will continue at the point it left off in the first run and update the file on tape17 until iteration 20. Do not attempt to use the IN= option before you have anything to **IN**put.

In a **SYSTEM**, the file can be quite large in large models. Be certain that the resulting disk files will not exceed your permanent file limits and that you can afford to pay the disk storage charges. In an **NL** problem the file will be quite small.

EXAMPLE 8

If you use **READ** commands to merge files, the setup might look like this:

attf dat1 tape11
attf dat2 tape12
attf dat3 tape13
shazam
SAMPLE *beg end*
READ(11) *vars*
READ(12) *vars*
READ(13) *vars*
(other commands)
STOP

RUNNING OUT OF MEMORY

When SHAZAM is unable to run a problem because of insufficient memory, you will usually get a message telling you how to set the **PAR** value. The **PAR** value specifies the amount of memory (in batches of 1024 bytes) that is needed. If you need to increase the **PAR** value you will need to ask your system programmer to recompile SUBROUTINE DOCDC and raise the amount of workspace.

USING SHAZAM INTERACTIVELY AT A TERMINAL

With a little care, you can easily run SHAZAM interactively at a terminal. The procedure is exactly the same as in batch, except some of the usual output will be deleted unless specifically requested. First, you willll probably need to assign files. This is usually done with the NOS/VE ATTF command. After all files are assigned, run SHAZAM by typing:

shazam

This statement will begin execution of the program. The prompt is now: ?. The first command to be entered when prompted will usually be **SET TALK.** This will tell SHAZAM that you are at an interactive terminal. The next command will usually be **SAMPLE.** At a terminal, it is almost always useful to have your data in a file. This is not necessary if you want to input your data directly. However, direct data input is not recommended since an error would require that you start over.

At a terminal, keep output to a minimum. If you are in the middle of a subproblem procedure and you want to stop execution, simply hit the ATTN or BREAK key. SHAZAM will then interrupt execution. To resume SHAZAM, press RETURN.

Unfortunately, once a SHAZAM option (for example, **OLS**) has begun execution, the only way to terminate execution of that option is to terminate SHAZAM completely.

To terminate SHAZAM completely, type CNTRL T (hold down the CNTRL key while typing T) then RETURN.

A nicer way to end a terminal session after running some subproblems is to type **STOP**.

If during an interactive SHAZAM session you wish to enter an SCL command to the system (for example, an ATTF command) it can be entered by preceding the command with a /. The command will be executed without leaving SHAZAM.

F. *HOW TO RUN* SHAZAM *ON HARRIS*

This section explains how to run SHAZAM on HARRIS computers using the VOS operating system Release 2.2 or later. SHAZAM commands may be up to 80 characters long. In the examples below HARRIS System commands are displayed in lower case to distinguish them from SHAZAM commands. WARNING: The instructions in this chapter may differ for each installation.

EXAMPLE 1

To run SHAZAM when your data is not in a separate file, type:

shazam
SAMPLE *beg end*
READ *vars*
(data goes here)
(other commands)
STOP

EXAMPLE 2

If your data is in a separate file assigned to unit 11, you should use the **as** command to assign it on the SHAZAM command as follows:

as 11 = *mydata*
shazam
SAMPLE *beg end*
READ(11) *vars*
(data is read from *datafile*)
STOP

EXAMPLE 3

You could have all your SHAZAM commands and data together in one file which should be read as follows:

shazam *myfile*

You could also have the output go into a file rather than come to the screen if you specify a name for the output file as follows:

shazam *myfile outfile*

EXAMPLE 4

You could have all commands in one file and data in another file, as follows:

as 11=*mydata*
shazam *commandfile*

EXAMPLE 5

Sometimes you will want to request **WRITE** output using some SHAZAM option and will want it placed in a file. In this case, you must assign unit 16 to the filename. This can be done with the **as** command.

as 16=*writefile*
shazam
SAMPLE *beg end*
READ *vars*
(other commands)
WRITE(16) *vars*
(other commands)
STOP

EXAMPLE 6

If you use the **OUT**= and **IN**= options in a **SYSTEM** or **NL** problem, the first run would ASSIGN unit 17 as follows:

as 17= *savefile*
shazam
SAMPLE *beg end*
READ *vars*
(other commands)
SYSTEM 3 / DN ITER= 10 **OUT**= 17
OLS *depvar indeps*
OLS *depvar indeps*
OLS *depvar indeps*
END
STOP

In the next run, to restart where you left off, you should add the **IN**= option. The **SYSTEM** command might read:

SYSTEM 3 / DN ITER= 10 **OUT**= 17 **IN**= 17

In this case, the model will continue at the point it left off in the first run and update the file on unit 17 (i.e. the contents of the file *savefile*) up to iteration 20. Do not attempt to use the **IN**=

option before you have anything to **IN**put. In a **SYSTEM**, the file can be quite large in large models. In an **NL** problem the file will be quite small.

EXAMPLE 7

If you use **READ** commands to merge files, the setup might look like this:

as 11 = *data1*
as 12 = *data2*
as 13 = *data3*
shazam
SAMPLE *beg end*
READ(11) *vars*
READ(12) *vars*
READ(13) *vars*
(other commands)
STOP

RUNNING OUT OF MEMORY

When SHAZAM is unable to run a problem because of insufficient memory, you will usually get a message telling you how to set the **PAR** value. The **PAR** value specifies the amount of memory (in batches of 1024 bytes) that is needed. For example, if you run SHAZAM and get the message:

RUN AGAIN WITH PAR = 64

you should then ask your local SHAZAM consultant to recompile SUBROUTINE DOHAR and raise the size of the workspace.

USING **SHAZAM** *INTERACTIVELY AT A TERMINAL*

With a little care, you can easily run SHAZAM interactively at a terminal. The procedure is exactly the same as in batch, except that some of the usual output will be deleted unless specifically requested. At a terminal, it is almost always useful to have your data in a file. This is not necessary if you want to input your data directly. However, direct data input is not recommended since an error would require that you start over.

At a terminal, keep output to a minimum. If you are in the middle of a subproblem procedure and you want to stop execution, simply hit the ATTN or BREAK key. SHAZAM will then stop.

G. *HOW TO RUN* SHAZAM *ON HONEYWELL CP-6*

This is most easily done by building job files at your terminal and submitting them via the !BATCH command, or you can run SHAZAM on-line. Additional information for on-line use is included later in this document. WARNING: The instructions in this section may differ for each installation.

The following examples show the Job Control commands required to run SHAZAM with various input and output options. Lower case letters are used to indicate places where you must substitute appropriate values. The substitutions are:

!JOB *acct#,acctname, pass* WSN = *workstation name*

where you replace *acct#* with your CP-6 account number, *acctname* with your CP-6 account name, *pass* with your CP-6 account password, and *workstation* with a CP-6 workstation name. By using the WSN = specification you can direct your printed output to a workstation.

!RESOURCE TIME = *tt*,MEM = *mm*

where you replace *tt* with minutes of CPU time required, and *mm* with the amount of memory required.

Most SHAZAM jobs will run within a time limit of TIME = 2, and a memory size of MEM = 40. Note that you can use the default memory allocation of 64, but you will pay for 64K words even if you did not need them. SHAZAM runs that include SYSTEM equations require substantially more memory than other types of runs.

Note: For those users familiar with standard program invocation, SHAZAM can be invoked using the form:

!SHAZAM *command fid* OVER *output fid*

EXAMPLE 1

To submit a SHAZAM job when your SHAZAM commands and your data are together in a file, use the following Job Control commands:

!JOB *acct#,acctname,pass* WSN = *workstation name*
!RESOURCE TIME = *tt*,MEM = *mm*
!SHAZAM
SHAZAM control commands and data
.
.
.

EXAMPLE 2

If your data is in a separate disk file assigned to unit 11, you should use the following Job Control commands:

!JOB *acct#,acctname,pass* **WSN** = *workstation name*
!RESOURCE TIME = *tt*,**MEM** = *mm*
!SET 11 *fid*
!SHAZAM
SAMPLE *beg end*
READ(11) *vars*
.
.
(other SHAZAM commands)
.
.

EXAMPLE 3

Sometimes you may want to request that output from the **WRITE** command be put in a file. You **must** supply a **!SET** command to direct the output to some destination. For example, to direct the output to a file, you need the following Job Control commands:

!JOB *acct#,acctname,pass* **WSN** = *workstation name*
!RESOURCE TIME = *tt*,**MEM** = *mm*
!SET 16 *fid*,**FUN** = **CREATE**
!SHAZAM
.
.
WRITE(16) ...
.
.

To direct the **WRITE** output to the lineprinter, use the following **!SET** command instead:

!SET 16 LO

EXAMPLE 4

If you use **READ** commands to merge files where you have specified units 11 and 12, you need the following Job Control commands:

!JOB *acct#,acctname,pass* **WSN** = *workstation name*
!RESOURCE TIME = *tt*,**MEM** = *mm*
!SET 11 *fid*
!SET 12 *fid*
!SHAZAM

.
.
READ(11) *vars*
READ(12) *vars*
.
(other SHAZAM commands)
STOP

EXAMPLE 5

If you use the **OUT=** option in a **SYSTEM** or **NL** problem the Job Control commands required are:

!JOB *acct#,acctname,pass* **WSN**=*workstation name*
!RESOURCE TIME=*tt*,**MEM**=*mem*
!SET 17 *fid*,**FUN**=**CREATE**
!SHAZAM
.
SHAZAM control commands and data

In the next run to restart where you left off, you use the **IN=** option and change your **SET** command as follows:

!SET 17 *fid*,**FUN**=**UPDATE**

It is possible to use both the **IN=** and **OUT=** options together, when your **!SET** specifies **FUN**=**UPDATE**. For example, the **SYSTEM** command might be:

SYSTEM 3 DN ITER=**20 OUT**=**17 IN**=**17**

In this case, the model will continue at the point it left off in the first run and update the file on unit 17 until iteration 20. Do not attempt to use the **IN=** option before you have anything to **IN**put. In a **SYSTEM** the file can be quite large in large models so you should be certain that you have enough disk space in your account and can afford to pay the disk storage costs. In an **NL** problem the file will be quite small.

RUNNING **SHAZAM** *ON-LINE*

You can run SHAZAM in *command file* mode as follows:

If your SHAZAM control commands and data are in one file, use:

!SHAZAM *fid*

If your data is in a separate file, use:

!SET 11 *fid*

If you want to capture the printed output in a file, use:

!SHAZAM *command fid OVER output fid*

To copy the *output fid* to the lineprinter at your workstation, use:

!COPY *output fid* **TO LPW***orkstation name***(VFC,FVFC)**

If you are making use of other SHAZAM input or output options, you must specify the appropriate **SET**s as discussed above, before invoking the program.

To exit SHAZAM when you are finished type **STOP**. To interrupt SHAZAM in the middle of execution type CTRL Y.

ADDITIONAL INFORMATION

LETTING SHAZAM *COUNT THE NUMBER OF OBSERVATIONS*

It is not necessary to specify on the **SAMPLE** command the number of observations in your data if your data is in a separate data file. If your data is in the same file as your SHAZAM control commands, you can omit the **SAMPLE** command and specify unit 11 on your **READ** command. Your data file would have previously been specified with the **!SET** command. When there is no **SAMPLE** command and the data is in a separate file, SHAZAM reads to the end of file on a **READ** command.

SAMPLE *beg end*
READ(11) *vars*
(other commands)
STOP

Note, however, that if you use the **BYVAR** option on the **READ** command, or if your data is being read in free-format, then you are cannot have SHAZAM do your counting for you and the correct number of observations must be specified on the **SAMPLE** command.

RUNNING OUT OF MEMORY

Whenever SHAZAM is unable to run a problem because of insufficient memory the program will print a message telling you this. You should then review the information on storage requirements in the manual. If this information does not help, you may be able to increase the MEM requested on your RES or ORES command. If SHAZAM has told you the amount of workspace required, subtract from this amount the workspace you are using for the run (this is reported at the beginning of the run). Add the calculated amount to the amount you had requested on your RES or ORES command and rerun the job.

Generally, the CP-6 version of the program will print an error message if you do not have enough memory, however, there may still be some problems on CP-6.

H. *HOW TO RUN* SHAZAM *ON ICL*

First, assign the SHAZAM OMF library with:

ALB(:PROD.SHAZAM.OMFLIBRARY,,E)

EXAMPLE 1

To run SHAZAM when your data is not in a separate file and you intend to enter the data and the SHAZAM commands during execution, use:

shazam
SAMPLE *beg end*
READ *vars*
(data goes here)
(other commands)
STOP

EXAMPLE 2

If your data is in a separate file assigned to unit 11 you would use:

shazam
FILE 11 *SRC.*datafile*
SAMPLE *beg end*
READ(11) *vars*
(other commands)
STOP

The above **READ(11)** command tells SHAZAM to get the data from *datafile*.

EXAMPLE 3

You could have all your SHAZAM commands and data together in one file: *infile*.

shazam(in = *infile*)

EXAMPLE 4

If you wish to place the output in a file use:

shazam(in = *infile*,out = *outfile)*

To print this file use:

listfile (*outfile*,des = *STDFORT) *outfile*

To obtain this output directly in a batch run, first create a file, say **"zap"**, which contains the following lines:

BEGIN
ALB(:PROD.SHAZAM.OMFLIBRARY,,E)
shazam(in = *infile*)
ej

This will make the file executable. To run the commands in *infile*, type:

RUNJOB(JOBNAME = myjob,**FILE** = zap)

EXAMPLE 5

You could have all commands in one file and data in another file as follows:

shazam(in = *commandfile*)

The first line in *commandfile* would be:

FILE 11 *SRC.datafile*

Within *commandfile* there will be a **READ(11)** command to indicate to SHAZAM that the data is to be found on unit 11 which is assigned to *datafile*.

EXAMPLE 6

If you wish to use the SHAZAM **WRITE** command to place data generated within a SHAZAM run in a new file, use:

shazam
FILE 16 ***SRC**.*datafile*
(other commands)
WRITE(16) ....
STOP

EXAMPLE 7

Users frequently wish to be relieved of counting the number of observations in their data. They do not want to have to put this number on the **SAMPLE** command. You can have SHAZAM do the counting for you by omitting the **SAMPLE** command. This can only be done when the data is in a separate file. SHAZAM then reads to the end of the file.

shazam
FILE 11 ***SRC**.*datafile*
READ(11) *vars*
(other commands)
STOP

Note: If you use the **BYVAR** option on the **READ** command you cannot omit the **SAMPLE** command.

EXAMPLE 8

If you use the **OUT**= and **IN**= options in a **SYSTEM** or **NL** problem, the first run will look like this (assuming unit 17 is used):

shazam
FILE 17 ***SRC**.*restartfile*
SAMPLE *beg end*
(other commands)
SYSTEM 3 / DN ITER = **10 OUT**= *unit*
OLS *depvar indeps*
OLS *depvar indeps*
OLS *depvar indeps*
STOP

In the next run, to restart where you left off, change the **SYSTEM** command to:

SYSTEM 3 / DN ITER = **20 OUT**= *unit* **IN**= *unit*

In this case, the model will continue at the point it left off in the first run and updating the information on restartfile until iteration 20. Do not attempt to use the **IN=** option before you have anything to **IN**put. Units 11-49 may be used. Note that the **SYSTEM** and **NL** dumps require UNFORMATTED files when the **FILE** command is used. Therefore, the unit number on the **FILE** command requires a period (.) next to it. See the chapter MISCELLANEOUS COMMANDS AND INFORMATION for details on the **FILE** command.

In a **SYSTEM**, the dump can be quite large in large models, so you should be certain that you have ample file space left in your computer account. In an **NL** problem the file will be quite small.

EXAMPLE 9

If you use **READ** commands to merge files, the run might look like this:

shazam
FILE 11 *SRC.data1
FILE 12 *SRC.data2
FILE 13 *SRC.data3
SAMPLE *beg end*
READ(11) *vars*
READ(12) *vars*
READ(13) *vars*
(other commands)
STOP

I. *HOW TO RUN* SHAZAM *ON PRIME*

This section explains how to run SHAZAM on PRIME computers with the PRIMOS Operating System. SHAZAM commands may be up to 80 characters. In the examples below PRIMOS commands are displayed in lower case to distinguish them from SHAZAM commands. WARNING: The instructions in this section may differ for each installation.

EXAMPLE 1

To run SHAZAM when your data is not in a separate file, type:

seg shazam
SAMPLE *beg end*
READ *vars*
(data goes here)
(other commands)
STOP

EXAMPLE 2

If your data is in a separate file assigned to unit 11, it should enter SHAZAM as follows:

seg shazam
FILE 11 *datafilename*
SAMPLE *beg end*
READ(11) *vars*
(data is read from *datafilename*)
(other commands)
STOP

EXAMPLE 3

You could have all your SHAZAM commands and data together in one file which should be read as follows:

seg shazam *myfile*

You could also have the output go into a file rather than come to the screen if you specify a name for the output file as follows:

seg shazam *myfile outfile*

EXAMPLE 4

You could have all commands in one file and data in another file, as follows:

seg shazam *myfile outfile*

The first line in *myfile* would be:

FILE 11 *datafile*

EXAMPLE 5

Sometimes you will want to request written output using some SHAZAM option and will want it placed in a file, e.g. on unit 16.

seg SHAZAM
FILE 16 *writefile*
SAMPLE *beg end*
READ *vars*
(other commands)
WRITE(16) *vars*
(other commands)
STOP

EXAMPLE 6

If you use the **OUT=** and **IN=** options in a **SYSTEM** or **NL** problem, the first run will appear as follows:

seg shazam
FILE 17 *restart*
SAMPLE *beg end*
READ *vars*
(other commands)
SYSTEM 3 / DN ITER=10 OUT=17
OLS *depvar indeps*
OLS *depvar indeps*
OLS *depvar indeps*
END
STOP

In the next run, to restart where you left off, you should add the **IN=** option. The **SYSTEM** command might read:

SYSTEM 3 / DN ITER=20 OUT=17 IN=17

In this case, the estimation will continue at the point it left off in the first run and updating the file on unit 17 (i.e. the contents of the file *restart*) up to iteration 20. Do not attempt to use the **IN=** option before you have anything to **IN**put.

In a **SYSTEM**, the file can be quite large in large models. In an **NL** problem the file will be quite small.

EXAMPLE 7

If you use **READ** commands to merge files, the setup might look like this:

seg shazam
FILE 11 *data1*
FILE 12 *data2*
FILE 13 *data3*
SAMPLE *beg end*
READ(11) *vars*
READ(12) *vars*
READ(13) *vars*
(other commands)
STOP

RUNNING OUT OF MEMORY

When SHAZAM is unable to run a problem because of insufficient memory, you will usually get a message telling you how to set the **PAR** value. The **PAR** value specifies the amount of memory (in batches of 1024 bytes) that is needed. For example, if you run SHAZAM and get the message:

RUN AGAIN WITH PAR=2640

you should then ask your local SHAZAM consultant to recompile SUBROUTINE DOPRIM and raise the size of the workspace.

USING SHAZAM INTERACTIVELY AT A TERMINAL

With a little care, you can easily run SHAZAM interactively at a terminal. The procedure is exactly the same as in batch, except some of the usual output will be deleted unless specifically requested. At a terminal, it is useful to have your data in a file. This is not necessary if you want to input your data directly. However, direct data input is not recommended since an error would require that you start over.

At a terminal, keep output to a minimum. If you are in the middle of a subproblem procedure and you want to stop execution, simply hit the ATTN or BREAK key. SHAZAM will then stop.

J. *HOW TO RUN* SHAZAM *ON UNIVAC*

This section explains how to run SHAZAM on UNIVAC series 1100 computers under the EXEC8 Operating System. SHAZAM commands may be up to 80 characters. WARNING: The instructions in this section may differ for each installation.

EXAMPLE 1

To run SHAZAM when your data is not in a separate file, use:

@SHAZAM
SAMPLE *beg end*
READ *vars*
(data goes here)
(other commands)
STOP

EXAMPLE 2

If your data is in a separate file, it should enter SHAZAM on unit 11 as follows:

@ASG,AZ *dataname.*
@USE 11,*dataname.*
@SHAZAM
SAMPLE *beg end*
READ(11) *vars*
(data is read from *dataname*)
(other commands)
STOP

EXAMPLE 3

You could have all your SHAZAM commands and data together in one file which should be read as follows:

@SHAZAM
@ADD,E *myfile.*

EXAMPLE 4

You could have all commands in one file and data in another file, as follows:

@ASG,AZ *dataname.*
@USE 11,*dataname.*
@SHAZAM
@ADD,E *myfile*

EXAMPLE 5

Sometimes you will want to request **WRITE** output with a SHAZAM command and will want it placed in a file. In this case, you must assign unit 16 to the filename:

@ASG,UP *writefile.*
@USE 16, *writefile.*
@SHAZAM
SAMPLE *beg end*
READ *vars*
(other commands)
WRITE(16) *vars*
(other commands)
STOP

Before you start using files you should know how they work.

EXAMPLE 6

Users frequently wish to be relieved of counting the number of observations in their data. They do not want to have to put this number on the **SAMPLE** command. You can have SHAZAM do the counting for you by omitting the **SAMPLE** command and by placing the data in a separate file. When there is no **SAMPLE** command and the data is in a separate file, SHAZAM reads all the data in the file specified on the **READ** command. For example:

@ASG,AZ *dataname.*
@USE 11,*dataname.*
@SHAZAM
READ(11) *vars*
(other commands)
STOP

Note that if you use the **BYVAR** option on the **READ** command then you cannot have SHAZAM do your counting, as the correct number of observations must be specified on the **SAMPLE** command.

EXAMPLE 7

If you use the **OUT=** and **IN=** options in a **SYSTEM** or **NL** problem, the first run will look something like this:

@ASG,UP *myshazam.,///***200**
@USE 17,*resfile.*   (Unit 17 is used for the RESTART file)
@SHAZAM
SAMPLE *beg end*
READ *vars*
(other commands)
SYSTEM 3 / DN ITER=10 OUT=17
OLS *depvar indeps*
OLS *depvar indeps*
OLS *depvar indeps*
END
STOP

In the next run, to restart where you left off, you should change **@ASG,AZ** and add the **IN=** option, so the **SYSTEM** command might be:

SYSTEM 3 / DN ITER=20 OUT=17 IN=17

In this case, the model will continue at the point it left off in the first run and update the file on unit 17 (i.e. the contents of the file *resfile*) up to iteration 20. Do not attempt to use the **IN=** option before you have anything to **IN**put.

In a **SYSTEM,** the file can be quite large in large models, so you should be certain that you have ample file space left in your computer account. In an **NL** problem the file will be quite small.

EXAMPLE 8

If you use **READ** commands to merge files, the setup might look like this:

@ASG,AZ *data1.*
@USE 11,*data1.*
@ASG,AZ *data2.*
@USE 12,*data2.*
@ASG,AZ *data3.*
@USE 13,*data3.*
@SHAZAM
SAMPLE *beg end*
READ(11) *vars*
READ(12) *vars*
READ(13) *vars*
(other commands)
STOP

RUNNING OUT OF MEMORY

Whenever SHAZAM is unable to run a problem because of insufficient memory, you will get a message telling you how to set the **PAR** value. The **PAR** value specifies the amount of memory (in batches of 1024 bytes) that is needed. Each **PAR** unit represents half of a Core Block and is used to allocate SHAZAM workspace. To change **PAR** you simply specify the desired amount when you first execute SHAZAM. For example, if you run SHAZAM and get the message:

RUN AGAIN WITH PAR=96

you should then use:

@SHAZAM,P 96

SHAZAM will inform you how much memory is taken by each subproblem so that you can alter the **PAR** value for efficiency. For small problems, the default (20) is sufficient.

USING SHAZAM INTERACTIVELY AT A TERMINAL

With a little care you can easily run SHAZAM interactively at a terminal. The procedure is exactly the same as in batch, except some of the usual output will be deleted unless specifically requested. At a terminal, it is almost always useful to have your data in a file. This is not necessary if you want to input your data directly. However, direct data input is not recommended since an error would require you that start over. To exit from SHAZAM at any time simply type **STOP**.

K. *HOW TO RUN* SHAZAM *ON UNIX*

EXAMPLE 1

To run SHAZAM when your data is not in a separate file and you intend to enter the data and the SHAZAM commands during execution, use:

% shazam
SAMPLE *beg end*
READ *vars*
(data goes here)
STOP

EXAMPLE 2

If your data is in a separate file assigned to unit 11 you would use:

% shazam
FILE 11 *datafile*
SAMPLE *beg end*
READ(11) *vars*
(other commands)
STOP

The above **READ(11)** command tells SHAZAM to get the data from *datafile*.

EXAMPLE 3

You could have all your SHAZAM commands and data together in one file: *infile*.

% shazam < *infile*

EXAMPLE 4

If you wish to place the output in a file, use:

% shazam < *infile* > outfile

To print this file, use:

% lpr *outfile*

To print this file with the carriage control in effect, use:

% **lpr -f** *outfile*

or

% **fpr** <*outfile*|**lpr**

To obtain this output directly in a batch run, create a file, say zap, which contains the following lines:

#
shazam <*infile*

Next, type:

chmod 744

to make the file executable. To run the commands in the *infile*, type:

% **batch zap**

EXAMPLE 5

You could have all commands in one file and data in another file as follows:

% **shazam**<*commandfile*

The first line in *commandfile* would be:

FILE 11 *datafile*

Within *commandfile* there would be a **READ(11)** command to indicate to SHAZAM that the data is to be found on unit 11 which is assigned to *datafile*.

EXAMPLE 6

If you wish to use the SHAZAM **WRITE** command to place data generated within a SHAZAM run in a new file use:

% shazam
FILE 16 *writefile*
(other commands)
WRITE(16) ....
STOP

EXAMPLE 7

Users frequently wish to be relieved of counting the number of observations in their data. They do not want to have to put this number on the **SAMPLE** command. You can have SHAZAM do the counting for you by omitting the **SAMPLE** command. This can only be done when the data is in a separate file. SHAZAM then reads to the end of file.

% shazam
FILE 11 *datafile*
READ(11) *vars*
(other commands)
STOP

Note: If you use the **BYVAR** option on the **READ** command you cannot omit the **SAMPLE** command.

EXAMPLE 8

If you use the **OUT=** and **IN=** options in a **SYSTEM** or **NL** problem, the first run will look like this (assuming unit 17 is used):

% shazam
FILE 17. *restartfile*
SAMPLE *beg end*
(other commands)
SYSTEM 3 / DN ITER= 10 OUT= *unit*
OLS depvar indeps
OLS depvar indeps
OLS depvar indeps
STOP

In the next run, to restart where you left off, change the **SYSTEM** command to:

SYSTEM 3 / DN ITER= 20 OUT= *unit* **IN=** *unit*

In this case, the model will continue at the point it left off in the first run and update the information on *restartfile*, until iteration 20. Do not attempt to use the **IN=** option before you have anything to INput. Units 11-49 may be used. Note that the SYSTEM and NL dumps require UNFORMATTED files when the **FILE** command is used. Therefore, the unit number on the **FILE** command requires a period (.) next to it. See the chapter *MISCELLANEOUS COMMANDS AND INFORMATION* for details on the **FILE** command.

In a **SYSTEM**, the dump can be quite large in large models, so you should be certain that you have ample file space left in your computer account. In an **NL** problem the file will be quite small.

EXAMPLE 9

If you use the **READ** command to merge files, the setup might look like this:

```
% shazam
FILE 11 data1
FILE 12 data2
FILE 13 data3
SAMPLE beg end
READ(11) vars
READ(12) vars
READ(13) vars
(other commands)
STOP
```

RUNNING OUT OF MEMORY

When SHAZAM is unable to run a problem because of insufficient memory you will usually get a message telling you how to set the **PAR** value. The **PAR** value specifies the amount of memory (in batches of 1024 bytes) that is needed. If you need to specify the **PAR** value, it should be done with the **PAR** command. For example, if you run SHAZAM and get the message:

RUN AGAIN WITH PAR=96

you should then use:

```
% shazam
PAR 96
(continue with the rest of the SHAZAM commands)
```

If used, the **PAR** command should be the first command in the SHAZAM run.

L. *HOW TO RUN* SHAZAM *ON VAX/VMS*

This section explains how to run SHAZAM on a VAX VMS operating system. In the examples below VMS commands are typed in lower case to distinguish them from SHAZAM commands. SHAZAM commands may be up to 80 columns. WARNING: The instructions in this section may differ for each installation.

EXAMPLE 1

To run SHAZAM when your data is not in a separate file, use:

$ shazam
SAMPLE *beg end*
READ *vars*
(data goes here)
(other commands)
STOP

EXAMPLE 2

If your data is in a separate file, it may enter SHAZAM on unit 11 as follows:

$ shazam
FILE 11 *dataname.dat*
SAMPLE *beg end*
READ(11) *vars*
(other commands)
STOP

EXAMPLE 3

You could have all your SHAZAM commands and data together in one file which should be read as follows:

$ assign *myfile* **for005**
$ shazam

EXAMPLE 4

Sometimes you will want to request **WRITE** output using some SHAZAM command and will want it placed in a file. In this case you must assign unit 16 to the filename:

$ shazam

FILE 16 *writefile.dat*
SAMPLE *beg end*
READ *vars*
(other commands)
WRITE(16) *vars*
(other commands)
STOP

EXAMPLE 5

Users frequently wish to be relieved of counting the number of observations in their data; they do not want to have to put this number on the **SAMPLE** command. You can have SHAZAM do the counting for you by omitting the **SAMPLE** command and by placing the data in a separate file to be read in on a **READ** command. In this case, SHAZAM will read to the end of the file. The following commands are appropriate:

$ shazam
FILE 11 *datafile.dat*
READ(11) *vars*
(other commands)
STOP

Using these commands SHAZAM will read all the data in *datafile.dat* and automatically set the appropriate **SAMPLE** size.

Note that the **BYVAR** option may not be used on the **READ** command if SHAZAM is doing the counting. The **BYVAR** option may only be used when there is a **SAMPLE** in effect.

EXAMPLE 6

If you use the **OUT=** and **IN=** options in a **SYSTEM** or **NL** problem, the first run will look something like this:

$ shazam
FILE 17 *resfile.dat*
SAMPLE *beg end*
READ *vars*
(other commands)
SYSTEM 3 / DN ITER = 10 OUT = 17
OLS *depvar indeps*
OLS *depvar indeps*
OLS *depvar indeps*
STOP

In the next run, to restart where you left off, you should change the **SYSTEM** command to read:

SYSTEM 3 / DN ITER = 20 OUT = 17 IN = 17

In this case the model will continue at the point it left off in the first run and update the file on unit 17 (i.e. the contents of the file *resfile.dat*) until iteration 20. Do not attempt to use the **IN=** option before you have anything to **IN**put.

In a **SYSTEM**, the file can be quite large in large models, so you should be certain that you have ample file space left in your computer account. In an **NL** problem the file will be quite small.

EXAMPLE 7

If you use **READ** commands to merge files, the setup might look like this:

$ shazam
FILE 11 *data1.dat*
FILE 12 *data2.dat*
FILE 13 *data3.dat*
SAMPLE *beg end*
READ(11) *vars*
READ(12) *vars*
READ(13) *vars*
(other commands)
STOP

EXAMPLE 8

When SHAZAM is unable to run a problem because of insufficient memory, you will usually get a message telling you how to set the **PAR** value. The **PAR** value specifies the amount of memory (in batches of 1024 bytes) that is needed. If you need to specify the **PAR** value, it should be done with the **PAR** command. For example, if you run SHAZAM and get the message:

RUN AGAIN WITH PAR = 96

you should then use:

$ shazam
PAR 96
(continue with the rest of SHAZAM commands)

If used, the **PAR** command must be the first command in the SHAZAM run.

USING **SHAZAM** *INTERACTIVELY AT A TERMINAL*

With a little care, you can easily run SHAZAM interactively at a terminal. The procedure is exactly the same as in batch, except some of the usual output will be deleted unless specifically requested. At a terminal, it is almost always useful to have your data in a file. This is not necessary if you want to input your data directly. However, direct data input is not recommended since an error would require that you start over. To exit SHAZAM at any time simply type **STOP**.

M. *HOW TO RUN* SHAZAM *ON THE MACINTOSH*

WARNING: THE INSTRUCTIONS IN THE VERSION 5.0-6.0 *SHAZAM USER'S REFERENCE MANUAL* SHOULD NOT BE USED. INSTEAD, USE THIS REVISED VERSION OF HOW TO RUN SHAZAM ON THE MACINTOSH. THE INSTRUCTIONS BELOW ONLY APPLY TO SHAZAM VERSION 6.1 AND LATER.

SHAZAM will run on all models of the Macintosh except the 128K Macintosh and possibly the LISA (Macintosh XL). In addition, an enhanced version of SHAZAM is available for the Macintosh II and machines that have the 68020/68881 processors to take advantage of the math co-processor although these machines can also run the regular version. If you try to run the enhanced version on other models of the Macintosh you will get a System error.

The best and easiest way to run SHAZAM is to use a Hard Disk to hold all your SHAZAM files. If you do not have a Hard Disk then it is possible to run SHAZAM with two double-sided floppy disk drives. If you are particularly clever and patient you can even run it with one double-sided drive although this is not recommended for heavy use. However, because SHAZAM is a large program you probably will not be able to put all the SHAZAM files on two floppy disks and you will have to configure your disks for your particular applications. A README file on the orginal SHAZAM disks contains valuable information required for installation.

HOW TO INSTALL SHAZAM ON A HARD DISK

If you have a Hard Disk you should create a New Folder called *SHAZAM* and copy all the files from the **SHAZAM** disk and **SYSDISK** into the *SHAZAM* folder. Next, open the *SUBROUTINES* folder on the hard disk and copy all the files in the folders from the **EXTRA** disk into the *SUBROUTINES* folder. The easiest way to do this is to open each folder from the **EXTRA** disk, for example, the *ARIMA* folder. Then choose *SELECT ALL* under the Finder's *EDIT* Menu to select all the files in the folder. Next, drag the entire set of files into the *SUBROUTINES* folder on the hard disk. Repeat this sequence for every folder on the **EXTRA** disk. The *SUBROUTINES* folder must *not* have any other folders inside it. If you do not copy the files in this manner SHAZAM will not be able to find the individual subroutines and you will be prompted for missing subroutines.

All your SHAZAM data files and SHAZAM command files should also be inside the *SHAZAM* folder. If not, they can be accessed with the SHAZAM **FILE** command and the complete **diskname:***foldername:filename* as discussed below. Note that SHAZAM will not tolerate blanks in any of the names so you may have to rename your disks, folders, and files to single word names. To run SHAZAM, open the *SHAZAM* folder then double click the *SHAZAM* icon (it looks like the world) and follow the examples later in this chapter.

HOW TO INSTALL SHAZAM ON A DOUBLE-SIDED FLOPPY DRIVE SYSTEM

Your copy of SHAZAM includes 3 disks called: **SYSDISK, SHAZAM,** and **EXTRA**. First make a backup copy of all 3 disks. There is no *System Folder* included so you should either boot up your machine with your own system disk or for convenience put a copy of your *System Folder* on **SYSDISK** in which case **SYSDISK** will be your startup disk. It is recommended that you use the most recent version of the System and Finder available for your machine. If you have a 512K or 512KE Macintosh this is System 3.2 and Finder 5.3. If you have a Mac-Plus, Mac-SE, or Mac II, use System 6.0 or later.

Insert **SYSDISK** in the internal disk drive and the **SHAZAM** disk in the external drive. The **SHAZAM** disk has all the file required to run **OLS** regressions and to use many other SHAZAM commands. The files necessary to use some commands are contained in folders on the **EXTRA** disk. The **EXTRA** disk contains folders with SHAZAM subroutines that will need to be placed in the *SUBROUTINES* folder on the **SHAZAM** disk if you wish to use them. For example, if you wish to use the **ARIMA** command you will need to place the files in the *ARIMA* folder into the *SUBROUTINES* folder on the **SHAZAM** disk following the procedure outlined above for Hard Disk users.

SYSDISK should also contain the three SHAZAM files (*SHAZMASTER*, *SHADEMO*, and *SHAHELP*).

Do not rename **SYSDISK** to any other name or SHAZAM will be unhappy.

When you receive SHAZAM it will have enough room for you to copy the files from 2 or 3 folders, from the **EXTRA** disks, depending on the command. By manipulating command folders in this way, you can have access to almost any SHAZAM command described in the SHAZAM manual. It might be useful to create several different **SHAZAM** disks with different purposes. For example, you might have one **SHAZAM** disk specifically designed for use with the **ARIMA** command and another **SHAZAM** disk to be used with the **PROBIT** command.

The following is a list of all the SHAZAM commands which require manipulation of folders from the **EXTRA** disk to the **SHAZAM** disk. Commands not included in this list are already available on the **SHAZAM** disk.

Command	*Folder Required*
ARIMA	*ARIMA*
AUTO	*AUTOBOX*
BAYES	*DISTRIB*
BOX	*AUTOBOX*
DISTRIB	*DISTRIB*
DLAG	*SYSTEMS*
GLS	*SYSTEMS*
INDEX	*SYSTEMS*
LOGIT	*PROBIT*
MATRIX	*MATRIX*
MLE	*NLIN*
NL	*NLIN*
OLS/METHOD = HH,EXACTDW	*DISTRIB*
OLS (Stepwise regression)	*DISTRIB*
PC	*DISTRIB*
POOL	*SYSTEMS*
PROBIT	*PROBIT*
ROBUST	*DISTRIB*
SYSTEM	*SYSTEMS*
TOBIT	*PROBIT*
2SLS	*SYSTEMS*

Most problems occur because there is insufficient room on one of your disks. If you get unexpected errors check whether your disks are full. You should also make sure that neither the **SHAZAM** nor **SYSDISK** disks are locked as the program needs to access both of these disks in an unlocked mode. All your SHAZAM command and data files should be on **SYSDISK**. If you run out of space on **SYSDISK** you remove the *SHAHELP* and *SHADEMO* files but the **HELP** and **DEMO** commands will no longer be available.

RUNNING **SHAZAM** *ON THE MACINTOSH*

When you first open SHAZAM, a standard Macintosh Menu Bar will appear on the screen. This contains the Apple menu with all your desk accessories. Most of these will be available at this point or anytime **TYPE COMMAND** appears on your screen.

The *FILE* menu contains *INPUT* and *OUTPUT* options to select the files to be assigned to your SHAZAM run. It is not recommended to use these; if you wish to assign input and output files it is more convenient to use the SHAZAM commands:

FILE OUTPUT diskname:*foldername:outputfile*
and
FILE INPUT diskname:*foldername:inputfile*

The *LIST* and *PRINT* options will be useful to display or print any text file. The *TRANSFER* option can be used to leave SHAZAM and start another application. Finally, the *QUIT* option will end SHAZAM and return to the finder. The SHAZAM STOP command will do the same thing.

The Menu bar includes the *EDIT* menu which is *not* used by SHAZAM (do not try to use it, or a bomb may occur).

The *COMMANDS* menu can be used to start execution or start a typing lesson.

The *MEMORY* menu contains 3 sections:

The first section sets the desired workspace size available to SHAZAM for internal use. The default is to grab all space available. This is the recommended procedure. If you have a Macintosh with a lot of memory you can select one of the other options to reduce the memory available to SHAZAM. In some cases, this may speed up execution slightly. Obtaining memory with this procedure replaces the **PAR** command (which does not work on the Macintosh) discussed in the manual.

The second section under the *MEMORY* menu sets the maximum number of variables allowed in a SHAZAM run. The default number of variables is 400 and can be increased to 1000 variables with the *SIZE* option under the *MEMORY* menu. This replaces the **SIZE** command (which does not work on the Macintosh) discussed in the manual.

The third section under the *MEMORY* menu indicates to SHAZAM whether you would like to use some of your memory to permanently load portions of SHAZAM in order to speed execution. The default is *LOAD SOME* which loads in a set of frequently used routines. If you select *LOAD NONE* you will free up some memory and SHAZAM may be able to run larger problems but execution will be slower. The *LOAD ALL* option requires a machine with at least 2 Meg of memory and will load the entire program in memory to obtain the fastest execution times. However, substantially less memory will be available for your data. The *LOAD SOME* option is probably the best way to use SHAZAM until you are familiar with memory requirements.

The *STYLE* menu can be used to set the background color if you have a Macintosh II. This is not a very useful option unless you wish to play with colors. In fact, even if you have color, it is recommended that you set your Monitor to 2 color Black and White as the use of Color substantially slows down most Macintosh programs EVEN IF THE PROGRAM ONLY USES BLACK AND WHITE. Try it if you do not believe it. The *STYLE* menu also contains an option to get the output in a 6 or 8 point font rather than the standard 9 point Monaco font. This works best if you actually have a 6 point Monaco font loaded in your system. Some users will find the 6 point font difficult to read.

The *HELP* menu can be used to obtain help on any SHAZAM command. It serves the same purpose as the SHAZAM **HELP** command.

After selecting the desired Menu options you can begin execution of SHAZAM by either typing a SHAZAM command, selecting *BEGIN* under the *COMMANDS* menu, or simply pressing the return key. SHAZAM will then start hunting for memory and loading routines. When SHAZAM displays: **TYPE COMMAND** you may begin with your actual SHAZAM commands. The maximum length of a command line is 255 characters but continuation lines will allow a maximum total length up to 1024 characters.

You will probably find it convenient to put a copy of an Editor such as the Apple TeachText or Edit program on **SYSDISK** or on your hard disk. It will also be useful to have the shareware Desk Accessories MOCKWRITE and SET PATHS available.

In the examples below, when reference is made to a file, it is *always* assumed that this file was created by a Text only Editor such as Apple's Edit or TeachText and was saved with the *SAVE AS...* option in the *FILE* menu with the *TEXT ONLY* option (if MacWrite is used). Using files that are not *TEXT ONLY* will result in error messages. If you are using **SYSDISK** then all of your files are assumed to be on **SYSDISK**. Files on other disks that have already been loaded can be accessed by using the diskname with a colon (:) on the SHAZAM **FILE** command. For example:

FILE 11 diskname:*diskfile*
or
FILE 11 diskname:*foldername:diskfile*

Be warned that SHAZAM will not tolerate disknames, foldernames, or filenames that have blank characters in the name. The shareware desk accessory SET PATHS is an excellent program to set default path names.

You will find the SHAZAM icon (it looks like the world) referred to in the examples below on the **SHAZAM** disk. To run SHAZAM, just click on it twice with the mouse. Once you have opened the SHAZAM icon and selected the desired Menu options you can use the commands and procedures described in the examples below.

It would be a good idea to type **DEMO** to learn how to use SHAZAM.

EXAMPLE 1

To run SHAZAM when your data is not in a separate file open SHAZAM and type:

SAMPLE *beg end*
READ *vars / options*
(data goes here)
(other commands)
STOP

EXAMPLE 2

If your data is in a separate file, it should enter SHAZAM on units 11-49. Open SHAZAM and type:

FILE 11 *datafilename*
SAMPLE *beg end*
READ(11) *vars / options*
(other commands)

EXAMPLE 3

You can have all your SHAZAM commands and data together in one file which should be read from unit **INPUT**. Open SHAZAM and type:

FILE INPUT *commandfilename*
(the output will appear on the terminal screen here)

After all output has finished, to leave SHAZAM type:

STOP

EXAMPLE 4

You could have all the commands in one file and the data in another. Open SHAZAM and type:

FILE 11 *datafilename* (You must assign unit 11 before unit **INPUT**.)
FILE INPUT *commandfilename*
(the output will appear on the terminal screen here)
STOP

In this case the **READ(11)** command would be contained in the command file. It would also be easier to put the **FILE 11** command in the command file. The **STOP** command should not be in the command file unless you want SHAZAM to automatically return to the Finder when finished.

EXAMPLE 5

Sometimes you will want to use the **WRITE** command to write data in a file. In this case you must assign units 11-49 to the file name. Open SHAZAM and type:

FILE 16 *writefilename*
SAMPLE *beg end*
(other commands)
WRITE(16) *vars / options*
(other commands)
STOP

EXAMPLE 6

Frequently, users want to be relieved of counting the number of observations in their data and wish they did not have to specify this number on the **SAMPLE** command. It is possible to have SHAZAM do the counting for you if you omit the **SAMPLE** command and your data is placed in a separate file. Open SHAZAM and type:

FILE 11 *datafilename*
READ(11) *vars*
(other commands)
STOP

The use of this feature saves a lot of trouble. SHAZAM will just read the whole file unless a **SAMPLE** command specifies the number of observations to be read. Note that if you use the **BYVAR** option on the **READ** command you are not allowed to have SHAZAM do your counting as the correct number of observations must be specified on a **SAMPLE** command.

EXAMPLE 7

You may use **READ** commands to read from several files. Open *SHAZAM* and type:

FILE 11 *datafile1*
FILE 12 *datafile2*
FILE 13 *datafile3*
READ(11) *vars / options*
READ(12) *vars / options*
READ(13) *vars / options*
(other commands)
STOP

EXAMPLE 8

If you are using the **OUT=** or **IN=** options in a **SYSTEM** or **NL** problem you will have to first create a restart file with the **FILE** command. Next, open SHAZAM and type:

FILE *unit. restartfile*
SAMPLE *beg end*
.
.
.
SYSTEM 3 / DN IT= 10 OUT= *unit*
OLS *depvar indeps*
OLS *depvar indeps*
OLS *depvar indeps*
STOP

where *unit* is any unit number from 11 to 49.

In the next run, to restart where you left off, you should add the **IN=** option. The **SYSTEM** commands might read:

SYSTEM 3 / DN IT= 20 OUT= *unit* **IN=** *unit*

In this case, the model will continue at the point it left off in the first run, updating the file on the specified unit (i.e. the contents of the file assigned to a unit) until iteration 20. Do not attempt to use the **IN=** option before you have anything to **IN**put.

In a **SYSTEM**, the file can be quite large in large models, so be sure you have lots of disk space available on your hard disk or **SYSDISK**.

SHAZAM GRAPHICS

If you use the **GRAPHICS** option on either the **PLOT** or **CONFID** commands, a PLOT window will appear on the screen to draw the graphics plot. Your regular text window will be under the PLOT window. You can make the plot go away by clicking the GO AWAY box in the upper left corner.

OBTAINING A HARDCOPY OF YOUR OUTPUT

At any time in an interactive SHAZAM run you can print the contents of the screen on an Imagewriter by pressing the *Command* key with the SHIFT key and 4 key simultaneously. The *Command* key is next to the space bar and is also known as the Apple Key and has a small symbol of a cloverleaf on it. This will print whatever is on the screen on your imagewriter. It does not work on a Laserwriter. If you press the *Command* key along with the SHIFT and 3 keys a MacPaint file will be created with a name like SCREEN 0 which is a snapshot of the screen. This is a useful way to save a copy of the PLOT window when using the **PLOT** or **CONFID** commands with the **GRAPHICS** option.

It is also possible to assign the **OUTPUT** unit to a file in which all of your output (except graphics plots) will be saved. You can then get a printed copy of your output on your printer by using the methods described below. To do this you must have a command file with all your SHAZAM commands in it. Open the SHAZAM application and type:

FILE OUTPUT *outputfilename*

After this command you will no longer see any output on the screen since all subsequent commands and output will be automatically stored in the output file. The next command will be:

FILE INPUT *commandfilename*

The commands in the command file will then be executed and the results will be stored in the **OUTPUT** file. Nothing will appear on the terminal screen except the Title Bar which indicates the name of each command as it executes. You will know when SHAZAM has finished executing all the commands in the command file when the machine noise ends and SHAZAM tells you that it has finished with the **INPUT** file.

If you wish to have your results come to the screen and go into a file at the same time, you should use:

FILE SCREEN *outputfilename*

instead of

FILE OUTPUT *outputfilename*

This provides additional flexibility, but the job will take longer to run. It is a good way to save a copy of your SHAZAM session. Note, that if your SHAZAM session bombs for some reason you may not see the last part of your output (and the reason for the bomb) if you use the **SCREEN** method.

You can print your output file (or any other file) by typing the command:

FILE PRINT *outputfilename*

This can also be done with the *PRINT* option on the *FILE* menu. Be sure to turn on your printer before executing this command. You could also print it as you would print any document by selecting its icon and choosing the *PRINT* option from the *FILE* menu.

To display a file from one of the loaded disks on screen use the *LIST* option on the *FILE* menu or type:

FILE LIST *filename*

Sometimes SHAZAM will not allow you access to a file that has previously been assigned. In this case you must close the file first with:

FILE CLOSE *filename*

If this does not work you may have to restart your machine. If SHAZAM displays Error 75 after a command it is most likely that the Subroutines for the Command are not on in the **SUBROUTINES** folder. In this case you will be prompted for a folder which does hold the missing subroutine. When you find it place the file in the **SUBROUTINES** folder.

If you get an Error 64 it means you have run out of memory. This could occur if you have attempted to run too many different kinds of commands in a single run. To solve this problem try to use the *LOAD NONE* option in the *MEMORY* menu. This will slow execution of your run, but provide slightly more memory. If you have more than 2 Meg of memory the *LOAD ALL* option may speed up execution.

HOW TO PAUSE OR BREAK OUT OF A SHAZAM RUN

If you have a long SHAZAM session running and for some reason you wish to temporarily "freeze" the screen, simply press the *Command* key with the *S* key. To resume the output press *Command-Q*. The proper use of *Command-S* and *Command-Q* will allow you to read your output if it is going too fast. If you wish to stop execution before the run finishes you should try pressing the *Command* key "." key simultaneously. *Command-.* will usually cause SHAZAM to stop and you will be able to return to the Finder with a carriage return. If this does not work then you can always simply turn off your machine. When the Mac says "CR TO EXIT" it wants you to just press RETURN. You might also be able to stop execution by pressing down the mouse in the menu bar. This occassionally works, but it depends on what SHAZAM is doing at the time.

USING STEPPING OUT II

SHAZAM works quite nicely with the program *Stepping Out II* by Berkeley System Design. This allows you to extend the size of your screen and hold a large amount of SHAZAM output after it has scrolled off the screen. The best size to use is 8.5 by 11 inches (or longer if you wish to hold more output). If you wish full screen output with the **SET WIDE** option then you should set the dimensions to 10.5 inches wide. The *Option-Command-R* feature in *Stepping Out II* should be used to keep the SHAZAM title bar from rolling off the screen.

USING SET PATHS

The Desk Accessory *Set Paths* by Paul F. Snively is a Shareware program that automatically sets the folder path name for your files so you can run SHAZAM from outside the SHAZAM folder or access files in other folders easily. After you install SET PATHS you should set the first path to **DISKNAME:SHAZAM:** where **DISKNAME** is the name of your hard disk. This will allow you to remove the SHAZAM icon from the *SHAZAM* folder and put it in another folder. Alternatively, you can use *Set Paths* to specify the **diskname** and *foldername* of another folder so you will not need to specify them on the SHAZAM **FILE** command. If SHAZAM has trouble finding files, or your machine bombs for some reason it is likely that the path has not been set properly or you have two folders with the same name.

USING MULTIFINDER

SHAZAM may work under Multifinder if sufficient memory and luck are available. If you click on the SHAZAM Icon once and press *Command-I* an Information Box will appear that allows you to set the Application Memory Size. It should not be set lower than 512. If you wish to increase the amount of memory available to SHAZAM (sometimes known as PAR) you will have to increase the Application Memory Size to a higher level. Then the *MaxK* option on the *MEMORY* menu will grab all the memory up to the Size specified. If you have difficulty running SHAZAM with Multifinder try turning off Multifinder.

SHAZAM SCRATCH FILES

Occasionally SHAZAM will need to create temporary scratch files during a run. SHAZAM will attempt to trash these files when it is finished with them, but they often will remain around on your disk. These files have names like: *00000000* or *00000001*. You can trash them yourself if you see them on your disk.

SYSTEM BOMBS

Do not try to use the *MEMORY* menu to select more memory than is available in your machine. If you try, you are likely to get (a) a blank screen, or (b) a weird and noisy pattern on your screen. If you think you have sufficient memory, but these things happen to you, it is likely that you set aside some of your memory for a Ram-Cache or other memory resident program.

SHAZAM often attempts to use every bit of memory it can find. Occasionally you may find that SHAZAM runs fine, but when SHAZAM attempts to return to the Finder, a System Bomb will occur. This happens when there is simply no memory left for the Finder to take control. In this case you may have to restart the machine.

Sometimes SHAZAM cannot return directly to the Finder and it will say:

ERROR 35 - CR to exit

This is harmless, so simply press the **RETURN** key to get back to the Finder.

MACINTOSH ERROR CODES

34 Disk full
43 File not found
49 File already assigned (restart system)
35 No such volume name
64 Insufficient Memory
65 Numeric Overflow
66 Divide by zero
75 Subprogram not found
76 FORMAT syntax error

MACINTOSH SYSTEM ALERT ERROR CODES (BOMBS)

 2 Address error (Usually Means Out of Memory)
 3 Illegal Instruction (Usually Means Out of Memory)
10 Possibly running 68020 version on 68000 machine 25 Out of Memory
28 Out of Memory
35 Make Block Free Error (Usually Means Out of Memory)

SUMMARY OF INPUT-OUTPUT UNITS FOR FILE COMMAND

1-10	Internal use. Not available to users.
11-49	Available to user.
INPUT	SHAZAM commands and input data stream; defaults to screen.
LIST	Output unit (Screen).
OUTPUT	Output unit; defaults to screen. If unit OUTPUT is assigned to a file that already exists the contents will be erased.
PRINT	Output unit (Printer).
SCREEN	Output to screen and file.
CLOSE	Closes a file.

N. *HOW TO RUN* SHAZAM *ON THE IBM PC*

"The computer has no commercial future."

IBM
1948

SHAZAM requires a hard disk system and at least 512K memory, MS-DOS 2.1 or higher, and the 8087, 80287, or 80387 Math Co-processor. A version of SHAZAM is available for those who do not have a Math Co-processor, but it runs much slower. All the files from the original SHAZAM disks should be in a directory on your hard disk called: SHAZAM. Specific instructions are contained with the original SHAZAM disks.

Most of the examples will have the SHAZAM commands (and sometimes the DATA) in a file. If the output is placed in a file then you will have a permanent record which you can observe by using the DOS command **print** or **type**. Note: The control-S and control-Q keys are useful for "freezing" and "unfreezing" output to the screen. The control-PrintSc key is useful for turning the printer on or off during an interactive session.

Due to DOS limitations you will probably not be able to use more than 14 files in any SHAZAM run. In the following examples commands typed in lower case are DOS commands. Commands typed in upper case indicate SHAZAM commands, although in actual practice you may type your commands in either upper or lower case.

You will want to obtain a good Editor for your computer. The DOS supplied Editor EDLIN is *not* a good Editor. In fact, it may be the worst excuse for an Editor in the history of computing. There are many commercial and public-domain shareware Editors which are very good. You can also use a Word Processing Program as an Editor if it has the capability to output a straight ASCII file, but a regular Edit program is preferred.

EXAMPLE 1

To run SHAZAM interactively when your data is not in a separate file type:

shazam
SAMPLE *beg end*
READ *vars / options*
(data goes here)
(other commands)
STOP

EXAMPLE 2

If your data is in a separate file, say *test.dat*, it should enter SHAZAM on unit 11-49 as follows:

shazam
FILE 11 *test.dat*
SAMPLE *beg end*
READ(11) *vars / options*
(other commands)
STOP

EXAMPLE 3

You could have all your SHAZAM commands in one file, say *command.sha*, which should be read as follows:

shazam
FILE INPUT *command.sha*

or

shazam <*command.sha*

(the output will appear on the terminal screen)

If you wish to have your output go into a file instead of the terminal screen you should also assign an output file as follows:

shazam <*command.sha* >*output.out*

If you wish, you can now send the file *output.out* to the printer with a DOS **print** command.

EXAMPLE 4

Suppose you want to use the **WRITE** command to write data in a file, say *out.dat*. In this case you must assign units 11-49 to the file name as follows:

shazam
FILE 16 *out.dat*
SAMPLE *beg end*
(other commands)
WRITE(16) *vars / options*
(other commands)
STOP

EXAMPLE 5

Users frequently wish to be relieved of counting the number of observations in their data; they do not want to have to put this number on a **SAMPLE** command. If you have your data in a separate file, you can have SHAZAM do the counting for you by omitting the **SAMPLE** command:

shazam
FILE 11 *test.dat*
READ(11) *vars* / *options*
(other commands)
STOP

When the data is in a file, SHAZAM will read the whole file unless the **SAMPLE** command specifies the number of observations to be read.

Note: You cannot the **BYVAR** option on the **READ** command, to do your counting as the correct number of observations must be specified on the **SAMPLE** command.

EXAMPLE 6

If you use the **OUT=** and **IN=** options in a **SYSTEM** or **NL** problem, you will have to first create a *restart.sav* file with the **FILE** command as follows:

shazam
FILE 17. *restart.sav*
SAMPLE *beg end*
(other commands)
SYSTEM 3 / DN IT= 10 OUT= 17
OLS *depvar indeps*
OLS *depvar indeps*
OLS *depvar indeps*
STOP

The output from the **OUT=** option of the **SYSTEM** command would be placed in the Binary file, *restart.sav*, attached to unit 17. Be sure to include a "." after the unit number on the **FILE** command to indicate that this is a binary file.

In the next run, to restart where you left off, you should use the **IN=** option, so the **SYSTEM** command might read:

SYSTEM 3 / DN IT= 20 OUT= 17 IN= 17

In this case, the model will continue at the point it left off in the first run and update the dump on unit 17 (i.e. the contents of the file *restart.sav*) until iteration 20. Do not attempt to use the **IN=** option before you have anything to **IN**put.

In a **SYSTEM**, the dump can be quite large in large models, so you should be certain that you have ample file space left. In an **NL** problem the file will be quite small.

EXAMPLE 7

If you use **READ** commands to merge data files, the setup in your SHAZAM program file might look like this:

shazam
FILE 11 *one.dat*
FILE 12 *two.dat*
FILE 13 *three.dat*
SAMPLE *beg end*
READ(11) *vars / options*
READ(12) *vars / options*
READ(13) *vars / options*
(other commands)
STOP

SHAZAM *GRAPHICS*

The SHAZAM **PLOT** and **CONFID** commands can create high resolution graphics rather than crude character plots. This requires either a CGA, EGA, or HERCULES graphics system on your machine. It is necessary for you to tell SHAZAM the type of graphics plot desired as an option which is discussed in the chapter *PLOTS*. The procedure is to add the appropriate graphics option to the **PLOT** or **CONFID** command. For example, if you have an EGA monitor you would use the **EGA** option. SHAZAM will draw the plot on your screen. If you are in **TALK** mode SHAZAM will leave the plot on the screen until you press RETURN. On many systems the plot can be transferred to a graphics printer by either typing a dot (.) before you press return or by following instructions with your graphics printer.

RUNNING OUT OF MEMORY

SHAZAM will automatically use all available memory on your machine up to the 640K DOS limitation so the **PAR** command will not provide any additional memory. You might be able to obtain additional memory by removing any space allocated to a RAM-DISK on RAM-CACHE on memory resident programs such as SIDEKICK, BACKSCRL, etc. The SHAZAM **SIZE** command is fixed at 300 variables.

SHAZAM *WITH A RAM-DISK*

It is possible to substantially speedup execution of SHAZAM by using some of your memory as a RAM-DISK. In this case you should put as many of the SHAZAM .OVL files on the RAM-DISK as you can. Specific details are in the README file on the installation disks.

FILE RECORD LENGTHS

If you get error message 3050 or 3086 it means the record length of one of your files (or an internal SHAZAM scratch file) exceeds the default length of 1024 characters. This can be raised by the /R nnnn option on the SHAZAM command line, for example:

SHAZAM /R 2048

would double the maximum record length. Note that this eats into the memory available for your data.

SHAZAM WITH A RAM-CACHE

Since SHAZAM grabs all available memory, many RAM-CACHE programs will find that no memory is left for caching so no increase in execution speed will result. In this case the RAM-DISK method described above is preferred.

DOS SYSTEM ERROR MESSAGES THAT MAY OCCUR

    194 Incompatible .OVL files
    195 Damaged .OVL file
    196 Damaged .OVL file
    197 Damaged .OVL file
    199 Missing or bad files in /SHAZAM/ directory or on wrong drive
    1009 EXP argument out of range (probably harmless)
    1013 LOG of non-positive number
    1025 SQRT of negative number
    2022 BINARY option used without "." on FILE command (ex FILE 7. fname)
    2504 Same as 3050
    2516 Invalid format used for input or output
    2525 Same as 2516
    2529 Same as 2516
    3000 Memory Allocation failure (too many files)
    3012 File Opening failure (too many files)
    3020 Read Error on unformatted sequential file
    3033 Write Error on unformatted sequential file (probably out of disk space)
    3039 Undefined Input-Output Unit
    3050 Record too long, use SHAZAM /R nnnn option (ex: SHAZAM /R 2048
    3072 PAUSE command not followed by RETURN key
    3073 PAUSE command not followed by RETURN key
    3074 Error in Releasing Memory (too many files)
    3086 Same as 3050, default is /R 1024
    4001 Missing Math coprocessor or switch not set
    4002 DOS Version below 2.1

SUMMARY OF INPUT-OUTPUT UNITS

1-3	Internal use. Not available to users
OUTPUT	Output unit
8-10	Internal use. Not available to users
11-49	Available for user files
50-99	Internal use. Not available to users
INPUT	SHAZAM commands and input data stream
LIST	Output unit (Screen)
SCREEN	Output to screen and file

Any questions about the IBM-PC version of SHAZAM should be addressed to:

SHAZAM Econometrics Limited
12 Varsdale Place N.W.
Calgary, Alberta
Canada T3A OG7

(403) 220-4096

OR

SHAZAM
Department of Economics
University of British Columbia
Vancouver, B.C. V6T 1W5
Canada

0. *HOW TO USE THE* SHAZAM *STUDENT VERSION ON THE IBM-PC*

The STUDENT Version of SHAZAM is available for purchasers of the *Gujarati Handbook* at low cost under a special arrangement. Because the available memory in the student version is intentionally limited, it will not be possible to use it for large size problems. However, the complete version of SHAZAM does not have these restrictions.

The SHAZAM Student Version for the IBM-PC or MS-DOS compatible computer is specifically designed to perform only the tasks which are needed for the textbook, *Basic Econometrics* by D. Gujarati. To use this program, an IBM-PC with at least 512K memory is necessary. This appendix is set up in two sections to describe how to use the SHAZAM Student Version on either a hard disk system or a two-drive floppy disk system.

HOW TO RUN THE SHAZAM *STUDENT VERSION ON A HARD DISK SYSTEM*

To run SHAZAM with the hard disk, create a new directory (called SHAZAM) and copy all of the SHAZAM files from the floppy disks to the hard disk. Both the command file and data file(s) (see the Introduction) for the examples must be in the same directory as the SHAZAM program. Then, to run SHAZAM, type:

SHAZAM <*comfile*

The above command will execute the command file named *comfile* and send the output to the terminal. If, however, you wish to send the output to an output file, the following command should be used:

SHAZAM <*comfile* >*outfile*

This will send the output to the file, *outfile*. Remember that it is not necessary to create *outfile* first on the DOS system. This will be done automatically.

SHAZAM may also be run interactively. This can be done by typing:

SHAZAM

Once you have done this, some information will appear on the screen and the following prompt will appear:

TYPE COMMAND
?

At this prompt, type your commands in one at a time.

To leave SHAZAM, type:

STOP

HOW TO USE THE SHAZAM STUDENT VERSION ON A TWO-DRIVE FLOPPY DISK SYSTEM

If a hard disk system is not available, a two-drive floppy disk system may be used, although it is slower. To run SHAZAM boot up the system with DOS Version 2.1 or higher. Then place the two SHAZAM disks in the A: and B: disk drives. The command and data file(s) (see the Introduction) must be placed on the B: disk. Start by switching to the B: directory and set the path with the following DOS commands:

B:
PATH = A:;B:

This will tell the computer to search the floppy in the A: disk drive if it cannot find the SHAZAM files on the B: disk. Once this has been done, you can run SHAZAM in the same manner as for the hard disk except that it will be necessary to indicate to DOS that your files are on the B: drive:

A:SHAZAM <*comfile* >*outfile*

Once again, it is not necessary to create *outfile* before running SHAZAM as it will be created automatically. However, remember that both the data file(s) and output file must be specified by both the name of the disk drive and its file name. For example, if the instructions say:

FILE 11 TABLE21

It will be necessary to type:

FILE 11 B:TABLE21

In the above example, *outfile* will be placed on the disk located in the B: disk drive. If you want the output to appear only on the terminal screen, just type:

A:SHAZAM <*comfile*

SHAZAM may also be run interactively on the two-disk drive system. Set the path to the B: drive as described above. Then, simply type:

A:SHAZAM

This command will load SHAZAM and put you into interactive mode.

Note that only limited space is available on the B: disk for your command and data files and there may not be enough room for output files. However, it is possible to run the examples in the *Gujarati Handbook* on a two-disk system.

LIMITATIONS OF THE STUDENT VERSION

The Student Version allows all problems in the *Gujarati Handbook* to be done with the exception of the **LOGIT** command and the **PC** command. The **GRAPHICS, EGA, HERCULES** and **TOSHIBA** options are **NOT** available for graphics plots in the Student Version. These commands require the complete SHAZAM version. If you get any of the following SHAZAM warnings or any similar warnings, your problem is too big for the Student Version:

**INSUFFICIENT MEMORY
TRY COMPRESS COMMAND
SORRY THIS OPTION NOT AVAILABLE IN STUDENT VERSION
USE "SET DISK" OPTION
VARIABLE LIMIT IS XXX RUN AGAIN WITH HIGHER LIMIT
USE SIZE COMMAND
STATEMENT TOO LONG
DISASTER - NO ROOM FOR THIS MANY PARAMETERS
GENR SPACE SHORTAGE
GENR TABLE FULL**

INDEX

INDEX

INDEX

INDEX

INDEX

INDEX

INDEX

326

INDEX

INDEX

INDEX

INDEX

THE SHAZAM FREQUENT REGRESSORS CLUB

SHAZAM is now the first Econometrics Computer Program to give bonus awards for Frequent Regressors.

Save all your old regressions for valuable awards. The more regressions you run the more awards you can receive. Members will receive 1 point for each regression run.

AWARD SCHEDULE

10,000 pts.: Regression upgrade. Run **OLS**; get output for **Two Stage Least Squares**.
20,000 pts.: One free Computer Handbook for Econometrics.
30,000 pts.: One free **SHAZAM** manual.
40,000 pts.: One free **SHAZAM** t–shirt.
50,000 pts.: 10% off on purchase of your next version of **SHAZAM**

Now for a limited time only you will start off with **3,000** points just for joining the Frequent Regressors Club.

Now, you can accumulate regressions even faster with SHAZAM bonus awards:

1. *Obtain double points for all regressions run in Version 5 (up to 100 bonus points allowed).*
2. *500 bonus points for regressions run while flying on United Airlines or Canadian Pacific Airlines (up to 1000 bonus points allowed).*
3. *Systems of equations yield multiple points. For example, a 3 equation system will yield 3 points.*
4. *1000 bonus points for running SHAZAM regressions at over 100 different SHAZAM installations. Select from over 500 worldwide.*
5. *Receive 1 bonus point for every R^2 over .99 (up to 100 bonus points allowed).*

Now, SHAZAM is the only program with penalty points:

1. *Subtract 1 point for every negative R^2 .*
2. *Subtract 2 points for every stepwise regression.*
3. *Subtract 3 points for every non–linear model that doesn't converge.*

How do I enroll?

It's easy! Simply fill out the application form on the reverse and mail it in. You may start running regressions as soon as your form is postmarked.

How do I claim my awards?

It's simple! When you have run enough regressions to qualify simply send copies of the regressions to the SHAZAM processing center. Your award will be mailed as soon as your output is verified. To receive your 10,000 point award regression upgrade you should also send your data.

What does it cost to join?

This is the best part! Enrollment is free.

How do I keep track of my points?

It's simple! Just count them.

Do all regressions count?

No. Only regressions run with **SHAZAM** *are eligible. Each regression must be different; duplicate results are not allowed. Regressions run in* **DO** *loops are also not eligible. All other regressions are eligible, even simple regressions.*

How much time do I have to accumulate regressions?

At present, there is no time limit. However **SHAZAM** *reserves the right to modify the rules and awards and introduce new award levels.*

ENROLL NOW! Don't let any of your regressions go to waste.

Date: _____

Name: _____

Address: _____

_____

_____

Phone: _____

Send this form to:

K.J. White
Department of Economics
University of British Columbia
Vancouver, British Columbia
Canada V6T 1W5

SHAZAM INFORMATION ORDER FORM

Name: _____

Address: _____

_____

_____

Phone: _____

Check off the items required.

_____ Send information about the IBM-PC Compatible Version of SHAZAM.
My computer model is: _____
I do _____ / do not _____ have a math co-processor (8087,80287,80387).
I do _____ / do not _____ have a hard disk.

_____ Send information about the Macintosh Version of SHAZAM.
My Macintosh model is: _____
I do _____ / do not _____ have a hard disk.

_____ Send information about the mainframe versions of SHAZAM.
My mainframe computer is:

_____

My operating system is:

_____

_____ Send information about Site Licenses for the IBM-PC Compatible and Macintosh
versions.

Please send information about the disks containing SHAZAM command and data files for the
following books:

_____ Berndt, E.R., *The Practice Of Econometrics*, Addison-Wesley, 1989.

_____ Gujarati, D., *Basic Econometrics*, McGraw-Hill, 1987.

_____ Judge, G., Hill, R., Griffiths, W., Lütkepohl, H., and Lee, T., *Introduction To The
Theory And Practice Of Econometrics*, Wiley, 1988.

_____ Judge, G., Griffiths, W., Hill, R., Lütkepohl, H., and Lee, T., *The Theory And
Practice Of Econometrics*, Wiley, 1985.

_____ Maddala, G.S., *Introduction To Econometrics*, Macmillan, 1988.

_____ Wallace, T., and Silver, J., *Econometrics: An Introduction*, Addison-Wesley, 1988.

Please send this completed form to the address given below:

SHAZAM   Telephone (604) 228-5062
Department of Economics
University of British Columbia
Vancouver, British Columbia V6T 1W5
CANADA